Economic Sociology

A SYSTEMATIC INQUIRY

Alejandro Portes

PRINCETON UNIVERSITY PRESS

PRINCETON AND OXFORD

Copyright © 2010 by Princeton University Press

Published by Princeton University Press, 41 William Street, Princeton, New Jersey 08540

In the United Kingdom: Princeton University Press, 6 Oxford Street, Woodstock, Oxfordshire OX20 1TW

Library of Congress Cataloging-in-Publication Data

Portes, Alejandro, 1944–
  Economic sociology : a systematic inquiry / Alejandro Portes.
      p. cm.
  Includes bibliographical references and index.
  ISBN 978-0-691-14222-7 (cl. : alk. paper) — ISBN 978-0-691-14223-4
  (pbk. : alk. paper) 1. Economics—Sociological aspects.   I. Title.
  HM548.P67 2010
  306.3—dc22   2009043506

British Library Cataloging-in-Publication Data is available

This book has been composed in Sabon

Printed on acid-free paper. ∞

press.princeton.edu

Printed in the United States of America

1 3 5 7 9 10 8 6 4 2

10 9 8 7 6 5 4 3 2 1

To the memory of my father

Contents

Figures and Tables

Preface

THE IDEA FOR THIS BOOK dates back to 2005 after a series of conversations with colleagues at Princeton, Cornell, and the University of Pennsylvania about the growing field of economic sociology and the direction, or lack thereof, that its development was taking. Over the years, I have published a series of essays on concepts and processes normally included among those of interest to specialists in this area. It occurred to me that assembling these in a single volume could be useful to those interested in economic matters and may help advance the sociological perspective on them. I also thought at the time that the project would not take too much effort—a question of stitching together published materials and highlighting the common threads among them.

Alas, that expectation proved to be most unwarranted. Reviewers of the first version of the manuscript, while polite and complimentary, could not see the common threads, nor figure out what the basic purpose of the volume was. A textbook? A collection of essays? Their well-taken critique forced me back to the writing table in an attempt to clarify the purpose of the project: no textbook intended, but no collection of essays, either. The motive for writing the book was grounded on the observation that contemporary economic sociology consists largely of exegeses of the classics, repetition of *one* of the founding notions of the field, and a growing number of individually valuable but disparate studies.

Earlier training in epistemology and the philosophy of science led me to the conclusion that such a disheveled state of affairs could not lead to sustained theoretical progress. Empirical studies in the field do not cumulate, in general, into new or refined theories and tend to conclude with a reassertion of the field's founding assumption: that sociability and social ties significantly mold economic behavior. My philosophical roots led me to a search for some order in this massed literature, seeking to identify what other elements existing studies have in common, and in what ways could they cumulate in theoretical progress beyond the classics. The readers will judge whether the proposed framework meets the test; ultimately, the success of this project will depend on whether other practitioners take the goal of theoretical growth seriously, either by adopting the ideas put forth in the coming chapters or proposing others to better fit the task.

In order to avoid repetition, I will not go into the argument here since it will be discussed in detail in the initial chapters and in the conclusion. I will use the remaining lines of this preface to acknowledge those who made this project possible. First, to my editors at Princeton University Press, initially Peter Dougherty, then Tim Sullivan, and finally Chuck Myers, who provided unwavering but critical support as the different stages of writing unfolded, and who identified extraordinary reviewers for successive versions of the manuscript.

To my Princeton colleagues, in particular Viviana Zelizer, Paul DiMaggio, and Martin Ruef, fellow economic sociologists, with whom I held many discussions and whose ideas inspired a number of substantive passages. They have my gratitude but certainly do not bear responsibility for any errors or for any polemical statements that others find objectionable. Beyond Princeton, I have benefited from conversations with other prominent colleagues, in particular Mauro Guillen at Penn and Victor Nee and Richard Swedberg at Cornell. They are also absolved of any responsibility for the contents.

With my wife, Patricia Fernández-Kelly, I had many talks at the dinner table, floating ideas past her and benefiting from her advice and most valuable intuitions. With her, I shared the disappointments inevitable in receiving less-than-glowing feedback on earlier drafts, and from her I drew the emotional energy required to learn from these critiques and seek to overcome them.

Finally, Barbara Lynch, my assistant, close collaborator, and friend of many years, patiently typed the many versions of each chapter, rendered the manuscript compliant with PUP requirements, and worked extensively on the graphics and the bibliography. She has my gratitude for her selfless dedication and my admiration for her multiple talents.

The substantive content, formatting, and organization of the book would not have been possible without the assistance of these persons. To all, once again, my thanks.

Alejandro Portes

Economic Sociology

CHAPTER ONE

Economic Sociology

PAST ACHIEVEMENTS AND PRESENT CHALLENGES

ECONOMIC SOCIOLOGY has experienced a remarkable rebirth. This trend has been chronicled and celebrated in a number of publications and reached its height with the appearance of two successive editions of a massive *Handbook*, edited by Neil J. Smelser and Richard Swedberg.[1] This feat, added to the influence achieved by Mark Granovetter's article on the social "embeddedness" of economic action, appeared to signal that the field was well underway.[2] Yet, in more recent years, there seems to have been a loss of direction. While purportedly sociological studies of economic activity have proliferated, basic texts in the field continue to chronicle its origins in the nineteenth century and to repeat notions that have become widely familiar by now. Above all, there is a disturbing return to "embeddedness" as if it were everything that, by way of theoretical contribution, contemporary economic sociology has to offer.

This impasse is not due, in my view, to the absence of an overarching theoretical framework, but to the lack of a precise understanding of the character and role that ideas at different levels of abstraction play in the organization of a given field. Overarching frameworks can do more harm than good, as sociology's experience with structural-functionalism and orthodox dialectical materialism can attest.[3] This is so because grand narratives tend to become self-referential, to approach reality deductively, and to force events into procrustean theoretical categories rather to than learn from them. Mercifully, economic sociology has no such grand narrative, but it simultaneously lacks a clear understanding of its constitutive elements.

In my view, these can be summarized into three broad categories: (1) meta-theoretical principles, (2) explanatory mechanisms, and (3) strategic sites of inquiry. The first component establishes the cognitive "lens" through which a particular field sees the world. This lens is neither superior nor inferior to others, it is simply distinct in privileging certain areas of empirical reality as worth investigating and in orienting ways of going about this enterprise. The second category includes ideas that can be invoked, in a variety of settings, to understand, clarify, and even predict concrete events. They represent the tool kit that those embracing a particular disciplinary perspective use to go about their work. Finally, the third category comprises the chosen locations for investigation and theoretical expansions of a particular field. Such sites are certainly not selected at random, but reflect the guiding orientations, the lens through which the field sees the world.

In current treatises in economic sociology, the three categories are mixed together so that "embeddedness" (a meta-theoretical assumption) appears right next to "firms" (a site for investigation) and "self-fulfilling prophecies" (an explanatory mechanism). A perusal of the two editions of the *Handbook* reveals that after its introductory section, labeled "General Concerns," it focuses mostly on sites of research such as firms, unions, the state, and the global economy.[4] The sites are very diverse, encompassing a wide variety of different topics and signaling that the field, at present, is anything but coherent. More disciplined is Richard Swedberg's *Principles of Economic Sociology*, which, after making a plea for the concept of "interest" as one such "principle" and chronicling the history of the field, goes on to review a tighter selection of research sites, headed by firms and markets.[5]

Strategic sites are not explanatory mechanisms, but rather instances where the latter can be applied. Successful explanation cannot be accomplished, however, by the mere invocation of the meta-theoretical principles because the latter are too abstract to provide sufficient causal guidance. Affirming, for example, that market transactors behave in particular ways because of their "social embeddedness" can be readily accepted without advancing, in any way, our understanding of that specific market or those particular transactions. For that, we need more proximate explanatory mechanisms, assimilable to what Max Weber labeled in his time *ideal types*.

The purpose of this book is to pursue this line of argument by first considering the key underlying principles or assumptions that guide the field and then examining a series of midlevel explanatory concepts that can be applicable in a variety of concrete situations. Those selected trace back to previously published work, which may convey the impression of a mere collection of essays. I seek to overcome this impression by showing how each chosen concept relates to the general assumptions of the field and how, in turn, they are usable for explanation and prediction in specific domains. Together they represent part, though not all, of the tool kit available to economic sociologists today. While these explanatory concepts and research sites reflect my personal interests, each is important enough to have spawned its own theoretical and research literatures, to be reviewed in the coming chapters.

THE WEBERIAN IDEAL TYPE

Weber is commonly cited as one of the fathers of economic sociology because of his substantive contributions, including his analyses of the role of religion in the economy, of forms of economic organization, and of the rise of modern rational capitalism.[6] Almost never discussed is his methodology, despite the fact that it contains elements crucial for the advancement of the field. A first such contribution is his skeptical stance toward the quest for universal laws and toward grand narratives in general and his emphasis on the fact that social science knowledge is historically bound. Happily, economic sociology has not been distracted by the search for an all-encompassing framework, but any movement in that direction should be finished off by Weber's cautionary warning:

> For the knowledge of historical phenomena in their concreteness, the most general laws, because they are most devoid of content are also the least valuable. The more comprehensive the validity—or scope—of a term, the more it leads us away from the richness of reality since, in order to include the common elements of the largest possible number of phenomena, it must necessarily be as abstract as possible and hence devoid of content.[7]

Second, Weber also gave us the ideal type as a mental construct based on past knowledge and designed to render meaningful specific areas of social reality. Grounded on past experience, ideal types describe how certain processes or events relate to one another and thus serve as explanations for specific historical phenomena: "[The ideal type] has the significance of a purely ideal limiting concept with which the real situation or action is compared and surveyed for the explication of certain of its significant components. Such concepts are constructs in terms of which we formulate relationships."[8]

As this citation makes clear, ideal types are "rubbed" against empirical evidence to put order in actual experience, highlight its most salient features, and establish whether theoretical expectations—implicit in the concept—actually hold. Thus, the ideal type *bureaucracy*, one of the most famous associated with Weber, can be compared with the ways particular states or corporations behave in order to clarify similarities and differences in probity, meritocracy, and esprit de corps from the expectations implicit in the concept.

Similarly, the ideal type *informal economy*, the subject of one of the following chapters, can be applied to a wide range of economic phenomena—from street vending in third world cities to complex chains of subcontracting in the developed world—to make sense of commonalities of what would initially appear as a Babel of disparate experiences.[9] Rubbing the ideal type against reality also leads to modifications, refinements, and qualifications of the concept itself, which is how scientific knowledge actually advances.

Weber's methodology is relevant to economic sociology because the field's explanatory mechanisms and even research sites are ideal types; that is, concepts at a midlevel of abstraction applicable to concrete historical phenomena and modifiable by the latter. While Weber himself cites as examples of ideal types such things as "city economy" and "handicraft system," which are research sites, their description shows that there are implicit causal propositions in each.[10] By contrast, concepts such as "inner-worldly asceticism" are explanatory mechanisms that can be invoked in a variety of contexts to highlight certain aspects of reality as causally relevant.[11] For ideal types to play this role, they must be neither too specific and tied to a particular time and place nor so general that they cannot be compared properly to any concrete process or event.

Low-level notions are linked to particular findings in certain bound localities and, while contributing to knowledge in such places, they do not travel beyond them. Thus the finding that immigrants' health deteriorates the longer they have been living in the United States is valuable in and of itself, but says nothing about what happens elsewhere or why the phenomenon occurs in the first place. Similarly the finding that, when confronted with unemployment, British workers resort to "self-provisioning" rather than informal trade is useful, but cannot be applied to other national contexts or historical periods.[12]

At the opposite end of the spectrum, concepts like *functional equilibrium*, *societal differentiation*, and *social systems* are so broad as to lack any clear empirical referent. When rubbed against reality, the common result is that they are found to be applicable to each and all situations, without advancing our understanding of any. Thus the statement that social change "proceeds through a process of differentiation, followed by integration" can be readily accepted without telling us anything about how specific historical processes of change take place. At the height of such theorizing in the United States, Robert K. Merton was one of the first to raise his voice against all-encompassing formulations. He proposed theories of the midrange as a more fruitful way to articulate ideas with empirical evidence.[13] In the context of his time, he contemporized with his grand theory mentors by defining midrange concepts as a necessary intermediate step for the formulation of broader systemic theories. With the wisdom of hindsight, we can confidently note that this is not the case. The midrange level of theoretical abstraction is the realm that useful ideal types inhabit, and they are not "preliminary" to anything. In my view, midrange ideal types represent the core of economic sociology. The following chapters will be organized accordingly.

PLAN FOR THE BOOK

Based on the preceding discussion, I plan to examine the meta-assumptions grounding economic sociology, some of its key explanatory mechanisms, and a few strategic research sites. As it happens, this tripartite classification also comes in threes: there are three general assumptions—socially oriented economic action, unexpected consequences of purposive action, and power. Selected explanatory mechanisms are also three: social capital, social classes, and social institutions. This will be followed by an analysis of three research sites: the informal economy, ethnic enclaves and middleman groups, and transnational communities. These sites have two characteristics in common. First, they are distinct from those most frequently discussed in the literature, such as firms and markets. Second, as ideal types, they also embody explanatory mechanisms, although less encompassing and at a lower level of abstraction than the first three. Selected explanatory mechanisms are not without their problems and these will be dealt with in the corresponding chapters. To anticipate: social capital has been intellectually "kidnapped" to play a role quite different from that contemplated by its original sociological creators; social class has been progressively abandoned as an explanatory tool in the wake of the general decline of Marxist political economy as an overarching perspective; by contrast, social institution has experienced a sudden rise of popularity, but its definition has become so vague and diverse as to threaten its heuristic value.

Finally, it may not be immediately obvious why the three cited meta-assumptions are so, that is, why they are held to be exhaustive of those grounding the field or why they are placed at a different level of abstraction than others mentioned. These questions will be addressed in the following chapters. For the time being, all that is asked from the reader is his or her preliminary assent to two points: (a) no all-encompassing general theory is necessary to move economic sociology forward; (b) to do so, however, a clear distinction is required among the different concepts that populate the field, their respective functions, and their relative levels of abstraction.

Since the time of its founding in the texts of Weber, Joseph Schumpeter, Thorstein Veblen, and others, economic sociology has shown enormous promise, both on its own and as a corrective to the orthodox marginalist tradition. Somehow that promise has never been quite fulfilled as texts in the field return, time and again, to the founding notions, and as a growing number of empirical studies invoke them as mantras, but without cumulating into theoretical advancement. To move us forward, empirical evidence should coalesce around a discrete set of midrange concepts, refining them and teasing out their heuristic value. Concepts (ideal types) are what we know and readily remember from our training and research experience. It is on their basis that this field, like any other in social science, can advance. Otherwise, we will be reduced to forever invoking the founding principles. If the rosary of concepts discussed in the following pages makes this argument persuasive, the goal of the book will have been fulfilled.

Explanation and Prediction

Conventionally, the goals of science consist in the explanation and prediction of phenomena in different areas of the world. The development of a discrete set of concepts, as described previously, has the exact purpose of facilitating these goals in the sociological study of the economy. No one would contest the assertion that a central purpose of the field is to render comprehensible the complexity of phenomena, past and present. In other words, explaining and interpreting economic reality is a major function to be met with the aid of a clear theoretical framework.

More questionable is the predictive function. Can the meta-assumptions and the set of ideal types so far developed in economic sociology predict anything? Here opinions are divided. Some theorists like Randall Collins have taken the bold position that the future, including major historical events, is predictable with the guidance of the proper theoretical tools. Collins offers as an example his own prediction of the demise of the

Soviet Union based on geopolitical principles and detailed information of the course of events in that country.[14]

A closer look at this assertion renders it questionable. While some predictive successes, such as Collins, may occur, the use of a particular set of theoretical principles does not guarantee this outcome in every case. Thus, about the same time that Collins was formulating his argument, another author using the same geopolitical principles plus "detailed information" predicted the likely demise of the United States. So far, that dramatic outcome has not materialized.[15] Disparities such as these have prompted authors like Charles Tilly to take the position that predicting the future on the basis of general "laws" or theoretical principles is a waste of time.[16]

Tilly's critique is compelling and reproduces, in all its essentials, Weber's classic argument about the impossibility of constructing a social science on the basis of universal laws. But before fully embracing this argument, which would confine social scientists to the exclusive role of interpreters of what has already happened, we should consider two issues: first, what are the phenomena to be predicted; second, what tools can be used for this task. There are, at least, three possible types of phenomena to be predicted in economic sociology, as elsewhere in the discipline: trends, steady states, and events.[17]

Most of the debate on prediction revolves around the third type and, especially, the subcategory of major, cataclysmic, and history-revamping events. The Russian Revolution of 1917, as well as the demise of the Soviet Union in the 1980s, would be good examples. Predicting such events would be akin to predicting the next Great Depression or the rise of Japan as the next hegemonic power in the capitalist world system. There are good reasons to doubt that such feats are possible, as attested by several recent attempts.[18]

However, macrosocial events of this kind do not exhaust all that there is to reality. With reasonable expectations of success, it is possible to predict certain trends at different levels of abstraction—from local communities to the world economy. It is hence feasible to transform the causes of major economic depressions or the determinants of the demise of core powers, as identified in the literature, into *trends* affecting the present and future. The ultimate outcome, however, would remain uncertain.

Marxist political economy made a specialty of predicting the end of the capitalist system, or strategic parts of it, on the basis of key social and economic indicators that should inevitably lead to its implosion. In

The Fiscal Crisis of the State, for example, the political economist James O'Connor predicted the financial breakdown of the American state under the dual strains of its accumulation and legitimation functions for sustaining advanced capitalism. This argument (which bears a close resemblance to Collins's geopolitical principles) held true as a trend. However, as did other Marxist analysts of the period, O'Connor confused *trend* with *outcome*. The strains were there and actually increased; the predicted final crisis never materialized.[19] The concept of social class, currently in abeyance because of its failure to predict revolutionary explosions, can be quite useful, nonetheless, when confined to the less ambitious role of detecting long-term trends.

Since functionalism fell into disrepute, most sociologists have been loath to focus on steady states and the processes contributing to their stability. Social ecologists, whose training leads them to focus on institutional survival, represent a partial exception but, for the most part, contemporary macrosociologists tend to avoid the issue. Although less exciting than big revolutionary explosions and catastrophic economic collapses, the *continuity* over time of normative structures and of institutions such as markets and corporate firms offer fertile ground for sociological inquiry. They also permit the formulation of predictions with a reasonable degree of accuracy. Although stable structures are commonly taken for granted, the question of how they arise and what keeps them going provides at least as solid a basis for theoretical development as the analysis of social change.[20] The concept of institutions is particularly relevant in this regard.

Finally, events that take place in restricted spatiotemporal contexts are also amenable to prediction. In a number of sociological fields, sufficient knowledge has accumulated to make possible this kind of bounded prediction. Theoretical advancements in economic sociology, for example, allow us to advance fairly accurate predictions about the organizational forms adopted by new corporations, the social consequences of industrial downsizing, the behavior of consumers in impersonal versus "embedded" transactions, the rise of entrepreneurial ethnic minorities, and employment decisions concerning different types of ethnically identified job applicants. The concept of social capital, as originally defined by Pierre Bourdieu, is especially useful in this restricted predictive role.

The theoretical tools to accomplish these predictive tasks are at hand and do not involve universal laws. Precisely because the midrange concepts just cited are fashioned in confrontation with reality and are responsive to its variations, they can be used with a measure of success to anticipate trends, steady states, and circumscribed events. While predicting the "big bang" and discovering the general laws behind it will continue to titillate the imagination and the ambition of scholars, progress in fulfilling the predictive function of sociology in general and economic sociology in particular will be achieved within those more restricted confines.

CHAPTER TWO

The Assumptions That Ground the Field

FIVE EXAMPLES

1. The operation of the Jewish informal economy in the former Soviet Republic of Georgia centered on the clandestine production and distribution of consumer goods.[1] Production took place in state-owned factories and with state-provided raw materials in direct violation of official rules. Heavy prison sentences awaited those caught. Despite this threat, the system flourished and functioned smoothly for years. It required securing low official production targets and a high wastage allowance to accommodate clandestine production. Bookkeeping was systematically altered. Production lines, for example, were declared "in maintenance" at times of peak unofficial production. Substandard parts and inputs were used to fulfill the official quota in order to increase the supply of parts going into clandestine goods.

Georgian Jews could sustain this complex system only through the operation of strong networks cemented in a common culture and history. Jonathan Altman, who studied the system, observed, "Trust is a fundamental requirement in the operation of the second economy. . . . A man's word has to be his bond." In case of trouble with the authorities, such as public raids, the network bailed out, threatened members, and obliterated incriminating evidence.[2]

2. In the indigenous villages surrounding the town of Otavalo in the Ecuadoran Andes, male owners of garment and leather artisan shops are often Protestant (or Evangelicals, as they are known locally) rather than Catholic. The reason is not that the Protestant ethic spurred them to greater entrepreneurial achievement, or that they found Evangelical doctrine to be more compatible with their own beliefs, but a rather more instrumental one. By shifting religious allegiance, these entrepreneurs remove themselves from the host of social obligations for male family heads associated with the Catholic Church and its local organizations. The Evangelical convert becomes, in a sense, a stranger in his own community, which insulates him from the religiously backed redistributional demands of his Catholic neighbors.[3]

3. The famed Italian industrial district in the central region of Emilia-Romagna is composed of small, highly dynamic firms, many of which started as informal enterprises and continue to use informally produced inputs and labor. According to Vittorio Capecchi, who studied the system, relationships of complicity rather than of exploitation or pure competition characterize the daily inter-

actions between employers and workers and among owners of firms. Small enterprises in textiles, ceramics, metallurgy, and others respond quickly to market demand, specializing in particular market niches, cooperating with one another in meeting sudden surges in demand, and resisting outside manipulations to undercut prices.[4]

Workers are hired informally but are paid reliably and are treated as apprentices eventually able to set up their own firms: "Many small firms concentrated on performing manufacturing operations or on producing certain parts of the machine. . . . Thus a subsystem of enterprises gradually evolved in which there was no leading firm. The factory that produced the final good did not necessarily constitute the center of the system because its role was often only that of assembling various parts produced by other firms."[5] This system of flexible specialization was explicitly opposed to the regulatory dictates emanating from the central government in Rome. The system was and is anchored in community networks identified with a common political culture. Emilia-Romagna is the core of the Italian "red belt" that witnessed militant opposition to the Fascist regime first and, subsequently, to the attempts by Christian Democratic governments to industrialize the nation on the basis of large-scale corporations concentrated in Turin, Milan, and other northern Italian cities. Instead, the communist regional governments of Emilia-Romagna encouraged and sponsored skilled workers and artisans to develop their own firms as an alternative to deskilling and mass migration north. The successful small firms thus created were not isolated, but coalesced into a mutually supportive system. The Emilian community of small producers promoted cooperative production and marketing, while ostracizing those who behaved individualistically as "real" market competitors.[6]

4. Chile has been hailed in recent years as the most successful Latin American economy and as an example of what "freeing the markets" can accomplish for a third world country. This much-touted success was the outcome of a trial-and-error process that saw young economists inspired by the neoliberal doctrines of Chicago professor Milton Friedman introduce radical reforms to open markets and stimulate foreign investments, only to see them go down into failure, producing economic stagnation and massive unemployment. Only because these "freedom" policies were introduced under the Pinochet dictatorship and sustained by army bayonets could they endure massive popular discontent.[7]

These failures led Pinochet to appoint a more pragmatic economy minister from the army's own ranks who took reform in a different direction. It consisted of creating new entrepreneurial groups by divesting the state of its vast industrial holdings. Chilean capitalism was not so much *liberated* by the Pinochet regime as *created* by it, through identification and sponsorship of selected entrepreneurial cliques. Pinochet's minister could undertake this massive divestment program because of the concentration of industrial holdings in the hand of the state. This was, in turn, a consequence of the large-scale nationalization program carried out by the previous socialist regime led by President Allende, who Pinochet deposed.

The socialists confiscated private industry in a bid to bring about a state-led model of development along the lines of Cuba and China. Little did they know that by putting industrial resources under state control, they were creating the means for neoliberal capitalism to finally take hold in the country. Without using these resources for empowering new and dynamic business elites, Pinochet and his minister would have been unable to launch Chile's economy into a sustained growth path. As Chilean sociologist Alvaro Díaz noted subsequently, "One never knows for whom, in the end, one works."[8]

5. At XXX International, a large American manufacturing conglomerate specializing in electronic games, toys, and computers, the behavior of corporate executives little resembles that of "economic man." Calvin Morrill conducted a study of corporate headquarters that revealed the development of an adversarial culture among executives in response to outside takeover pressures and managerial innovations. Public confrontations between executives became commonplace and led to the creation of an elaborate ritual as well as a rich imagery to describe these encounters. Executives engaged in "shootouts" and entire departments "went to war," with initial skirmishes followed by the tossing of "hand grenades" toward the adversary camp.[9]

In this highly competitive environment, opportunistic behavior—known as "ambushing" or "flying low" to avoid open confrontation—was possible, but only at the cost of serious status loss. "Honor" became the executives most prized good and was earned through straight conduct, making strong presentations in public debates, and learning how to win or lose with grace. Those who adhered to this normative code became "white knights" or "white hats." Less honorable executives could earn a skirmish or a duel through guile, but were promptly dubbed "black hats" and were often forced to move to a different department or resign from the company—"jump ship."

The pursuit of honor in corporate joustings became so dominant that the substance of debates commonly took a backseat to the etiquette of the encounter:

> challenges and counterchallenges indicated that a "duel" would occur at the next team meeting. Besides carefully preparing their presentations, each of the principals prepared themselves through rituals common in such situations. All of the principals wore their lucky ties and "flack vests" to fend off "bullets" from the opposition. . . . As was customary, an uninvolved team member spun a gold ballpoint pen flat on the meeting table; the principal to whom the ink end pointed was allowed to choose the order of presentation.[10]

The sociological study of the economy has evolved rapidly in recent years encompassing both exotic and unique phenomena and those at the very center of the capitalist system. The apparently disparate examples just summarized play a role as illustrations of this diversity, as well as examples of a distinct point of view on economic trends and events. The point of view that these examples, each in its own way, illustrate is formed by five orientations:

- A skeptical stance toward the notion that legally regulated exchanges and markets comprise all that there is, or even the principal part of real economic activity.
- An equally skeptical eye to the idea that unbridled self-interest is the sole or the primary motivator of economic action.
- A general recognition that economic transactions do not occur in a vacuum but are inserted into cultural systems and webs of sociability.
- An appreciation of the fact that rational means directed toward explicit goals frequently end up producing consequences different or even opposite to those originally intended.
- An overall rejection of the image of the economy as a level laying field and an emphasis on the role of power.

The first two orientations differentiate the analytic point of departure of economic sociology from economics proper, particularly its neoclassical version. The last three define the key meta-assumptions from which the sociological study of the economy departs: the social embeddedness of the economy, the unexpected consequences of purposive action, and the pervasive influence of power.

In the remainder of this chapter, I consider these assumptions as they set the framework for the emergence of more specific explanatory mechanisms and the identification of relevant sites for investigation. The choice of meta-assumptions differs from those conventionally presented in texts on the "new" economic sociology that identify only the first as its point of departure. Although embeddedness is certainly important, it does not exhaust all that there is in the way of orienting strategies for this field. As we shall see, all three assumptions possess a common status because of their high level of abstraction and general unfalsifiability. They are not hypotheses to be tested, but "lenses" through which reality is grasped and explored.

Socially Oriented Economic Action

Economists and sociologists agree that economic action refers to the acquisition and use of scarce means. All activities required for the production, distribution, and consumption of scarce goods and services are conventionally characterized as economic. There is less agreement, however, on the array of motives of economic actors and on the socially patterned influence of others upon their activities. The triumph of the neoclassical perspective in economics hinged on the adoption of a set of simplifying assumptions about human nature that allowed the construction of complex mathematical models. Rationality in this system is defined as the unimpeded pursuit of gain by economic actors, be they individual or collective. Many neoclassical economists are aware that these are only heuristic assumptions that, they argue, lead to internally consistent and predictively powerful models of economic events. While agreeing that this is the case, other social scientists have observed that there are many situations where these assumptions neither hold nor lead to accurate prediction. The field of behavioral economics has focused on the assumption of individual rationality and has shown its untenability in a number of contexts. Most of this work has been conducted from the standpoint of individual psychology.[11]

Economic sociology has been less concerned with psychological constraints on individual self-centered rationality than with those created by the social environment. Research in this field has focused on the ways in which external influences modify the assumed maximizing behavior of individuals and lead to predictions different from those of conventional economic models. This perspective assumes that actors are rational, in the sense of pursuing goals through deliberately selected means, but that they are not socially atomized. On the contrary, relationships enter at every stage of the process, from the selection of economic goals to the organization of relevant means to achieve them.

The most succinct classical formulation of this approach is found in Max Weber. In *Economy and Society*, as is well known, Weber distinguished three types of action: those guided by habit, by emotion, and by the deliberate pursuit of certain goals. The last type, described as "rational" action, is differentiated by whether its means-end structure is oriented toward the pursuit of individual ends (*zweckrational*) or the pursuit of some transcendental value (*wertrational*). These distinctions identified the type of action assumed by neoclassical theory as simply one ideal construction among several, all of equal stature. Moreover, Weber also assumed that rational instrumental action is socially oriented in the sense that "it takes into account the behavior of others" and is thereby oriented in its course.[12]

"Taking account of others" is not meant by Weber solely in the sense of formal considerations attending market transactions but, more importantly, in the sense of substantive expectations linked to sociability. By virtue of membership in human groups—from families to churches and associations—individuals acquire a set of privileges and associated obligations that simultaneously further and constrain their selfish pursuits. Even more importantly, every interaction, including market interaction, creates sociability in the sense of generating over time a complex set of stable expectations, status rankings, and emotions.

The postulate of socially oriented economic action, therefore, is not simple but contains several related subarguments. For the sake of clarity, it is convenient to list them as separate forms, although this does some violence to reality:

1. Economic action is socially oriented in the sense that it can be governed, in whole or part, by value introjection. Included in this category is not only the type of behavior dealt with in economics and sociology under the label "altruism" but also, and more generally, every action guided by moral considerations. Morality, or the acting out of collectively held values, may influence both the character of personal goals and the selection of means to attain them.

2. Economic action is also socially oriented in the sense that the pursuit of material gain interacts with other self-centered goals such as the quest for approval, status, and power, all of which depend on the opinions of others. Wholly unrestricted maximizing behavior meets with disapproval by others in the same social milieu, especially if it is pursued without regard to their own interests.

The accumulation of the valued goal, wealth, may thus come into conflict with the realization of another valued goal, social status, and with the unhampered exercise of the power that wealth itself confers. The accumulation of material means compels others to do one's bidding, but it does not by itself create the *auctoritas* that lead others to do so willingly. The Weberian distinction between power and authority thus bears directly on how economic action is conducted, insofar as authority is guided by concerns for legitimacy.[13]

3. Finally, economic action is socially oriented in the sense that even the unrestricted pursuit of gain is constrained by reciprocity expectations built up in the course of social interaction. The accumulation of social "chits" is central to the pursuit of economic advantage insofar as they facilitate access to information, capital, and other scarce resources. By the same token, such access is granted in the course of everyday transactions with full expectation that it will be reciprocated. Over time, each economic actor becomes surrounded by a dense web of expectations built in this manner. Nonobservance of reciprocity expectations carries the threat of immediate or delayed retribution, either by the aggrieved party or by his/her associates. The existence of such social obligations does not guarantee that economic actors will not pursue their own

self-interests, but it insures that they will conceal, as much as possible, those aspects of their actions that carry the threat of sanctions. Their behavior will be modified accordingly.[14]

The various forms of social influence on economic action, of course, combine in a multiplicity of ways in concrete situations. Their analytic separation remains useful, however, both because of their implications for the prediction of actual behavior and because they help identify different stages of sociological theorizing about the economy. An "over-socialized" conception of action in which individual conduct is guided primarily by value introjection was the focus of functionalist economic sociology. As elaborated by Talcott Parsons and Neil Smelser, the economy was portrayed as existing to fulfill one of the key functional prerequisites of society, with economic actors oriented fundamentally by moral imperatives.[15]

This conceptualization did not prosper because its theoretical categories were so abstract and its implications for individual action so stereotyped. Critics had no trouble pointing out systematic deviations from the expected behavioral patterns, and many lost no time in debunking what they saw as sociologists' "naive" view of human nature. The reemergent field of economic sociology has not abandoned moral considerations as an aspect of social influence on economic behavior but has focused, to a greater extent than earlier schools of thought, on the remaining forms described above, both of which assume self-interested actors. It has thus paid closer attention to criteria for social approval and reciprocity expectations.

Socially oriented economic action is not an explanatory mechanism but an orienting strategy—a meta-assumption. Like all concepts at a similar level of abstraction, it is unfalsifiable and vacuously applicable to a number of settings. Its value consists in calling attention to features of economic structure and exchange that otherwise may pass unnoticed and to their potential effects in the behavior of relevant actors. The concept of socially oriented economic action leads naturally to that of embeddedness of the economy. The latter was pioneered by Karl Polanyi in his efforts to demonstrate that markets were neither natural creations nor omnipresent. Instead, the road to markets had been opened and kept open by deliberate governmental intervention.[16] Polanyi emphasized, in addition, that there were forms other than markets to organize the economy, including reciprocity and redistribution. However, once the road to markets was opened, he acknowledged that market actors tended to operate according to the rational maximizing logic assumed by mainstream economics.

The concept of *embeddedness* was redefined by Mark Granovetter in the article responsible, in large part, for the rebirth of the sociological study of the economy.[17] Granovetter was not ready to concede that, once established, markets operated autonomously, as at least tacitly conceded by Polanyi. Instead, he emphasized that markets are themselves social entities and that recurrent interactions by market actors create networks, reciprocity expectations, sympathies, and aversions that consistently modify what are supposed to be economically "rational" actions. Not only markets but also hierarchical corporate structures are subject to the same problem. In a sustained dialogue with economist Oliver Williamson, Granovetter emphasized that corporate structures constructed to internalize market operations and thus reduce "transaction costs" are themselves subject to the perennial influence of sociability. Formal hierarchies are not what they seem, and orders coming from the top are not always executed as intended. Instead, informal status systems emerge, based on the differential levels of approval and respect granted to various actors, and hierarchical commands are followed, modified, or ignored, according to this alternative logic.[18]

Granovetter's reworking of Polanyi thus extended the sway of social influence to *all* areas of economic life and opened them to sociological analysis based on the embeddedness argument. Several of the examples that open this chapter illustrate, in different ways, the nature of the forces at play: the direct contravening of Soviet economic directives by Georgian Jewish managers and operators; the alternative logic guiding central Italian informal entrepreneurs successfully resisting capture by larger northern firms; and the social games engaged in by New York corporate executives obsessed with "honor" are all instances of the mobilization of socially grounded resources and the power of status considerations, altering predictions about the expected behavior of economic actors.

For additional empirical support, Granovetter turns toward examples drawn from observational studies of managerial behavior in American industry. Among others, he cites the classic study by Melville Dalton of the ways in which departmental heads in a large industrial corporation tipped one another in advance of the "surprise" visits of central auditing staff and helped one another conceal what they did not want auditors to see or count: "Notice that a count of parts was to begin provoked a flurry of activity among the executives to hide certain parts and equipment. . . .

As the practice developed, cooperation among the chiefs to use each other's storage areas and available pits became well organized and smoothly functioning. Joint action of a kind rarely, if ever, shown in carrying on official directives enabled the relatively easy passage of laborers and truckers from one work area to another."[19]

For a contemporary illustration, drawn from the core of the capitalist market economy, I turn to Mitchell Abolafia's study of traders on Wall Street:

> Opportunism on the trading floor, like all other economic behaviors, is embedded in a specific social and cultural milieu. This perspective explicitly rejects the dominant economic notion that levels of opportunism are nothing more than the sum of individual actors' independent preferences. Market makers, stock and futures exchange officials, and regulators at all levels are embedded in cultures that define tolerance levels for opportunism and for restraint.
>
> Recruits to investment banks receive very different socialization than do recruits to the New York Stock Exchange. As a result, social relationships and cultural definitions differ from trading floor to trading floor and the levels of opportunism differ in relationship to them.[20]

The different cultural expectations in which economic actors are socialized, the need for sociability and the quest for approval, the webs of reciprocity expectations created by repeated interaction are all factors that affect not only the social framework within which economic transactions occur, but also the very nature of the latter. Through this analytic lens, the level market field of neoclassical economics becomes much "bumpier" and the behavior to be expected from presumable utility maximizers more problematic.

UNANTICIPATED CONSEQUENCES OF RATIONAL ACTION

The second orientation underlying modern economic sociology is a skeptical stance toward the notion that individual or collective action involving the purposive selection of means leads normally to the desired goals. Precisely because such actions are socially embedded, the end point may be quite different from that originally anticipated. Efforts to build systems of sociology have a history of almost two centuries; for the most part, early system builders grounded their treatises in a linear logic that identified certain master principles from which a series of predictable consequences would follow.

But along with these efforts, there has always been an alternative tradition that questions the validity of explicitly stated intentions and of linear predictions. This alternative camp has always been heterogeneous—ranging from theorists who gave primacy to nonrational and charismatic factors to those who elevated conflict to the motor of history. This second and diverse tradition encompasses Marx and Engels's materialist dialectic and Georg Simmel's analysis of the functions of social conflict, all the way to C. Wright Mills's critique of the Parsonian system.[21]

Written more than sixty years ago, Robert Merton's article, "The Unanticipated Consequence of Purposive Social Action" synthesizes the core of this skeptical perspective. That article accomplished two things: first, it summarized the tradition of sociological skepticism from the classics to its time; second, it drove a wedge into the ambitions of sociological system builders who were grounded on the assumption of linear purposive action. By so doing, the essay opened the door to a number of modern concepts, all highlighting the paradoxical nature of social life. Merton himself was a prime contributor to this literature, adding the "self-fulfilling prophecy," "latent functions and dysfunctions," and "the serendipity pattern" to this literature.[22]

Unlike Granovetter's, Merton's article did not relaunch economic sociology, becoming incorporated instead into the framework of general sociological theory. It is invoked as a guiding perspective for this field because of its singular affinity with the concept of socially oriented economic action and the related fact that a number of prominent studies in the field conclude by highlighting how embeddedness leads to unexpected consequences of the most diverse sorts.[23] Among our opening stories, the link is illustrated, at the microlevel, by the religious conversion of Andean entrepreneurs the better to escape the host of onerous obligations associated with the Catholic Church; and, at the macrolevel, by the mass industrial confiscations in socialist Chile, paving the way for state-sponsored, liberal capitalism under the new regime.

"Unexpected consequences" is a meta-assumption because it cannot be tested directly due both to its generality and to the very condition of uncertainty that it highlights. Possible alternative outcomes to purposive action can be systematized, however, in ways that bring the concept closer to explanatory mechanisms and, hence, empirically testable propositions. If we think of purposive action as represented by a straight arrow between the explicit goal of actors—individual or collective—and the achieved end state, it is possible to identify five different alternatives to this rational schema:

1. The announced goal is not what it seems—that is, it is not what the actor or those in authority in a collectivity actually intend.
2. The announced goal is intended by the actors, but their actions have other real consequences of which they are unaware.
3. The goal is what it seems—but the intervention of outside forces transforms it midcourse into a qualitatively different one.
4. The goal is what it seems—but the intervention of outside forces produces unexpected consequences different and sometimes contrary to those intended.
5. The goal is what it seems—but its achievement depends on fortuitous events, entirely outside the original plans.

In summary form, these alternatives represent different end states from those assumed by a purposive logic as follows: (1) the real goal is not the apparent one; (2) the real goal is not what the actors actually achieve; (3) the real goal emerges from the situation itself; (4) the original goal is real, but the end state is contrary to its intent; (5) the original goal is real, but it is achieved by an unexpected combination of events. Figure 2.1 summarizes this typology, and the examples that follow illustrate each type.

1. Marxist and neo-Marxist analyses of social structure made a specialty of unearthing the real ends of capitalism behind its political facade and cultural superstructure. This is the "hidden abode" that Marx described in such poignant detail and that Richard Edwards documented a century later in his analysis of labor market segmentation.[24] More recent Marxist analyses of the cultural su-

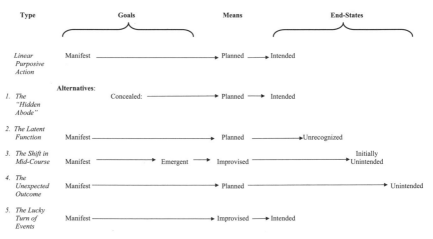

Figure 2.1 Linear Purposive Action and Alternative Behavioral Patterns

perstructures of advanced capitalism portray them either as a deliberate tool for legitimating the existing class structure or as having an autonomous origin, but unwittingly serving that end. Thus, David Harvey's *The Condition of Postmodernity* sometimes depicts postmodern cultural forms as the deliberate creation of advanced capitalism in its latest incarnation—that of "flexible specialization"—but at other times presents them as an autonomous growth that functions the same way that superstructures have always done, namely to mystify the economic realities underneath.[25] Outside the orthodox Marxist camp, Bourdieu's study of cultural "distinction" and the consumption of high art goes beyond the apparent enjoyment of such activities to unearth their real significance as markers of status and symbolic dividers between the masses and the elites.[26]

2. Consequences that are not recognized but are real find their classical expression in Émile Durkheim. Religious rituals organized to propitiate the divinities have the real, albeit unrecognized, consequence of strengthening collective solidarity. Marriage and extended families organized around various manifest goals actually function to protect individuals from the destructive consequences of anomie. An entire school of anthropology operated on these theoretical premises, seeking to uncover the unrecognized functions of primitive cultural practices.[27]

The study of modern organizational forms has also been based on looking for real outcomes underneath formal announced goals. The research program of John Meyer and his associates suggests, for example, that modern institutional structures, like research institutes and programs of advanced education transplanted to the remote confines of the less developed world have the manifest goal of promoting scientific advancement, but the latent one of serving as symbols of the country's modernity and, hence, relative parity with the advanced nations.[28]

3. The third departure from linear purposive action in figure 2.1 has to do less with the existence of concealed or latent ends beneath manifest ones than with the actual *shift* of goals in the course of a given activity. Weber's classic thesis of the role of Puritanism on economic behavior derives its appeal precisely from this type of account, namely how "preferences" are not stable at all but can change under the press of events. In Weber's account, actions originally intended to bring about certainty of otherworldly salvation end up reoriented, by the power of external forces, into a search for business success and wealth accumulation. The analysis of this midcourse shift—from the ascetic puritan to the rational capitalist entrepreneur—remains one of the most intellectually appealing arguments left from sociology's classic period.[29]

Nor is it the only one. Robert Michels's Iron Law of Oligarchies is grounded on a similar process. This is the logic that prompts idealistic bands of reformers and revolutionaries to shift goals over time: from the single-minded pursuit of altruistic aims to the selfish defense of privileges acquired in the course of the struggle. If for Pareto history is but a cemetery of elites, for Michels it is the scenario for the continuous degeneration of lofty undertakings into selfish material pursuits.[30]

4. The next departure from linear purposive action is arguably the most important. It involves end states that are qualitatively distinct, if not opposite to, those originally intended. The concept of *cumulative consequences* finds in this fourth family of events its exact opposite. Instead of the past leading in linear incremental steps to the present, events take unexpected turns, sometimes coming full circle. Among sociological classics, Simmel displayed the keenest eye for this type of outcome.

For Simmel, the formal facts of numbers and space play havoc with purposive action leading to multiple unexpected forms. Thus, the peaceful assembly turns into the violent mob under the influence of numbers and contagion; and the success of a religious sect in recruiting new members leads necessarily to dilution of its original radicalism, under the influence of dispersion and growing heterogeneity. For Simmel social conflict is not the unmitigated disaster that it seems because it possesses certain emergent and positive consequences, a theme recovered for contemporary theory in Lewis Coser's *The Functions of Social Conflict*.[31]

This fourth type comes closest to Merton's original treatment of unintended effects. In his article, Merton stressed the role of the paradoxical in social life, a perspective that came into full bloom in his subsequent analyses of self-fulfilling prophecies and the clash between cultural ends and structural opportunities to attain them.[32] The influence of the original concept is pervasive in modern economic sociology, even among those who endorse a rational means-ends paradigm. Thus, James Coleman notes that when a number of actors pursue their goals without institutional restraints, their actions often lead to consequences that are exactly the opposite of those intended. He offers market "bubbles," "stampedes," and "panics," as examples of such events.[33]

A final example comes from Manuel Castells's analysis of how, in its quest for military parity with the United States, the former Soviet Union ended up deeply dependent on its rival's technological capacity. As the pace of innovation in electronics accelerated, Soviet military planners became increasingly worried that their scientific establishment would miss a crucial step, leaving the country behind in the arms race. Hence, they opted for the safer approach of copying the latest Western computer equipment, bought or stolen by KGB agents. In the process, the Soviet government succeeded in hollowing out their country's own autonomous technological capacity. Castells puts their reasoning as follows:

> let us have the same machines as "they" have, even if we take some extra time to reproduce their computers. After all, to activate Armageddon, a few years' technological gap in electronic circuitry would not really be relevant. . . .

Thus the superior military interests of the Soviet state led to the paradox of making the Soviet Union dependent on the United States in [this] crucial field.[34]

5. This example also helps introduce the fifth departure from linear purposive action in Figure 2.1. Tilly introduced this type, illustrating it with a vivid example from eighteenth-century France.[35] He tells us how, by the end of his long reign, Louis XIV was able to reflect on his achievements in bringing peace and internal order to the realm. With the wisdom of hindsight, he presented his achievement as the outcome of a foresighted, well-thought-out plan. Closer scrutiny reveals, however, that it was nothing of the kind. Instead the king and his minister, Colbert, engaged in "determined, but often desperate improvisation in the face of unexpected reactions—both popular and elite—to royally sanctioned initiatives."[36] As is still common today, history was reconstructed in neat means-ends narratives when the actual process required on-the-spot decisions, sudden improvisation, and numerous departures from the intended course. To the Smithian faith in the "Hidden Hand" of the market, Tilly opposes the "Hidden Elbow" of adaptive intuition and improvisation.[37]

This also happened to Colonel Jimmy Doolittle and his "marauders" as their aircraft carrier, the *Hornet*, approached Tokyo Bay in 1942. After Pearl Harbor, the United States stood in dire need of a psychological uplift and this is what Doolittle and his men intended to deliver by bombing the Japanese capital. The raid was scheduled to take place at night and was meticulously planned. Unfortunately, hundreds of miles before the planned takeoff, the *Hornet* was spotted by Japanese fishing trawlers, destroying the key element of surprise. Doolittle decided to attack immediately to prevent the Japanese from strengthening their defenses. The raid took place in broad daylight, starting at great distance from its target. Against all odds, it was successful because the trawlers never actually alerted Japanese air defenses and because, by an extraordinary coincidence, that day had been singled out in Japan for civil defense exercises against the very threat that Doolittle's planes posed. The planes reached their target undetected in part because they were initially assumed to be part of the fake maneuvers.[38]

The analysis of latent consequences, midcourse shifts, unexpected effects, and improvised means are part of a disciplinary tradition unique among the social sciences. It represents one of sociology's distinct contributions and grounds its contemporary approach toward the analysis of economic events and processes. Placed next to each other in a typology of alternatives to the rational means-ends paradigm, they serve to flesh out the concept of unexpected consequences and facilitate the formulation of propositions of the sort: Given determinants *A* or *B*, outcome types *X* or *Y* outcomes can be expected, These outcomes may include the fulfillment of manifest goals by the intended means, but also any of the other five alternatives described. The assumption of unexpected consequences orients the sociologist to look for conditions leading to these alternatives, rather than simply being taken by surprise by them, as it occurs regularly among adherents of the rational linear paradigm.

POWER

The third general assumption grounding economic sociology is that power represents an omnipresent factor in economic transactions and organizations. This assumption negates the classical economic view of markets as level playing fields and its general neglect of the role of coercive arrangements capable of imposing their logic on individuals. Power may be defined as one component of embeddedness, that is, of the social structures that frame and constrain economic action. However, the concept of power is qualitatively distinct from the networks, values, and reciprocity expectations that normally comprise discussions of embeddedness. Indeed, some authors have faulted the "new" economic sociology and specifically the school of neoinstitutionalism for its relative neglect of this last dimension.[39] The desire to establish a dialogue with mainstream economists may have led to this neglect, which necessarily entails distancing the field from political economy, especially the Marxist-inspired kind.

As we will see in a subsequent chapter, there is no contradiction between the analysis of embeddedness focused on social networks and reciprocity and the investigation of power differentials. The two can be actually located within the same conceptual schema.[40] For the time being, the crucial point is that restoring power to the status of a core assumption prevents this unnecessary split and allows the field to retain and benefit from key insights in the classical sociological tradition.

Power is defined by Weber as the relative ability of individuals or associations of individuals to impose their will on others "despite resistance."[41] The term *impose* in this definition is crucial for it underlies the nonconsensual, coercive nature of this element of social life. Power that depends on the consent or agreement of those subject to it is meaningless. While its use may be masked by a consensual veneer, it must ultimately be able to force compliance on individuals and groups.[42]

Among the classics, Durkheim emphasized the external and coercive character of social phenomena that compel actors to follow certain paths of action and not others, despite their own wishes or inclinations. Durkheim located the source of this power in a diffuse "collective will" whose origin and modus operandi were never fully clarified.[43] Marx and his followers sought to tear this conceptual veil by locating the possession of power in the capitalist bourgeoisie and its source in the effective control of the means of production. For Marx, "collective will" and similar "laws" of society claimed as scientific discoveries by many of his nineteenth-century contemporaries were just fantasies. They simply masked the reality underneath—the "hidden abode"—where holders of wealth compelled not only the workers but also the rest of society to do their bidding.[44]

Weber essentially accepted Marx's definition of power, but extended its sources beyond the means of production to the possession of scarce skills that confer differential levels of "market power."[45] Weber also emphasized that dominant elites seek to veil and legitimize their control over the levers of power in order to persuade the masses to acquiesce to their situation. Power thus legitimized becomes "authority," which is the form in which most actors in normal times perceive its effects. Not incidentally, mainstream economists who have chosen to venture into this realm generally go no further than "authority" in their own analyses. This is, for instance, the case of Oliver Williamson's well-known discussion of corporate "hierarchies."[46]

In modern sociology, Bourdieu has arguably been the most prominent follower of this tradition by distinguishing sources of power attached to various forms of "capital." Bourdieu's main emphasis is on the "fungibility" of these various sources—material, cultural, and social—as they reinforce one another to consolidate the dominance of elites and the stable subordination of the masses.[47] In the Marxist camp, Antonio Gramsci and his followers have gone furthest in exploring the crucial antinomy between "power" and "authority"—the latter relabeled "hegemony"— as it explained the political stability of modern capitalist society, but also identified potential sources of revolutionary change.[48]

Like the two preceding assumptions, the concept of power inhabits a high level of abstraction, rendering general assertions about its existence and importance unfalsifiable. As such, it also possesses the status of a guiding perspective, a lens through which reality can be perceived. An emphasis on the significance of power in society leads logically to a search for its sources and its effects. As in Weber and Bourdieu, sources are identified with different forms of capital; consequences are reflected in durable and patterned inequalities crystallized in social classes and the class structure. Such lower-level concepts—social capital and social classes, among them—become, in turn, explanatory mechanisms for investigating a number of economic phenomena. These will be explored in subsequent chapters.

Jointly, socially embedded economic exchange, social power, and unexpected consequences of purposive action comprise, in my view, the three conceptual pillars of economic sociology. Their influence is pervasive, being present in various degrees, in all or most empirical studies in this field. Jointly, they produce a distinct point of view for the analysis of economic phenomena. As noted previously, they also lead into a series of lower-level concepts that represent explanatory mechanisms, as well as into a series of strategic research sites. Several of these are examined next.

CHAPTER THREE

Social Capital

THE CONCEPT of social capital and the related one of social networks have become key explanatory mechanisms in the field of economic sociology, fleshing out the implications of its meta-theoretical assumptions.[1] It is in networks that much (although not all) economic action is socially embedded, and one of the most important outcomes of that embeddedness is social capital. A commonly accepted sociological definition of social capital is the ability to gain access to resources by virtue of membership in networks or larger social structures.[2] Clearly, such ability flows out of embeddedness, becoming one of its most tangible manifestations.

Similarly, unexpected consequences of rational purposive action are commonly provoked by social capital because it gives rise to a number of commitments and loyalties running parallel to formal blueprints. The sequence is graphically portrayed, in stylized form, in figure 3.1. While formal economic enterprise usually develops mechanisms to police and control the unpredictable effects of networks and sociability, these controls are not always effective, faced with the pervasiveness of these phenomena.

As seen in the previous chapter, social capital is also a power-conferring resource "fungible" (in Bourdieu's terminology) with other

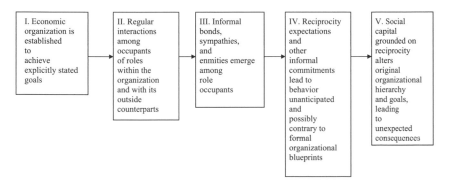

Figure 3.1 Social Capital and Unexpected Consequences in Economic Organizations

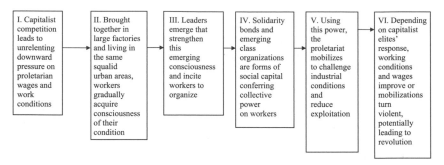

| I. Capitalist competition leads to unrelenting downward pressure on proletarian wages and work conditions | II. Brought together in large factories and living in the same squalid urban areas, workers gradually acquire consciousness of their condition | III. Leaders emerge that strengthen this emerging consciousness and incite workers to organize | IV. Solidarity bonds and emerging class organizations are forms of social capital conferring collective power on workers | V. Using this power, the proletariat mobilizes to challenge industrial conditions and reduce exploitation | VI. Depending on capitalist elites' response, working conditions and wages improve or mobilizations turn violent, potentially leading to revolution |

Figure 3.2 Social Capital and Working-Class Mobilization

resources. Unlike wealth, however, social capital is within reach of everyone, becoming, theoretically, one of the means by which subordinate classes can resist the coercive power of elites. This is what Marx and Engels had in mind when they invoked a proletarian "class for itself" in which consciousness of a common fate led to solidarity bonds and collective action.[3] Those bonds were indeed the proletariat's "social capital," conferring upon it a form of power beyond the reach of its individual members. Figure 3.2 graphically portrays this sequence.

Unlike the meta-assumptions discussed in the previous chapter, social capital, as defined, is measurable and its consequences are testable. As such, it can become a major tool for theoretical advancement in economic sociology, provided that it can overcome a powerful attempt at intellectual kidnapping. This attempt and its consequences are discussed next.

THE TWO MEANINGS OF SOCIAL CAPITAL

Social capital is arguably one of the most successful exports from sociology to other social sciences and to public discourse during the last two decades. It has been used to explain the differential performance of children raised in intact versus broken families, the success of housing programs in some communities but not others; and the economic development and government efficiency of cities and even entire nations. That success has come at a price, however, since the original meaning of the concept was subverted, as pundits and politicians effectively kidnapped it to their own ends.

Much of the controversy surrounding social capital has to do with its application to different types of problems and its use in theories involving different units of analysis. The original development of the concept by the French sociologist Pierre Bourdieu and the American sociologist James Coleman centered on individuals or small groups as the units of analysis. With some significant variations, both scholars focused on the benefits accruing to individuals or families by virtue of their ties with others.[4] Bourdieu's treatment of the concept, in particular, was instrumental, going as far as noting that people intentionally built their relations for the benefits that they would bring later on. In a few brilliant pages, the French sociologist dealt with the interaction between money capital, social capital, and cultural capital, the latter defined as the formal educational credentials that an individual possesses and the more intangible complex of values and knowledge of cultural forms in his or her demeanor.[5]

The subsequent research literature followed, for the most part, these theoretical guidelines focusing on the types of resources that accrue to persons by virtue of their social ties. In sociology, in particular, a tripartite family of effects evolved as researchers explored the implications of the concept. Social capital became defined as: (1) a source of social control, (2) a source of family mediated benefits, and (3) a source of resources mediated by nonfamily networks.[6] The latter usage, exemplified by personal connections that facilitate access to jobs, market tips, or loans, comes closest to Bourdieu's original definition of the concept. By contrast, family-mediated benefits approach his analysis of "cultural capital" since what families do, above all, is to facilitate children's access to education and transmit a set of values and outlooks, variously classified as "low" to "high-brow" culture.

On his part, Coleman paid particular attention to the first usage of the term, that is, as a source of control. He became preoccupied by the disintegration of what he called "primordial" social ties guaranteeing the observance of norms. A whole gamut of pathologies followed from this state of affairs—from crime and insecurity in the streets to freeloading by teachers and students in American public schools. In seeking remedies to these ills, Coleman pursued a double path: first, he wrote in defense and celebration of the community ties that still remained in place; second, he advocated the replacement of primordial social structures that had disappeared elsewhere with "purposively constructed" organizations where economic incentives took the place of vanishing social capital. Thus, he devised a whole series of schemes through which parents and teachers would be economically rewarded for the "value added" to society produced by their child-rearing and educational efforts.[7]

But it was the celebration of community that caught the eye of scholars in other disciplines. For Coleman, community ties were important for the benefits they yielded to *individuals*. Old people could walk the streets at night without fear, and children could be sent to play outside because tight community controls guaranteed their personal safety. A subtle but major transition took place as the concept was exported into other disciplines, primarily political science, where social capital became an attribute of the community itself. In this new garb, its benefits accrued not so much to individuals as to the collectivity as a whole in the form of reduced crime rates, lower official corruption, and better governance. Social capital became synonymous with "civicness" and, thus redefined, emerged as the new darling of a popularized literature bemoaning the loss of civic spirit in modern society, particularly in America.

This conceptual stretch was initiated by the political scientist Robert Putnam. It made possible to speak of the "stock" of social capital possessed by cities and even nations and the consequent structural effects on their development.[8] To be sure, individual and collective benefits derived from social ties are not necessarily incompatible, and, perhaps for this reason, Coleman never openly challenged the new use of the term by Putnam. But social capital as a property of cities or nations is quite distinct from its original definition. In effect, the concept was kidnapped for its rhetorical value and public appeal in metaphors such as "bowling alone."[9]

This redefinition of the concept gave rise to the present state of confusion about the meaning of the term. In one sentence, social capital is an asset of children in intact families; in the next, it is an attribute of networks of traders; and in the following, it becomes the explanation of why entire cities are well-governed and economically flourishing, while others stagnate. The heuristic value of the concept disappears as it ceases to be an explanatory mechanism to become a value, a synonym of all that is positive and good in social life. The confusion becomes evident when we realize that the two definitions of the concept, though compatible in some instances, are at odds in many others. For instance, the right connections allow certain persons to gain access to profitable public contracts and bypass regulations binding on others. "Individual" social capital in such instances consists precisely in the ability to undermine "collective" social capital—defined as civic spirit grounded on impartial application of the law.

Causes and effects of social capital as a public value were never disentangled, giving rise to much circular reasoning. The theoretical spadework done by Bourdieu and his successors prevented this from happening to the original version of the concept. At this level, the sources of social capital were clearly associated with a person's networks, including those that she explicitly constructed for that purpose, while effects were linked to an array of material and informational benefits. These were separate and distinct from the social structures that produced them.[10]

The ideologized version of the concept lacks this distinct separation. As a property of cities and nations, measurable in "stocks," social capital is said to lead to better governance and more effective policies, and its existence is simultaneously inferred from the same outcomes. When not entirely circular, the argument takes the form of a truism:

> For every political system (city, nation, etc. . . . .),
> If authorities and the population at large are imbued with a sense of collective responsibility and honesty;
> Then, the system will be better governed and its policies will be more effective.

It is difficult on the one hand to see how it could be otherwise. Indeed, it would be extraordinary if the opposite turned out to be the case. On the other hand, this self-evident character of the argument led to its growing popularity in policy circles. The truth that such statements convey is immediately graspable without need for additional explanation: Why are some cities better governed and richer than others? Because they are "blessed" with substantial stocks of social capital. Why does democracy work in Western European countries, but not in East European countries? Because the first possess the requisite "stocks," while the second have not acquired them. This intuitive appeal of social capital as a public value conceals but does not remove its basic circularity.

Whatever its current popularity among pundits and the public at large, the important fact is that social capital defined as "civic spirit" and as a property of cities and nations takes it away from the realm of economic sociology and into that of political ideology. For this reason, we will not concern ourselves further with this definitional strand. While remaining skeptical about its alleged blessings, we will leave the ideologized version of social capital to follow its fate and return to its original meaning and its bearing on economic sociology. This will be done by examining the sources of social capital as a property of individuals and small groups and its consequences at this level.

Sources of Social Capital

In its original version, social capital embodies an analytic distinction of potential importance in determining individual and group economic outcomes. Both Bourdieu and Coleman emphasize the intangible character of social capital relative to other forms. Whereas economic capital is in people's bank accounts and human capital is inside their heads, social capital inheres in the structure of their relationships. To possess social capital, a person must be related to others, and it is those others, not herself, who are the actual source of advantage. As mentioned before, the motivation of others to make resources available on concessionary terms is not uniform. At the broadest level, one may distinguish between consummatory versus instrumental motivations to do so.

As examples of the first, people may pay their debts in time, give alms to charity, and obey traffic rules because they feel an obligation to behave in this manner. The internalized norms that make such behaviors possible are then appropriable by others as a resource. In this instance, the holders of social capital are other members of the community who can extend loans without fear of nonpayment, benefit from private charity, or send their kids to play in the street without concern. Coleman refers to this source in his analysis of norms and sanctions: "Effective norms that inhibit crime make it possible to walk freely outside at night in a city and enable old persons to leave their houses without fear for their safety."[11] As is well known, an excessive emphasis on this process of norm internalization led to the "oversocialized" conception of human action in sociology so trenchantly criticized by Dennis Wrong.[12]

An approach closer to the "undersocialized" view of human nature in modern economics sees social capital as primarily the accumulation of obligations from others according to the norm of reciprocity. In this version, donors provide privileged access to resources in the expectation that they will be fully repaid in the future. This accumulation of "social chits" differs from purely economic exchange in two respects. First, the currency with which obligations are repaid may be different from that in which they were incurred and may be as intangible as the granting of approval or allegiance. Second, the *timing* of the repayment is unspecified. Indeed, if a schedule of repayments exists, the transaction is more appropriately defined as market exchange than as one mediated by social capital. This instrumental treatment of the term is quite familiar in sociology, dating back to the classical analyses of social exchange by Simmel, more recent ones by George Homans and Peter Blau, and extensive work on the sources and dynamics of reciprocity by authors of the rational action school.[13]

Two other sources of social capital exist that fit the consummatory versus instrumental dichotomy, but in a different way. The first finds its theoretical underpinnings in Marx's analysis of emergent class consciousness in the industrial proletariat, as described in figure 3.2 above. By being thrown together in a common situation, workers learn to identify with one another and support one another's initiatives. This solidarity is not the result of norm introjection during childhood, but represents an emergent product of a common situation. For this reason, the altruistic dispositions of actors in this case are not universal, but are bounded by the limits of their community. Other members of the same community can then appropriate such dispositions as "their" source of social capital.

Bounded solidarity is the term used in the recent literature to refer to this mechanism. It is the source that leads wealthy members of a church to anonymously endow church schools and hospitals; members of a suppressed nationality to voluntarily join life-threatening military activities in its defense; and industrial workers to take part in protest marches or sympathy strikes in support of their fellows. Identification with one's own group, sect, or community can be a powerful motivational force. Coleman refers to extreme forms of this mechanism as "zeal" and defines them as an effective antidote to free riding by others in collective mobilizations.[14]

The final source of social capital finds its classical roots in Durkheim's theory of social integration and the sanctioning capacity of group rituals.[15] As in the case of reciprocity exchanges, the motivation of donors of these gifts is instrumental, but in this case the expectation of repayment is not based on knowledge of the recipient, but on the insertion of both actors in a common social structure. The embedding of a transaction into such structure has two consequences. First, the donor's return may not come directly from the recipient, but from the collectivity as a whole in the form of status honor or approval. Second, the collectivity itself acts as guarantor that debts incurred will be repaid.

As an example of the first consequence, a member of an ethnic group may endow a scholarship for young coethnic students, not expecting repayment from the direct beneficiaries, but rather approval and status in the collectivity. The students' social capital is not contingent on direct knowledge of their benefactor, but on membership in the same group. As an example of the second effect, a banker may extend a loan without collateral to a member of the same religious community in full expectation of repayment because of the threat of community ostracism. In other works, *trust* exists in this situation precisely because obligations are *enforceable*, not through recourse to law or violence but through the sanctioning power of the community.

In practice, these two effects of enforceable trust are commonly mixed, as when someone extends a favor to a fellow member in expectation of both guaranteed repayment and group approval. As a source of social capital, enforceable trust is, hence, appropriable by both donors and recipients: for recipients, it obviously facilitates access to resources; for donors, it yields approval and expedites transactions because it guarantees against malfeasance. No lawyer need apply for transactions underwritten by this source of social capital.

The left side of figure 3.3 summarizes this discussion. It is worth noting again how the various sources of social capital flesh out the meta-assumptions of economic sociology and allow them to be put to use in testable propositions. Reciprocity expectations and enforceable trust flow out of the embeddedness of transactions into dyadic relationships or larger social structures. Value introjection and, especially, bounded solidarity can be transformed into power insofar as they compel members of a population to act selflessly and even sacrifice for the collective good. Finally, as illustrated in figure 3.1, the development of reciprocity expectations and emergence of bounded solidarity among subordinates in formal organizations can play havoc with their original blueprints and goals.

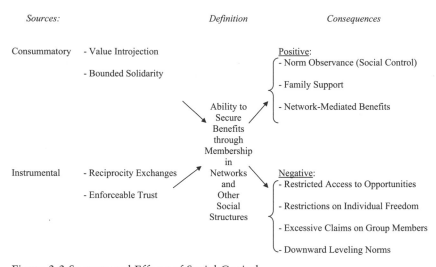

Figure 3.3 Sources and Effects of Social Capital

CONSEQUENCES OF SOCIAL CAPITAL

Just as the sources of social capital are plural, so are its consequences. A review of the relevant sociological literature points toward three general consequences of the phenomenon. As seen previously, they include: (a) social control, (b) family support, and (c) nonfamily benefits. As examples of the first function, we find a series of studies that focus on rule enforcement. The social capital created by tight community networks is useful to parents, teachers, and police authorities as they seek to maintain discipline and promote compliance among those under their charge. Sources of this type of social capital are commonly found in bounded solidarity and enforceable trust, and its main result is to render formal or overt controls unnecessary. The process is exemplified by Min Zhou and Carl Bankston's study of the tight-knit Vietnamese community of New Orleans: "Both parents and children are constantly observed as under a 'Vietnamese microscope.' If a child flunks out or drops out of a school, or if a boy falls into a gang or a girl becomes pregnant without getting married, he or she brings shame not only to himself or herself but also to the family."[16]

The influence of Coleman's writings is also clear in the second function of social capital, namely as a source of parental and kin support. Intact families and those where one parent has the primary task of rearing children possess more of this form of social capital than do single parent families or those where both parents work. The primary beneficiaries of this resource are, of course, the children whose education and occupational achievement are promoted accordingly. Coleman thus cites approvingly the practice of Asian immigrant mothers who not only stay at home but also often purchase second copies of school textbooks to help their offspring with their homework.[17]

A second example is Lingxin Hao's analysis of kin support and out-of-wedlock motherhood. Like financial capital, social capital influences transfers made by parents to children and behavioral outcomes such as teen pregnancy, educational attainment, and labor force participation. Social capital is greater in two-parent families, those with fewer children, and those where parents have high aspirations for their young. These conditions foster greater parental attention, more hours spent with children, and the emergence of an achievement orientation among adolescents.[18]

Along the same lines, Steven Gold highlights the change in parental roles among Israeli immigrant families in the United States. In Israel, close community bonds facilitate supervision and rearing of children because other adults know the young and assume responsibility for their well-being. In the more anomic American environment, mothers are assigned the role of compensating for the lack of community ties with exclusive dedication to their children. Thus, female labor force participation is much greater in Israel than among Israelis in the United States as mothers endeavor to preserve an appropriate cultural environment for their young.[19] Note that in this example, reduction of the first consequence of social capital—community bonds and control—is partially compensated by an increase in its second consequence, familial support.

By far, however, the most common function attributed to social capital is as a source of network-mediated benefits beyond the immediate family. The most common manifestation of this consequence is promoting the economic and occupational opportunities of the beneficiaries. The idea that "connections" are instrumental in furthering individual mobility is found among a number of authors, even those who do not conceptualize them explicitly as social capital. Granovetter for example coined the term "strength of weak ties" to refer to the power of indirect influences outside the immediate circle of family and close friends to serve as an informal employment referral system. The idea was original because it ran contrary to the commonsense notion that dense networks, such as those available through family circles, would be more cost effective in finding jobs.[20] Almost two decades later, Ronald Burt built on Granovetter's insight by developing the concept of "structural holes." Burt did employ the term "social capital" and, like Bourdieu's, his definition is instrumental. In Burt's case, however, social capital is based on the relative *scarcity* of network ties rather than on their density.[21]

Another noteworthy early effort was by Nan Lin and colleagues in their article "Social Resources and Strength of Ties," which points precisely in the opposite direction.[22] Although Lin and his colleagues did not use the term *social capital*, Coleman cites their work approvingly because of a common emphasis on dense networks as a resource. This alternative stance, which, in contrast to Granovetter and Burt, may be labeled "the strength of strong ties," is also evident in other areas of the social-networks-and-economic-mobility literature. One of the most noteworthy is the study of immigrant and ethnic entrepreneurship, in which networks and the social capital that flows through them are consistently identified as a key resource for the creation of small businesses. Ivan Light, for example, has emphasized the importance of rotating credit associations (RCAs) for the capitalization of Asian immigrant firms in the United States. RCAs are informal groups that meet periodically, with every member contributing a set amount to a common pool that is received by each in turn. Social capital in this case comes from the trust that each participant has in the continuing contribution of others even after they receive the pooled funds. Without such trust, no one will contribute and each will be deprived of this effective means to gain access to finance.[23]

The role of social networks is equally important in studies of ethnic business enclaves. Enclaves are dense concentrations of immigrant or ethnic firms that employ a significant proportion of their coethnic labor force and develop a distinctive physical presence in urban space. Studies of New York's Chinatown, of Miami's Little Havana, and of Los Angeles's Koreatown consistently highlight the role of community networks as a source of vital resources for these ethnic firms.[24] Such resources include but are not limited to start-up capital; others are tips about business opportunities, access to markets, and a pliant and disciplined labor force.

The opposite of this situation is the dearth of social connections in certain impoverished communities or their truncated character. Since publication of Carol Stack's *All Our Kin*, sociologists know that everyday survival in poor urban communities frequently depends on close interaction with kin and friends in similar situations.[25] The problem is that such ties seldom reach beyond the inner city, thus depriving their inhabitants of sources of information about employment opportunities elsewhere and ways to attain them. Loic Wacquant and William Wilson emphasize how the departure of both industrial employment and middle-class families from black inner city areas left the remaining population bereft of social capital, a situation leading to high levels of unemployment and welfare dependency.[26]

The same point is central to Mercer Sullivan's comparative ethnographies of Puerto Rican, black, and working-class white youths in three New York communities. Sullivan challenges blanket assertions about youth subcultures as determinants of deviant behavior by showing that access to regular jobs and participation in deviant activities are both network mediated.[27] As Granovetter had noted earlier, teenagers seldom find jobs; instead, "jobs come to them" through the mediation of parents and other adults in their immediate community.[28] Sullivan shows how such networks are much feebler in the case of black youths because of the scarcity of occupants of influential positions in the adult generation. Thrown back on their own resources, black adolescents are seldom able to compete successfully for good regular jobs; hence, they become available for alternative forms of income earning.

In her analysis of teenage pregnancy in Baltimore's ghetto, Patricia Fernández-Kelly notes how the dense but truncated networks of inner city black families not only cut off members from information about the outside world but also simultaneously support alternative cultural styles that make access to mainstream employment even more difficult.[29] In this isolated context, teenage pregnancy is not the outgrowth of carelessness or excess sexuality but, more commonly, a deliberate means to gain adult status and a measure of independence.

The popularity of the concept, subsequent to its transformation into a value, has led some international organizations, particularly the World Bank, to promote social capital as a means to bring about development to third world communities.[30] The mixed record of such attempts attests to the difficulty of seeking to create social capital from the outside and to the importance of identifying and calibrating sources of the phenomenon. In the absence of strong bounded solidarity among members of a particular community, external exhortations to act selflessly for the collective good are bound to fall on deaf ears. This is what has happened to a number of programs prompted by the naive belief that *consequences* of social capital can be brought about without a detailed investigation of its *sources*.[31]

The three consequences of the phenomenon described in this section should be kept in mind both to avoid confusion and facilitate understanding of their interrelationships. It is possible, for example, that social capital leading to social control may clash with social capital leading to network-mediated benefits, if the latter consists precisely on the ability to bypass existing norms. The capacity of authorities to enforce rules (social control) can hence be jeopardized by the existence of tight networks whose function is precisely to facilitate violation of those rules for private benefit. These outcomes point to the need of a closer look at the actual and potential gainers and losers in transactions mediated by social capital. The right side of figure 3.3 summarizes the previous discussion.

The Downside of Social Capital

The research literature on social capital strongly emphasizes its positive consequences. Indeed it is our sociological bias to see good things emerging out of sociability; bad things are more commonly associated with the behavior of *Homo economicus*. However, the same mechanisms appropriable by individuals and groups as social capital can have other, less desirable consequences. It is important to emphasize them for two reasons: first, to avoid the trap of presenting community networks, social control, and norms as unmixed blessings; second, to keep the analysis within the bounds of serious sociological analysis rather than moralizing statements. Recent studies have identified at least four negative consequences of social capital: exclusion of outsiders, excess claims on group members, restrictions on individual freedoms, and downward leveling norms. It is worth examining each in turn as a necessary complement to the positive effects discussed in the prior section.

First, the same strong ties that bring benefits to members of a group commonly enable it to bar others from access. Roger Waldinger describes the tight control exercised by white ethnics—descendants of Italian, Irish, and Polish immigrants—over the construction trades and the fire and police unions of New York. Other cases include the growing control of the produce business by Korean immigrants in several East Coast cities, the traditional monopoly of Jewish merchants over the New York diamond trade, and the dominance of Cubans over numerous sectors of the Miami economy. In each instance, social capital generated by bounded solidarity and trust are at the core of the group's economic advance. But, as Waldinger points out, "the same social relations that . . . enhance the ease and efficiency of economic exchanges among community members implicitly restrict outsiders."[32]

Ethnic groups are not the only ones to use social capital for economic advantage. Two centuries ago, Adam Smith complained that meetings of merchants inevitably ended up as a conspiracy against the public. The "public," of course, are all those excluded from the networks and mutual knowledge linking the colluding groups.[33] Substitute for "merchants" white building contractors, ethnic union bosses, or immigrant entrepreneurs, and the contemporary relevance of Smith's point becomes evident.

The second negative effect of social capital is the obverse of the first because group or community closure may, under certain circumstances, prevent the success of business initiatives by their members. In his study of the rise of commercial enterprises in Bali, Clifford Geertz observed how successful entrepreneurs were constantly assaulted by job- and loan-seeking kinsmen. These claims were buttressed by strong norms enjoining mutual assistance within the extended family and among community members in general.[34] The result was to turn promising enterprises into welfare hotels, checking their economic expansion.

Granovetter, who calls attention to this example, notes that it is an instance of the problem that classic economic development theory identified among traditional enterprises. Weber made the same point when he stressed the importance of impersonal economic transactions guided by the principle of universalism as one of the major reasons for Puritan entrepreneurial success.[35] Thus, cozy intergroup relations of the kind found in highly solidaristic communities can give rise to a gigantic free-riding problem, as less diligent members enforce on the more successful all kinds of demands backed by a shared normative structure. For claimants, "their" social capital consists precisely of privileged access to the resources of fellow members. In the process, opportunities for entrepreneurial accumulation and success are dissipated. The "conversion" of successful Ecuadoran artisan-entrepreneurs to Protestantism, one of the opening stories in chapter 2, represented an effective antidote against the weight of such demands.

Third, community or group participation necessarily creates demand for conformity. In a small town or village, all neighbors know one another, one can get supplies on credit at the corner store, and children play freely in the streets under the watchful eyes of other adults. The level of social control in such settings is strong and also quite restrictive of personal freedoms, which is the reason why the young and the more independent-minded have always left. Jeremy Boissevain reported such a situation in his classic study of village life in the island of Malta. Dense, "multiplex" networks tying inhabitants together created the ground for an intense community life and strong enforcement of local norms. The privacy and autonomy of individuals were reduced accordingly.[36]

This is an expression of the age-old dilemma between community solidarity and individual freedom analyzed by Simmel in his classic essay on "The Metropolis and Mental Life." In that essay, Simmel came out in favor of personal autonomy and responsibility.[37] At present, the pendulum has swung back, and a number of authors are calling for stronger community networks and norm observance in order to reestablish social control. This may be desirable in many instances, but the downside of this function of social capital must also be kept in mind. Constraints on individual freedom may be responsible for Rubén Rumbaut's findings that high levels of familistic solidarity among recent immigrant students are negatively related to four different educational outcomes, including grades and standardized test scores. According to this author, "family ties bind, but sometimes these bonds constrain rather than facilitate particular outcomes."[38]

Fourth, there are situations in which group solidarity is cemented by a common experience of adversity and opposition to mainstream society. In these instances, individual success stories undermine group cohesion because the latter is precisely grounded on the alleged impossibility of such occurrences. The result is *downward leveling norms* that operate to keep members of a downtrodden group in place and force the more ambitious to escape from it. In his ethnographic research among Puerto Rican crack dealers in the Bronx, Phillippe Bourgois calls attention to the local version of this process, which singles out for attack individuals seeking to join the middle-class mainstream:

> When you see someone go downtown and get a good job, if they be Puerto Rican, you see them fix up their hair and put some contact lenses in their eyes. Then they fit in and they do it! I have seen it! Look at all the people in that building, they all "turn-overs." They people who want to be white. Man, if you call them in Spanish it wind up a problem. I mean like take the name Pedro—I'm just telling you this as an example—Pedro be saying [imitating a whitened accent] "My name is Peter." Where do you get Peter from Pedro?[39]

Similar examples are reported by Alex Stepick in his study of Haitian American youths in Miami and by Marcelo Suarez-Orozco and Maria Eugenia Matute-Bianchi among Mexican American teenagers in Southern California.[40] In each instance, the emergence of downward leveling norms has been preceded by lengthy periods, often lasting generations, in which the mobility of a particular group has been blocked by outside discrimination. That historical experience underlines the emergence of a solidarity grounded in a common experience of subordination. Once in place, however, this normative outlook has the effect of helping perpetuate the very situation it decries.

Note that social capital in the form of social control is still present in these situations, but its effects are exactly the opposite of those commonly celebrated in the literature. Whereas bounded solidarity and trust provide the sources for socioeconomic ascent and entrepreneurial prowess among some ethnic groups, among others, they have exactly the opposite effect. Sociability cuts both ways: while it can be the source of public goods, such as those celebrated by Coleman and others, it can also lead to public "bads." Mafia families, prostitution and gambling rings, youth gangs offer so many cases of how embeddedness in social structures can be turned toward socially less desirable ends. The value of social capital as an explanatory mechanism for economic sociology lies precisely in its capacity to address these paradoxical outcomes, a capacity that is lost in exclusively celebratory versions of the concept.

SOCIAL CAPITAL AND IMMIGRATION

Having reviewed the range of consequences of social capital, it is appropriate to return to its sources outlined in figure 3.3, in order to illustrate the two that have been less theorized in the classical and contemporary sociological literatures. These examples come from the field of immigration, which, for analysis of events linked to the effects of sociability, is invaluable. Because of their very recency in the host society, their lack of institutionalization, and their paucity of material resources, immigrant groups are commonly forced to rely on their own networks for a host of needs—from sheer survival to entrepreneurial initiatives. In that sense, the activities of immigrant communities can provide a strategic field site for theoretical development in economic sociology.

Bounded Solidarity

In 1989, a riot was triggered in Miami by the shooting of two African American cyclists by a Colombian-born policeman. The officer, William B. Lozano, was suspended without pay from the Miami police force and found himself facing the wrath of the entire black community. To defend himself in the face of the hostility of much of the local population, he hired one of Miami's best criminal attorneys. As his legal bills mounted, the unemployed Lozano found that he had no other recourse but to go to the local Spanish-language radio stations to plead for help from his fellow Colombians and other Latinos. Lozano had no means of verifying his claims to innocence and, as a potential felon, he should have received little sympathy from most citizens. However, he counted on the emergent feeling among Colombians that he was being turned into a scapegoat and on the growing sympathy toward that position in the rest of the Latin community. After his first radio broadcast, Lozano collected $150,000 for his legal bills; subsequent appeals also yielded substantial sums.[41]

The source of social capital at work in this case is bounded solidarity because it is limited to members of a particular group who find themselves affected by common events in a particular time and place. Its fundamental characteristic is that it does not depend on enforceability, but on the moral imperative felt by individuals to behave in a certain way.

The confrontation with the host society has historically created solidarist communities among immigrants. Victor Nee and Brett de Bary Nee, Terry Boswell, and Zhou describe the plight of nineteenth-century Chinese immigrants in New York and San Francisco who were subjected to harsh forms of discrimination and lacked the means to return home. Barred from factory employment by nativist prejudice and prevented by the Chinese Exclusion Act from bringing their wives and other family members into the country, these hapless seekers of the "Mountain of Gold" had no recourse but to band together in tight-knit communities that were the precursors of today's Chinatowns.[42] Solidarity born out of shared adversity is reflected in the "clannishness" and "secretiveness" that outsiders were later to attribute to these communities. Such communities also provided the basis for the rapid growth of fledgling immigrant enterprises. Today, Chinese immigrants and their descendants have one of the highest rates of self-employment among all ethnic groups, and their enterprises are, on the average, the largest among both native and foreign-born minorities.[43]

All immigrant groups do not experience equal levels of confrontation. The cultural and linguistic distance between home country and receiving society, and the distinctness of immigrants relative to the native-born population govern, to a large extent, the magnitude of the clash between the two groups. A second factor critical to forging solidarity is the possibility of "exit" from the host society to return home. Immigrants for whom escape from nativist prejudice and discrimination is but a cheap ride away are not likely to develop as high levels of bounded solidarity as those whose return is somehow blocked. Turn-of-the-century Chinese immigrants are an example of the latter, as were the Russian Jews who came to America to escape czarist persecution at home.[44] Today, blocked return is characteristic of many political refugees, and higher levels of internal solidarity have repeatedly been noted among these groups.[45]

Enforceable Trust

The Dominican immigrant community in New York City has been characterized until recently as a working-class ghetto composed mostly of illegal immigrants working for low wages in sweatshops and menial service occupations. A study conducted under the auspices of the U.S. Congressional

Commission for the Study of Immigration contradicts this description and points to the emergence of a budding entrepreneurial enclave among Dominican immigrants. The city-within-a-city that one encounters when entering the Washington Heights area of New York, with its ethnic restaurants and stores, Spanish-language newspapers, and travel agencies, is, to a large extent, a Dominican creation built on the strength of skills brought from the Dominican Republic, ready access to a low-wage labor pool, and the development of informal credit channels.[46]

While New York City hosts several formally registered Dominican finance agencies (*financieras*), networks of informal loan operations also grant credit with little or no paperwork. And although some of the Dominican capital represents profits from the drug trade, it also comes from established ethnic firms and from the savings of workers who obtain higher interest rates from the ethnic finance networks than from formal banking institutions. These sources are reinforced by flight capital from the Dominican Republic. Money circulates within community networks and is made available for business start-ups because recipients are expected to repay the loans made to them. This expectation is based on the reputation of the recipient but also on the knowledge that there will be swift retribution against those who default. Such punishment may include coercive measures but is more often based on ostracism from ethnic business opportunities.[47]

As a source of social capital, enforceable trust varies greatly with the character of the community. Since the relevant behaviors are guided by utilitarian expectations, the likelihood of their occurrence is conditioned by the extent to which the community is the sole or principal source of certain rewards. When immigrants can draw on a variety of valued resources—from social approval to business opportunities—from their association with outsiders, the power of their own community becomes weaker. Conversely, when outside prejudice denies them access to such rewards, observance of community norms and expectations becomes much more likely. After reviewing studies of business behavior among the overseas Chinese in the Philippines and Asian Indians in Kenya, Granovetter arrives at essentially the same conclusion, noting that "the discrimination that minority groups face can actually generate an advantage. . . . Once this discrimination fades, intergenerational continuity in business is harder to sustain."[48]

What happens outside the community must be balanced, however, with the resources available within the ethnic community itself. It may be that the second- or third-generation Chinese Americans or Jewish Americans face no great prejudice in contemporary American society, yet they may still choose to preserve ties to their ethnic community because of the opportunities available through such networks. The durability of institutions created by successful immigrant groups may have less to do with the long-term persistence of outside discrimination than with the ability of these institutions to compete effectively for the loyalty of their own with rewards unavailable in the broader society. Conversely, a resource-poor immigrant community will have trouble enforcing normative patterns, even if its members continue to face severe outside discrimination.

The Tense World of Social Capital

Throughout this chapter, we have seen how the concept of social capital and the realities underneath are fraught with tension. At least three sources of tension can be identified: (a) between the original and ideologized definitions of the concept, (b) between its consequences in the form of social control and in the form of network-mediated benefits, (c) between its positive and negative consequences at the individual and collective levels. These multiple tensions explain why a seemingly easy-to-grasp idea has proven so difficult to handle. They are indeed at the source of confusion about the meaning, effects, and applicability of the concept.

Even after restricting social capital to its original definition in Bourdieu and Coleman, tensions persist. Ultimately, they have to do with the dual presence required for the effects of this mechanism to materialize: the individual and the group. Both individuals and communities can derive gains from social capital, but their interests do not necessarily coincide. For example, the operation of strong bounded solidarity benefits Balinese kinsmen and Andean Catholic peasants, but at the expense of hardworking entrepreneurs in the same collectivities. Similarly, the benefits of enforceable trust in the form of tight social controls accrued to Maltese villages and Vietnamese immigrant communities as a whole, but at the cost of restricting the freedom of their individual members.

Nowhere is this tension more evident than in the contrasting treatment of the concept by Burt and Coleman. As seen throughout this chapter, the latter emphasizes the benefits of social control and thus advocates dense and multiplex social networks similar to those portrayed in the bottom panel of figure 3.4. Dense networks in this case lead to "closure" of parental networks allowing greater control over children and, hence,

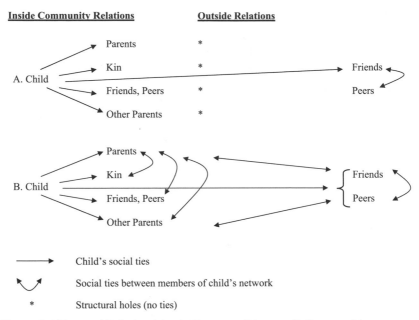

Figure 3.4 Types of Relationships in Dense vs. Dispersed[1] Communities
[1]Adapted from Portes, *The Economic Sociology of Immigration*, p. 261.

greater academic achievement and lesser chances for wayward behavior among the latter.

For Burt, individual social capital depends on the *absence* of these controls and the presence of "structural holes" promoting ties beyond family, neighborhood, and ethnic community. Structural holes are not good for community closure and norm enforcement, but they may be positive for individuals. Thus, the dispersed community portrayed in the top panel of figure 3.4 may offer youths more chances to explore career options and sources of information absent in their own closed group. The benefits of social capital, according to this view, lie in the individual's ability to exploit weak points in the social structures enforcing normative controls.

Social capital is double edged and failure to recognize this intrinsic tension has serious consequences, both at the analytic and practical levels. These realities should also give pause to those who insist on the un-mitigated celebration of community.

CONCLUSION

Economic sociology has in social capital one of its most valuable explanatory tools. Perhaps because of its heuristic value, vigorous attempts have been made to appropriate it, subverting in the process its original intent and meaning. Despite the appeal of these versions, serious analysts should not lose sight of their conceptual shortcomings, not the least of which is to do away with the scientific value of the term. Like some high-tech engineering invention, social capital requires delicate handling.

While the sudden fame of the concept stems from its promise of a ready remedy for a host of social ills, the reality is far more complex as its underlying dynamics are riddled with contradictions: at the individual level, "my" social capital gain may be "your" loss; at the community level, social control and the pursuit of collective values may sacrifice individual autonomy to explore alternative paths. It is precisely these complexities that render the concept valuable for the scientific study of economic life. As a midrange ideal type, social capital is not only operationalizable but also transportable, rendering service as an explanatory tool in a number of different settings and for a wide variety of phenomena. We will see many additional examples of its applicability in the following chapters.

CHAPTER FOUR

The Concept of Institutions

THIS CHAPTER INTRODUCES a second explanatory mechanism that, like social capital, is applicable to a wide range of economic and economically relevant phenomena, but whose heuristic value is also under threat for different reasons.[1] Recent years have brought a significant change in economics and sociology, including an unexpected convergence in their approaches to issues like firms and economic development. This convergence pivots around the concept of institutions, a familiar term in sociology and social anthropology but something of a revolution in economics, dominated so far by the neoclassical paradigm.[2]

This trend has been accompanied by much confusion about what the new master term means and, importantly, by a failure to mine prior theoretical work that sought to order, classify, and relate multiple aspects of social life that are now brought under the same umbrella concept in a rather disorderly fashion. This chapter seeks to reverse these trends by recalling key distinctions in sociological theory and illustrating their analytic utility with examples from the recent research literature. My argument is that recourse to these distinctions provides the means to situate the concept of institutions within a proper theoretical framework. This, in turn, allows its use as a midrange ideal type in the explanation of a variety of economic and economically relevant phenomena.

INSTITUTIONALISM IN ECONOMICS

As Peter Evans has pointed out, the long-held consensus in economics that equated increasing capital stocks with national development has given rise to an emerging view that the key role belongs to "institutions." He approvingly quotes Karla Hoff and Joseph Stiglitz to the point that "development is no longer seen as a process of capital accumulation, but as a process of organizational change."[3] Sociologists of development, including Evans himself and several nonorthodox economists, have been saying the same thing for decades without their arguments swaying the economic mainstream.[4] It was necessary for two Nobel prizes in economics, Joseph Stiglitz and Douglass North, to take the lead in order to accomplish this feat. When North finally declared that "institutions matter," they actually started to be taken into account.

By 2004, the Berkeley economist Gerald Roland could declare that "we are all institutionalists now."[5] Sociologists have generally welcomed this "institutional turn" as a vindication of their own ideas, albeit with an important omission. Swayed perhaps by the promise of interdisciplinary dialogue in the wake of North's declaration, they have commonly overlooked a fundamental fact: economists are not professionally equipped to deal with the multiple elements of social life and, in ad hoc attempts to do so, they confuse them, producing impoverished or simply erroneous diagnoses of reality.

Other observers have noted the same problem and put it in still more critical terms. Geoffrey Hodgson, for example, states: "The blindness may be partial, but the impairment is nevertheless serious and disabling. What is meant by this allegation of blindness is that, despite their intentions, many mainstream economists lack the conceptual apparatus to discern anything but the haziest institutional outlines . . . [they] have not got adequate vision tools to distinguish between different types of institutions, nor to appraise properly what is going on in them."[6] This judgment may be too harsh because, after all, some economists have taken the first steps toward incorporating different aspects of social reality into their analyses. However, the level of interdisciplinary collaboration needed to do this properly and efficiently is still lacking. The first obvious question is what institutions are and the collective answer coming from economics is a rather disparate set of factors that range from social norms, to values and traditions, all the way to "property rights" and complex organizations, such as corporations and agencies of the state. North defined institutions as "any form of constraint that human beings devise to shape human interaction,"[7] a rather vague definition that encompasses everything from norms introjected in the process of socialization to physical coercion.

From this definition, all that can be said is that institutions exist when something exerts external influence over the behavior of social actors: the same notion that Durkheim identified as "norms"[8] more than a century ago and certainly not all there is to social life. To convey the flavor of the ad hoc sociology being developed from economics, two quotes from a recent essay by a development economist will suffice:

[I]n general social norms and values change slowly. Even individual social norms, such as attitudes towards the death penalty or acceptance of corruption tend to change rather slowly, possibly because many norms are rooted on religion whose precepts have changed remarkably little for centuries.[9]

Whatever group holds power will use that power in its own best interest. Thus, ruling elites who have a vested interest in maintaining their power in societies with inefficient institutions may not agree to give up that power because the winners of institutional change may not be able to commit to compensation schemes for the losers.[10]

Norms are indeed rooted in values that tend to resist change, and power structures also change slowly because power holders prefer not to give up their privileges. Confronted with such commonplaces, sociologists have politely demurred, accepting them as perhaps the price to pay for interdisciplinary dialogue. In the enthusiasm for the "institutional turn," some sociologists have even turned to the same practice of lumping together under the same umbrella term distinctions developed over decades of theoretical work. Richard Scott's excellent review of the development of institutionalism makes clear that much selective forgetting has taken place, with ideas such as regulatory mechanisms and normative constraints presented as "new" when they were already present and well developed among the sociological classics.[11]

From the field of socioeconomics have come additional attempts to impose some order on this conceptual chaos. Rogers Hollingsworth, for example, distinguishes among "institutions" (norms, rules, conventions, values, habits, etc.); "institutional arrangements" (markets, states, corporate hierarchies, networks, etc.); "institutional sectors" (financial systems, systems of education, business systems); organizations; and "outputs and performance" (quantity and quality of products, etc.).[12] This typology is, unfortunately, ad hoc, suffering again from the tendency to lump very disparate elements under the same umbrella concept.

Neoinstitutionalism has also traveled to the realm of politics, where it has been used, as in economics, to denote the constraints that the social context puts on the actions of "rational man," thus leading to "bounded rationality."[13] This assertion leaves open the question of what are the features of social context that actually "bound" rational action. Saying simply that everything depends on time and place leads nowhere theoretically. Elinor Ostrom has moved things further by proposing a neoinstitutional analysis of the "Commons" that seeks to solve the dilemma between self-interest and the collective good among users of the same readily available, but exhaustible common resources.[14] Ostrom argues that neither the state nor the market do a very good job in these situations, since they seek to impose external rules. Rather, actors can devise their own enforceable institutional arrangements to escape the tyranny of atomized self-interest. These arrangements are a product of the specific situation and, hence, can vary widely.

In synthesis, the enthusiasm in development economics and related fields for the explanatory value of the new concept has led to a proliferation of definitions and improvised typologies that threaten its usefulness. For without a theoretically rigorous and empirically measurable definition, the power of "institutions" as an explanatory mechanism dissipates. The basis for such a definition already exists and consists of a set of well-established distinctions in sociology, social anthropology, and social psychology. These distinctions allow for an identification of separate elements of social life, their proper placement in the same conceptual framework, and the situations of the idea of institution within it. Only in this manner can the insight that the concept "matters" be put into motion for explanation of economic and economically relevant phenomena.

CULTURE AND SOCIAL STRUCTURE: A PRIMER

From its classic beginnings, modern sociology developed a central distinction, consolidated by the mid-twentieth century, between culture and social structure. There are good reasons for this distinction. Culture embodies the symbolic elements crucial for human interaction, mutual understanding, and order. Social structure is composed of actual persons enacting roles organized in a status hierarchy of some kind. The distinction is analytical because only human beings exist in physical reality, but it is fundamental to understand both the motives for their actions and their consequences. It provides the basis for analyzing, among other things, the difference between what *ought to be* or is *expected to be* and what actually *is* in multiple contexts.

The diverse elements that compose culture and social structure can be arranged, in turn, into a hierarchy of causal influences from "deep" factors, often concealed below everyday social life but fundamental for its organization to "surface" phenomena, more mutable and more readily perceived. Language and values are deep elements of culture, the first as the basic instrument of human communication and means to develop cognitive frames and the second as the motivating force for moral action.

The importance of values ranges, in turn, from fundamental imperatives of a society to traditions prized mostly out of custom. In every instance, values point toward a clear continuum between the desirable and the abhorrent.[15] Values are deep culture because they are seldom invoked in the course of everyday life. Yet they underlie, and are inferred from, aspects of everyday behavior that are the opposite of unrestrained self-interest, the constraints that North and others refer to.

Norms are such constraints. Values represent general moral principles, while norms embody concrete directives for action.[16] These rules can be formal and codified into constitutions and laws, or they can be implicit and informally enforced. The concept of norms has been used, at least since Durkheim, to refer to this restraining element of culture. The significance of the values embodied in norms is reflected in practice in the level of sanctions attached to the latter. Thus life in prison or the death penalty awaits those found guilty of deliberate murder, while loud protest and insulting remarks may be the lot of those seeking to sneak ahead of a queue.[17]

Norms are not free-floating but come together in organized bundles known as *roles*. This sociological and social psychological concept has been widely neglected in the economic literature, which thus deprives itself of a key analytic tool. For it is as role occupants that individuals enter into the social world and as role occupants that they are subject to the constraints and incentives of norms. Roles are generally defined as the set of behaviors prescribed for occupants of particular social positions.[18]

An extensive literature in both sociology and social psychology has analyzed roles as one of the lynchpin concepts linking the symbolic world of culture to real social structures. The same literature has examined in depth such dynamics as the "role set" enacted by individual actors and the "role conflict" or "role strain" created when normative expectations in an actor's role sets contradict one another.[19] None of these analytic concepts has made its appearance in the ad hoc sociology being created from economics or in the neoinstitutionalism as currently practiced in political science. Roles are an integral part of institutions, but they are *not* institutions, and confusing both concepts weakens the heuristic power of both.

Along with normative expectations, roles also embody a cognitive repertoire of skills and "scripts" necessary for their proper enactment. Language is the fundamental component of this repertoire for, without it, no other cognitive skill can be developed. As Paul DiMaggio and Walter Powell properly noted, the most innovative aspect of the new institutionalism in sociology has been its emphasis on cognitive frameworks and scripts as determinants of individual and collective action.[20] Swidler coined the related notion of cultural "tool kits" applicable in a variety of situations, an idea with identifiable parallels to Bourdieu's concept of cultural capital.[21] These theoretical developments have elevated the cognitive elements of culture to a plane comparable to the evaluative/ normative complex in framing and guiding the behavior of actors in roles.[22]

POWER, CLASS, AND STATUS

Parallel to the component elements of culture are those of social structure. These are not made up of moral values or cognitive frames, but by the specific and differentiated ability of social actors to compel others to do their bidding. This is the realm of power, which, like that of values, is situated at the deep level of society influencing a wide variety of outcomes. As seen in chapter 2, Weber's definition of power as the ability of an actor to impose his/her will despite resistance is appropriate, for it highlights the compulsory and coercive nature of this basic element of social structure. It does not depend on the voluntary consent of subordinates and, for some actors and groups to have it, others must be excluded from it.[23] Naturally, elites in control of these resources seek to stabilize and perpetuate their position by persuading others of the fairness of the existing order.[24]

In Marx's definition, power depends on control of the means of production, but in the modern postindustrial world this definition is too restrictive. Power is conferred as well by control of the means of producing and appropriating knowledge, by control of the means of diffusing information, as well as by the more traditional control of the means of violence.[25] In the Marxist tradition, a hegemonic class is one that has succeeded in legitimizing its control of the raw means of power, thus transforming it into authority. Power is not absent from contemporary institutionalist writings, but the emphasis is on authority relations within firms, what Oliver Williamson denominates "hierarchies."[26] Although these analyses are important, they neglect more basic forms of power, including the power to bring firms into being in the first place.

Just as values are embodied into norms, so power differentials give rise to social classes—large aggregates whose possession of or exclusion from resources leads to varying life chances and capacities to influence the course of events. As we shall see in the following chapter, classes need not be subjectively perceived by their occupants in order to be operative, for they underlie the obvious fact that people in society are ranked according to what they can or cannot do or, alternatively, by how far they are able to implement their intentions when confronted with resistance. Class position is associated with wealth, but it is also linked to other power-conferring resources such as human capital or the "right" connections linked to different amounts of social capital.[27]

Class position is not readily transparent and it is a fact, repeatedly verified by empirical research, that individuals with very different means and life chances frequently identify themselves as members of the same "class."[28] Legitimized power (authority) produces, in turn, status hierarchies, which is how most social actors actually perceive the underlying structure of power and how they classify themselves. In turn, status hierarchies are commonly linked to the enactment of occupational roles, as shown in figure 4.1.[29]

The various elements of culture and social structure, placed at different levels of causal importance, all occur simultaneously and appear, at first glance, like an undifferentiated mass. Their analytic separation is required, however, for the proper understanding of social phenomena and economic phenomena, and for reliable predictions of the course that

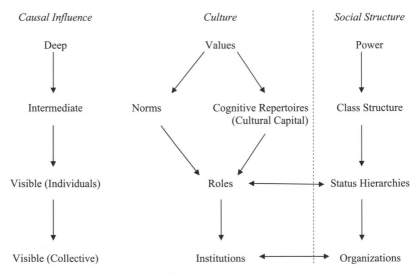

Figure 4.1 Elements of Social Life

they are likely to take. This conceptual spadework has not been done by institutional economics, which has limited itself to some basic typologies without making use so far of the sociological framework already at hand. The result is the present state of confusion about the meaning of institution and the concept's explanatory reach.

The framework presented in this section is summarized in figure 4.1. As the citation supporting it indicates, this framework is neither new nor improvised, but forms part of an intellectual legacy built over the course of more than a century and neglected in the current enthusiasm for the "institutional turn."

INSTITUTIONS IN PERSPECTIVE

As suggested in figure 4.1, status hierarchies do not generally occur in isolation, but form part of social organizations. Organizations, economic and otherwise, are what people normally inhabit in the routine course of their lives, and they embody the most readily visible manifestations of the underlying structures of power. *Institutions* are the symbolic blueprint for organizations. They comprise the set of rules, written or informal, governing relationships among role occupants in organizations like the family, the schools; and the other major institutionally structured areas of social life: the polity, the economy, religion, communications and information, and leisure.[30]

This definition of institutions is in closer agreement with everyday usages of the term, as when one speaks of "institutional blueprints." Its validity does not depend, however, on this overlap but on its analytic utility. My position concerning this and other concepts in this sociological framework is entirely nominalist. I claim no intrinsic reality for any of them, outside of their collective capacity to guide our understanding of social phenomena, including the economy. If, backed by the aura of the Nobel Prize and well-earned fame, North and his followers wish to call individual norms *institutions*, they are certainly entitled to do so, but then they would have to cope with the conceptual problem of the relationship between such *institutions* and the roles in which they coalesce, as well as the symbolic blueprints specifying relationships among such roles and, hence, the actual structure of organizations. As Anthony Giddens has noted, institutions are not social structures, they *have* social structure (i.e., organizations) as the actual embodiment of the symbolic blueprints guiding relationships among roles.[31]

The relationships between organizations and institutions have been treated in sociology in ways more complex than as simple mechanisms for social control. John Meyer and Brian Rowan, among others, have emphasized the influence of institutional environments composed of "powerful rules which function as highly rationalized myths."[32] In Philip Selznick's classic formulation, "to institutionalize is to infuse with value beyond the technical requirements of the task at hand."[33] Such myths and values in the external environment lead, in turn, to isomorphism, as organizations increasingly copy one another seeking ways to adapt to these pressures.[34] In our conceptual framework, external pressures shaping institutional blueprints and leading to adaptive behavior by organizations stem from the deep causal levels of culture and social structure: roles and rules reflect alternative value commitments, cognitive frames, and the power of different actors, individual or collective, to impose their will.

The distinction between organizations and the institutions that underlie them is important because it provides us with a tool for understanding the actual character of social and economic organizations. It is not the case that, once established, role occupants blindly follow institutional rules. Instead, they constantly modify them, transform them, and bypass them in the course of their daily interaction. No doubt, "institutions matter," but they are subject to "the problem of embeddedness": the fact that the human exchanges that institutions seek to guide in turn affect these institutions.[35] This is why formal rules and prescribed hierarchies of organizations come to differ from how they operate in reality. Absent this analytic separation, everything becomes an undifferentiated mass where the recognition that contexts matter produces, at best, descriptive case studies and, at worst, circular reasoning.

The meta-theoretical assumptions of economic sociology are well reflected in this conceptual framework in ways that transform them into usable tools for explanation. Not only does the analytic distinction between institutions and organizations embody the assumption of embeddedness, but it also points to the likely unexpected consequences of rational action. For it is at this level where institutions as "highly rationalized myths" confront the power of social interaction to modify them and set them into alternative paths.[36] As symbolic blueprints for organizations, institutions exist at a midlevel of abstraction that makes them useful for explanation of concrete phenomena. The following sections put this conceptual framework into motion, applying it to the analysis of three specific examples.

The Failure of Institutional Monocropping

One of the most tangible results of the advent of institutionalism to the field of economic development has been the attempt to transplant the institutional forms of the developed West, especially the United States, into the less developed world. The definition of "institutions" employed in such attempts is in close agreement with that advanced here: blueprints specifying the functions and prerogatives of roles and the relationships among their occupants. Institutions and the resulting organizations may be created from scratch—as a central bank, a stock exchange or an ombudsman office—or they may be remolded—as in attempts to strengthen the independence of the judiciary or streamline the local legislature.

Many authors have noted that these attempts to put North and other institutionalists' ideas into practice have not yielded the expected results and have frequently backfired. Peter Evans, in particular, calls these exercises in transplantation "institutional monocropping," in which the set of rules constructed by trial and error over centuries in the advanced countries are grafted into different societies and expected to have comparable results.[37] Gerard Roland diagnoses the cause of these failures as lying in the gap between "slow-moving" and "fast-moving" institutions, but the actual forces at play are much more complex.[38]

Institutional grafting takes place at the surface level of social life and faces the potential opposition of a dual set of forces grounded in the deep structure of the receiving societies: those based on values and those based on power. Within the realm of culture, and to keep the argument simple, consider the different bundles of norms and tool kits that go into formally similar roles. That of "policeman" may entail, in less developed societies, the expectation to compensate paltry wages with bribe taking, a legitimate preference for kin and friends over strangers in the discharge of duties, and skills that go no further than using firearms and readily clubbing civilians at the first sight of trouble. The role of "government minister" may similarly entail the expectation of particularistic preferences in the allocation of jobs and government patronage, appointment by party loyalty rather than expertise, and the practice of using the power of the office to insure the long-term economic well-being of the occupant through variable levels of graft.

Such role expectations are commonly grounded in values that privilege particularistic obligations and ascriptive ties and that encourage suspicion of official bureaucracies and seemingly universalistic rules. When imported institutional blueprints are grafted onto such realities,

results are not hard to imagine. It is not the case that these plans necessarily backfire, but they can have a series of unexpected consequences
following from the fact that those in charge of their implementation and
the presumed beneficiaries view reality through very different cultural
lenses.[39] Figure 4.2 illustrates these dynamics, as well as the argument
that follows.

Institutional grafting has the purpose of strengthening certain branches
of the state, promoting a more efficient allocation of resources, and en-
hancing the attractiveness of the country to foreign investors. These are
worthy goals, but they commonly clash with the interests of those in positions of power. Dominant classes seldom willingly give up their positions
or their power-conferring resources. A struggle almost invariably ensues
in which the advantages of incumbency confer on entrenched elites the
upper hand. This is why it is so difficult to implement agrarian reforms in
the face of organized opposition by landowners, or to increase the international competitiveness of local industries owned by elites accustomed
to protection.[40]

Economists who have analyzed these dynamics recognize the importance of power. Hoff and Stiglitz note, for example, that imposing new

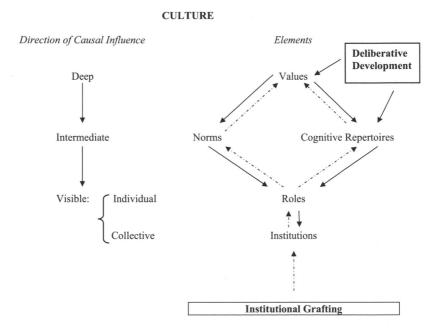

Figure 4.2 Participatory Democracy and Institutional Monocropping

sets of formal rules without simultaneously reshaping the distribution of power is a dubious strategy.[41] Less well understood is another relevant feature discussed previously, namely that the existing class structure may be legitimized by the value system in such a way that change is resisted not only by those in positions of privilege, but by the mass of the population as well. As Weber and the line of Marxist theories inspired by Gramsci recognized, legitimized power is particularly hard to dislodge because the masses not only acquiesce to their own subordination but also stand ready to defend the existing order.[42]

Following the argument of another Nobel Prize winner, Amartya Sen, Evans then offers an alternative to institutional monocropping that he labels "deliberative development." Sen's argument for participatory democracy starts with the notion that "thickly democratic" initiatives, built on public discussion and free exchange of ideas, offer the only way to reach viable developmental goals.[43] For Sen, democratic participation is not only a means to an end but also a developmental goal in itself. Evans agrees, and cites such instances as the "participatory budgeting" process in Brazilian cities dominated by parties of the left as examples of the viability of deliberative development.[44]

Elinor Ostrom's analysis and solution to the "tragedy of the commons," discussed previously, follow parallel lines. She, too, criticizes state attempts to impose external rules and deems them doomed to failure for reasons similar to those described by Evans. Instead, she advocates institutional blueprints that grow out of dialogue and commitments among users of common property resources. Thus, fishers using the same ocean grounds have been able to come up with better and more durable solutions to the depletion of stocks than the set of rules dreamed up by state bureaucrats.[45]

The conceptual framework outlined previously is useful to envision the contrast between institutional grafting and deliberative development. As shown in figure 4.2, the idea of importing institutions begins at the surface level and tries to push its way upward into the normative structure and value system of society. For reasons already seen, such efforts are likely to meet resistance and failure. The participatory strategy begins at the other end, by engaging the population in a broad discussion of developmental goals (values) and the rules (norms) and technical means (skill repertoires) necessary to attain them. Although messy and complicated, the institutional blueprints that eventually emerge from such discussions are likely to be successful because they correspond to the causal directionality of culture itself.

As with institutional grafting, a key problem for deliberative development is presented by the right-side elements of figure 4.1, namely those grounded on power and crystallized in the class structure. Unless dominant classes are somehow persuaded to go along with deliberative experiments, they are not likely to succeed. If implemented against elite resistance, they can be derailed into just talk—deliberation as an end in itself. As Sen recognizes, technocrats (i.e., technically trained elites) prefer to impose institutional blueprints that enhance their power and image rather than subordinate themselves to the messy deliberations of ordinary people. Evans acknowledges, as well, that the dynamics of power are likely to be the biggest impediment to the "institutionalization of deliberative institutions" [sic].[46] Not surprisingly, only when parties of the left have gained solid control of state or regional governments have experiments in participatory democracy had a chance of succeeding. This occurs because authorities can then mobilize the resources of government to neutralize those possessed by elites, persuading them that it is "in their interest" to join the deliberative process.

The Privatization of the Mexican Economy

Starting in 1982, the Mexican state started a massive program of divestiture of the many companies it had created and owned. This program amounted to a radical departure from the previous state-centric model of development and touched the interests and life changes of almost everyone in the country. The shift came in the aftermath of the Mexican default of 1982 and the conditions imposed by the International Monetary Fund (IMF) and the U.S. Treasury to bail out the country. Over the next three *sexenios* (presidential terms), the Mexican state divested itself of almost everything—from the telecommunications company to the banks to the two national airlines (Mexicana de Aviación and Aeroméxico).[47]

This massive economic realignment could not have been accomplished without resistance. There was a great deal of money to be made in state privatization, but there were also a number of actors who lost power, wealth, or their jobs. In a recent study, Dag MacLeod examined how the program was implemented and with what results.[48] Mexico's privatization of the economy amounted to drastic institutional change—a profound modification of the legal/normative blueprints under which firms operate and their internal status hierarchies. This transformation, however, could not have been accomplished at the level of the institutions, for it required the intervention of much deeper social forces.

State-owned enterprises operated with a logic of their own, creating constituencies around themselves. Though frequently inefficient, they gave secure employment to many and political capital to the line ministers and managers who operated them. Thus, Aeroméxico operated with a staff of two hundred employees per airplane at a time when the inefficient and about-to-be-bankrupt Eastern Airlines had 146. Yet, the minute that plans for Aeroméxico's restructuring were announced, its employees struck, arguing that the firm would be profitable "if only" management were more efficient.[49]

The battle for divestment and market opening pitted the unions, managers of state-owned industries, and the ministries that supervised them against a group of reformers imbued with the new neoliberal doctrines at the Treasury Ministry and other strategic places in the government bureaucracy. On the outside, large Mexican capitalists, foreign multinationals, and the IMF supported divestiture and opening; while small firm owners who had much to lose with the removal of state protection opposed it: "Although Mexican capitalists had united briefly—they were soon divided again between large and small, internationally oriented and domestically focused. As President de la Madrid began lowering tariff barriers and allowing greater foreign investment, it soon became clear that labor would not be the only casualty of restructuring."[50]

During President de la Madrid's *sexenio*, only smaller and relatively marginal firms were privatized. Defenders of the status quo could still keep faith that the strong corporatist traditions of the ruling party, the PRI, would in the end prevail. Despite sustained external pressure, institutions (i.e., state-owned corporations) would not reform themselves and attempts to do so were effectively resisted:

> When it became clear during the de la Madrid administration that the very source of political power and patronage—the parastate firm—might actually be taken away, officials within the bureaucracy quickly developed strategies to resist privatization. . . . From their positions on the executive committees and boards of directors of parastate firms, line ministers could keep a watchful eye on the efforts of would-be reformers. Line ministers withheld data or presented contradictory or incorrect data, making it virtually impossible to evaluate the company.[51]

True reform, as the IMF and the multinational corporations envisioned it, could only come from the top of the power structure. This actually happened during the next *sexenio* under President Carlos Salinas de Gortari. A convinced free marketeer, Salinas appointed economists of the same persuasion to key positions in the Central Bank and the Treasury Ministry. Once there, they created new, compact, and powerful agencies to ensure that privatization would move forward. The president shifted the balance of power, abandoning erstwhile allies in the unions, the smaller industrialists, and farmers to establish a firm alliance with the larger and more internationalized sector of the Mexican capitalist class.

Not willing to believe that things would take such a turn for the worse, union leaders and national firm owners bypassed the new bureaucratic structures to take their case directly to the president. To no avail: "When the UDEP [Unit for the Divestiture of Parastate Entities] began the process of privatizing parastate firms, labor leaders, line ministers, and executives of parastate firms often sought to circumvent the authority of UDEP by appealing directly to the President. President Salinas regularly sent these supplicants back to the director of UDEP . . . this process quickly consolidated UDEP's authority within the Mexican bureaucracy."[52]

The "sale of the state" engineered by UDEP in subsequent years amounts to a major case of institutional transformation; it also represents a clear example of the dynamics of power. As shown in figure 4.3, reforms initiated from the outside and from below barely made a dent in the Mexican corporatist structure. It was necessary for the top political and economic leadership of the country to get involved in order to overcome the strong resistance of organized social classes and interest groups. Unionized workers and national entrepreneurs became the losers in this giant power struggle that saw the Mexican labor market become far more "flexible" and the Mexican corporation far more open to external competition and takeover.[53] As elsewhere, significant institutional and organizational change did not originate with organizations, but required major transformations at deeper levels of the social structure.

This example makes clear the significance of power, as embodied in the state and the class structure, and its capacity for radical institutional transformation. As we shall see next, institutions seldom transform themselves. Drastic institutional change commonly requires the intervention of forces buried deep in the culture or the class structure. In the particular case of the Mexican privatization program, change was imposed from the heights of the power structure but without much consensual support, as it took place against a background of public skepticism about the need to denationalize the economy and strong opposition from several sectors of

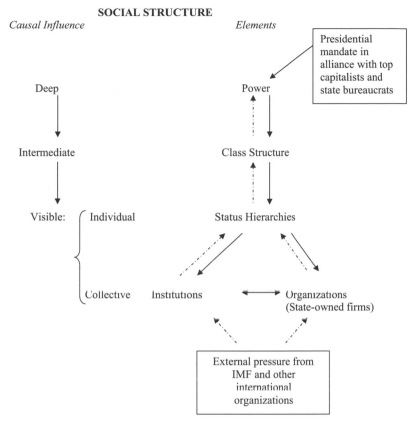

Figure 4.3 The Divestiture of Parastate Corporations in Mexico

society. This lack of legitimacy was to have consequences: Salinas ended his term in disgrace, becoming an unpopular figure and being eventually forced to leave the country. While the course in which he set the Mexican economy remains unchanged, there have been growing signs of resistance from large segments of the population as the announced benefits of privatization have failed to materialize.[54]

The Problem of Change

In his book *Institutional Change and Globalization*, John Campbell describes the different schools of institutional analysis that exist today. These he labels "Rational Choice Institutionalism," associated primarily with economics; "Organizational Institutionalism," associated with the sociology of organizations; and "Historical Institutionalism," based on political economy and certain strands of political science.[55] Depending on the school, social change is seen primarily as an evolutionary process, developing gradually over time, or as a combination of evolution and "punctuated evolution" when drastic shifts occur.

Despite these differences, all three schools are identified by Campbell as favoring two major forces as determinants of change. These are "path dependence," meaning the tendency of events to follow a set course where "what existed yesterday" largely determines what happens today and what is likely to occur tomorrow; and "diffusion" meaning the tendency of established institutional patterns to migrate, influencing the course of events in other societies. Diffusion is identified by the school led by John Meyer as a master process in the contemporary global system in which the institutions of the advanced nations, particularly the United States, are commonly reproduced in weaker, poorer societies, either under the aegis of international agencies or out of the desire of local rulers to imitate the modern world.[56]

Campbell argues that "the problem of change" has been a thorny one for institutional analysis. This is not difficult to understand. First, with a vague and contested definition of "institution," the analysis of change confronts a moveable target. When institutions can be anything—from the incest taboo to the central bank—we do not have a sufficiently delimited object to examine how it changes over time. The proposed sociological definition—blueprints that govern the patterned, regular relationships among role occupants in organizations—is sufficiently specific to allow consideration of how processes of change in this sector of social life takes place. Thus defined, institutional change is *not* the same as change in the class structure or in the value system, processes that ultimately affect institutions, but that occur at deeper levels of society.

Second, with concepts such as path dependence and diffusion as its main tools for the analysis of change, it is not difficult to understand how the predicted course of events for institutional analysis would be evolution or, at most, "punctuated evolution." Indeed, at the surface of social life, change tends to be gradual, with patterned ways of doing things largely determining the course of events. Cross-national diffusion of culture may operate at a deeper level, affecting not only institutional blueprints but also the normative and skill contents of specific roles. Diffusion of new technologies (skills repertoires) and patterns of consumption (norms) from the advanced world to the less developed countries is indeed one of the most common and most important sources of change in these countries.[57]

However, the determinants of change are not limited to diffusion and path dependence, for they can also affect deeper levels of the culture and social structure, producing drastic, nonevolutionary outcomes. To be sure, as sometimes argued by institutionalists, radical events often have long periods of gestation, but, once they burst into reality, consequences for the affected society can be abrupt and frequently traumatic. Technological change, to take one example, can be endogenous and not only brought about by diffusion. Once they occur, technological breakthroughs can affect, in a very short time, the skills repertoires and the roles played by social actors. One such example is the advent of the Internet, an innovation that has altered the content of occupational roles and the rules linking them in most institutions of modern society.[58] Figure 4.4 summarizes the discussion so far, as well as the points that follow.

Religion and religious prophecies can affect the culture in still more profound ways because they impinge directly on the value system. Weber's theory of social change focuses on the history of religion and, specifically, on the role of charisma and charismatic prophecy as forces capable of breaking through the limits of reality, as hitherto known, and providing the impetus necessary to tear down the existing social order and rebuild it on a new ideological blueprint. The influence of the

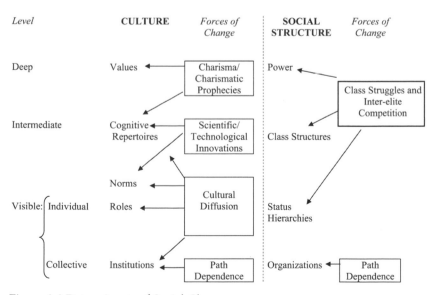

Figure 4.4 Determinants of Social Change

Reformation and, especially Calvinism, in revolutionizing economic life in Western Europe is perhaps the best-known illustration of the effects that charismatic prophecy can have on society.[59]

The advent of charismatic prophecy capable of revolutionizing the value system and, hence, an entire civilization, occurs after a long period of historical gestation, but this does not prevent it from having an immediate and profound effect once it bursts onto the scene. After Calvinism had transformed the social order of much of Western Europe, historians had little difficulty in tracing the concatenation of events that led to it. But they would not have bothered to engage in such an exercise had Luther not nailed those theses at Wittenberg and had Calvin not come to power in Geneva. Post-hoc reconstruction of revolutionary social change can always be "evolutionary."

For those who dismiss the role of religious charisma as a thing of the past, one only needs to point to the decisive influence that Evangelical Christianity continues to have in transforming large portions of American society and to the emergence of a fundamentalist brand of Islam set on ultimate confrontation with the West. The radical Islamist threat that is today one of the overriding concerns of states in North America and Western Europe is interpretable as a direct consequence of a reenergized, charismatic religious prophecy seeking to remake the world in its own image.[60]

Revolutionary change can also come from the right side in figure 4.4, as when power is wrested away from its current possessors and vested on a new elite. The question of power, and its embodiment in the class structure, will be addressed in the following chapter. For the time being, it suffices to note that the significance of power, as a meta-assumption, is reflected in the capacity of those in control of the necessary resources to implement radical changes at the more visible levels of social life, including institutions. The privatization of Mexican parastate institutions provides a suitable example. The attempt by left-wing elites to legitimize drastic changes through "deliberative development" provides another.

Seen from the perspective of the profound consequences wrought by transformations of a society's value system or class structure, a theory of social change based on path dependence and cultural diffusion looks limited indeed. Change—whether revolutionary or not—at more profound levels filters downstream to the more visible components of social life, including institutions and organizations. Thus it is possible to distinguish at least five sets of forces impinging on institutions and leading to their transformation: path dependence, producing evolutionary change at the more visible level; diffusion also leading to evolutionary and sometimes "punctuated" change at the intermediate levels of culture; scientific/ technological breakthroughs affecting the cultural skills repertoire and normative order. At a deeper level, charismatic prophecy—religions or secular—capable of transforming the value system and, hence, the rest of the culture; and interelite and class struggles with the capability for radically changing the distribution of power. The last three sources hold the potential for profound social change, of the type seen in the aftermath of social revolutions and epoch-making inventions.

Figure 4.4 summarizes this discussion. John Campbell concludes his review of institutional change by recommending that we consider such processes only within well-limited time frames and "in its multiple dimensions."[61] These recommendations are unobjectionable, but do not go far enough. While limited time frames are a way of preventing infinite regress into history, they do not distinguish between evolutionary change over a given period and abrupt, revolutionary transformations. Similarly, the "multiple dimensions" to be considered in the analysis of change are left unspecified. An institutional analysis of change limited to institutions themselves and the organizations that they underlie would produce a rather impoverished account of these processes. Institutions do not transform themselves in radical ways. As an explanatory ideal type, their value lies in embodying the interplay between deeper levels of culture and social structure in ways that directly impinge on social actors and the organizations that they inhabit.

CONCLUSION: EMBEDDEDNESS, INSTITUTIONALISM, AND THE CLASS STRUCTURE

The conceptual framework outlined in this chapter may perform double duty in providing a way to reconcile conflicting positions on the scope of economic sociology and its proper object of study. Granovetter's article on embeddedness was a polemic against both functionalist descriptions of human behavior in sociology, that overemphasized the role of values, and their counterparts in neoclassical economics, that overemphasized the role of interests. In their place, Granovetter proposed a "relational" approach in which the influence of both, values and interests, is conditioned by the social context in which they are enacted. Embeddedness of economic action in networks, communities, and other stable forms of human interaction takes the edge away, for example, from the sharp distinction between "markets" and "hierarchies" proposed by the economist Oliver Williamson.[62]

The embeddedness argument has been subsequently criticized from a Marxist-inspired political economy perspective for neglecting the importance of power and asymmetrical class relations.[63] For Fred Block and other critics, Granovetter was too influenced by the "level field" imagery of markets used by economists so that the constraints on self-interested behavior that he describes arise more from interactions among social equals than from the will of the powerful. From a political economy perspective, the debate about "markets" and "hierarchies" conveys a sanitized view of the economy consisting of buyers, sellers, managers, and employees, obscuring the harsh realities of exploitation and inequality.

From closer theoretical quarters came the critique that the influence of social interaction that the embeddedness approach emphasizes neglects the true significance of institutions, defined, as here, as rules and their embodiment in legal codes and legally sanctioned organizations. North's claim that "institutions matter" is taken seriously by these critics. Their point, as advanced by Victor Nee and others, is that formal rules, like constitutions and property rights, have an important influence on economic life, regardless of social networks or the gradual build-up of reciprocity expectations.[64]

The conceptual framework proposed here makes clear that the critiques of Granovetter by both political economists and neoinstitutionalists are misplaced. This is the case because these critics address aspects of social and economic life other than those highlighted by the embeddedness argument. While, as seen in chapter 2, this argument provides a core meta-assumption for economic sociology, it never claimed to offer a comprehensive description of everything that goes on in society or the economy. Its substantive scope, as well as those of its critics, can be perfectly accommodated within the same conceptual framework. From this perspective, both "markets" and "hierarchies" are *institutions* representing blueprints for the patterned interaction among role occupants in their respective organizational fields. As summarized in figure 4.5, political economy concerns itself with the right-side dynamics of social structure—power, inequality, and the formation and interplay of classes. As seen previously, these dynamics significantly affect institutions and organizations, but they do not exhaust what actually takes place in them.

In turn, sociological neoinstitutionalists concern themselves with the left-side realm of "crystallized culture"—the interplay of norms and legal codes governing market exchange and the internal structuring of

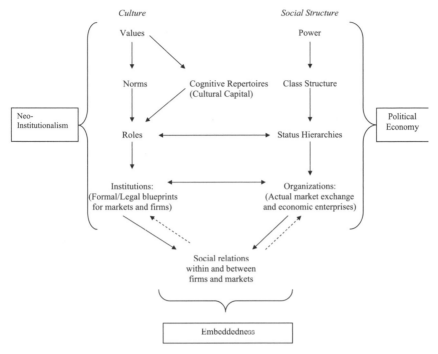

Figure 4.5 Topical Emphases on Economy and Society

economic organizations. Nee defines institutions, for example, as "a dominant system of interrelated formal and informal elements—custom, shared beliefs, conventions, norms, and rules—which actors orient their actions when they pursue their interests."[65] The focus of Granovetter and the embeddedness argument is on how social interactions *within* markets and other organizations can modify, condition, and often alter their original institutional logic by creating networks, reciprocity expectations, and emergent norms not envisioned originally.

Figure 4.5 situates each of these specific concerns in conceptual space. In my view, each of them is valid and economic sociology can properly encompass all of them. The apparent contradictions arise from terminological confusion, in particular the vague and changing definitions of *institution*, and the fundamental fact that the complexity of social and economic life cannot be captured by one single concept or, for that matter, a single perspective. Much space has been wasted criticizing what are, in effect, alternative topical lenses. While it is true that an exclusive focus on the left side of figure 4.5 may lead to an oversocialized image of human action and an exclusive focus on the right side to an undersocialized view, this need not happen because the two approaches are, in fact, compatible.

The critiques of political economists and neoinstitutionalists on the embeddedness argument boil down to the point that it too can be exaggerated into an extreme form of relationism. This is true, but again need not happen. The social sciences in general and sociology, in particular, should have progressed to the point that the discovery that different areas of social life—values, classes, and institutions—"matter" need not lead us to neglect others or deny their significance. In this sense, an economic sociology grounded on meta-assumptions that include both social embeddedness and power and guided by a set of midrange ideal types is perfectly reconcilable with the alternative thematic foci represented in figure 4.5.

CHAPTER FIVE

The Concept of Social Class

MARSHAL MICHEL NEY, one of Napoleon Bonaparte's greatest generals, was approached on a social occasion by a countess of the old French nobility who, wanting to poke fun at the parvenu nobles created by the Bonapartist regime asked him, "And Marechal, who are your ancestors?"[1] Raising his towering figure over the assembled audience, Ney replied, "Madame, I am my own ancestor."[2] The answer was, no doubt, influenced by the winds of egalitarianism whistling from the all-too-recent Jacobin past and the example of the newly crowned emperor, in military obscurity one day and onto the French throne the next. Despite these extraordinary events, the social order of France and the concert of Europe were eventually restored: Louis XVIII came back in the wagons of the English-led European coalition; Metternich convened the Quadruple Alliance and set out to suppress popular rebellions. Ancestors, once again, counted.[3]

In the wake of another historical demise, that of the Soviet Union and its satellites, Ney's bold stance against the *ancien régime* has been revindicated. The way in which it was, is both curious and instructive. The defeated Leninist regimes were precisely based on a critique of modern capitalist societies as dedicated to the perpetuation of class privilege. In lieu of them, Lenin and his followers promised a world where the door would be opened wide to the energies and achievements of all. The failure of this project brought down the analytic premises that had sustained it. Because the defeated communists had affirmed that capitalist societies were structured by class inequalities, their failure meant that these inequalities did not really exist or that they did not count for much. In the newly assertive capitalist societies of the West, each man could indeed be "his own ancestor."

Class analysis is on its way out, largely as an outgrowth of this curious process. Former Marxist scholars have rushed to disassociate themselves from its premises and to proclaim a brave new world where cultural trends and lifestyle issues will be the prime molders of public opinion and collective movements. In a steadier vein, American stratification scholars have reaffirmed the primacy of finely grained hierarchies of skills and prestige over alleged major cleavages in power. Thus, Meyer and his associates have repeatedly emphasized the significance of educational differences, while analysts of social inequality have focused their attention on racial and gender gaps in the otherwise continuous distributions of income and occupational prestige.[4]

This chapter is dedicated to an analysis of social class as a third explanatory mechanism for economic sociology. Unlike the first two, discussed in prior chapters, which are quite fashionable these days, social class is not. The political events leading to this situation are comprehensible but, by themselves, do not justify abandonment of social class as a midrange ideal type. This is especially the case since it directly reflects and fleshes out the third meta-assumption of economic sociology, namely power.

The contemporary attacks on this concept come from multiple theoretical and ideological quarters. In unison, however, detractors of class analysis have emphasized the lack of correspondence between alleged class differences and the self-identities of people. They have also noted that popular mobilizations seldom occur around broad class issues, but around more circumscribed concerns of lifestyle and occupational privileges.[5] Seeking to salvage what they can from this debacle, David Grusky and Jesper Sørensen present a defense of class analysis redefined to exclude broad social aggregates, and restricted to occupationally defined groupings. By "ratcheting down" (their term) class categories to the level of specific occupations, Grusky and Sørensen hope to bring the analysis into closer correspondence with a realist definition, based on the perceptions and behavior of actual people: "The class analytic fallacy amounts then to insisting on aggregate models even when the underlying categories are no longer so deeply institutionalized. By contrast, a disaggregate mapping preserves this correspondence between lay and scholarly understandings."[6]

Supporters of classic Marxist and Weberian theories may justly respond that, with friends like these, who needs enemies. Indeed, bringing down the definition of social class to the level of specific occupations removes the raison d'être of the concept, as it becomes lost in a kaleidoscope of endless identities and occupational concerns at a low level of abstraction. It is undoubtedly the case that individual self-identities, organizational "closure," and uniform lifestyles are more evident among members of occupations, but the analysis of such patterns can be perfectly advanced without invoking the concept of class. The latter inhabits a midlevel of abstraction that aims at bringing order into this empirical chaos by identifying a set of broad categories and bringing it to bear on the explanations of a variety of economic and social phenomena.

Contrary to Grusky and Sørensen's argument, I seek to demonstrate that the concept, defined according to its original Marxian and Weberian roots, continues to occupy a key role for sociological theory. For economic sociology, in particular, class is a central element in the analysis of the ways in which economic phenomena are socially embedded. Classes reflect differentials of power that, in turn, affect interactions among actors situated within each of these broad categories.

The argument in favor of the concept of class comprises three interrelated points:

1. The validity of the concept for explanation and prediction does not depend on personal self-definitions.
2. A class framework is required to clarify the deep causes of multiple economic processes. Absent such framework, causal accounts are often swayed by surface manifestations of these processes.
3. The utility of class analysis does not depend on dogmatic adherence to nineteenth-century typologies, but on the use of the concept as a heuristic tool, modifiable according to evolving conditions.

CLASS ANALYSIS IN THE PAST

The Realist Fallacy

Critics of class analysis request not only that the concept provide plausible explanations, but that actors actually endorse them. Thus, when Wall Street investment bankers mount a campaign to weaken federal regulations of corporate mergers, their actions count against class analysis insofar as they are undertaken by "managers and administrators" in the name of the "stock-owning public's" welfare. Similarly, when public schoolteachers mobilize against the use of vouchers for private schooling or American health workers seek to restrict the hiring of immigrants, their actions are defined as "occupational closure" rather than as reflecting any underlying pattern of class struggle. Theoretical analysis is thus put at the mercy of the conscious definitions of participants in particular events.

In Marxist terminology, only a mobilized class—a "class-for-itself"— is deserving of the name; otherwise class represents a useless construct.[7] It is true that classical Marxism and most of its revisionist versions sought the transformation of latent class interests into actual forces of revolutionary struggle, but the ultimate validity of the concept does not hinge on these expectations. That validity depends, instead, on its ability to make sense of macrosocial trends and to anticipate the behavior of economic actors. A conscious mobilization of social classes on the basis of broadly shared interests represents *one* such outcome, but not necessarily the only one.

The desire for a protagonical role for social classes, especially the proletariat, assumes what must be investigated. It has also placed generations of Marxist scholars in the uncomfortable position of disappointed prophets, forever waiting for the masses to vindicate their predictions.[8] For economic sociology, the utility of a class perspective depends on the development of typologies and classificatory criteria that are neutral with respect to their final outcome. A useful parallel can be established with the concepts in modern demographic analysis. Demographic concepts, such as population density, rate of population growth, ratio of economically active to dependent population, fertility transitions, and the like are routinely and successfully used in analyses of numerous phenomena by *failing* to make the assumption that participants are self-aware of these constructs or that they lead to some preordained outcome. Rural-urban migrants, those affected by low life expectancies, and those living in dense areas are not expected to become conscious of their common plight and act in unison; nor are these demographic indicators assumed to lead to some inevitable future.

Class analysis has been notably bereft of this sort of neutrality. Instead, the passion for revolutionary change and the urge to bring it about consistently obscure the analytic detachment required for proper evaluation of the facts. Since Lenin, a number of class theorists have taken to scolding the proletariat for failing to fulfill its "historical" revolutionary role and, in the process, contradicting their prophecies.[9] This is surely a dead end. Not surprisingly, the predictive failures of this tradition opened the way for such sad remedies as turning the analysis of social classes into the analysis of occupations.

The Classless Fallacy

Not long ago, the National Research Council (NRC) commissioned a distinguished panel of social scientists to prepare a report on the consequences of contemporary immigration for American society. Formed primarily by economists, the panel focused mainly on the "costs" of immigration measured in terms of fiscal outlays by the federal and state government and the countervailing "benefits," measured in terms of tax contributions. The final report featured a series of highly sophisticated models where, depending on the assumptions used by the author, immigration ended up costing the nation several dozen billion dollars a year or contributing to its fiscal health by a similar hefty sum.[10]

The panel spent no time in examining how immigration affected different sectors of the American population. Instead, its implicit "map" of American society consisted of a level field of isolated individuals paying taxes to the state and receiving benefits from it. Immigrants just added to this number and their aggregate impact depended on the specific ratio of taxes to benefits. There is no hint in the NRC report of the major cleavages splitting the nation on the question of immigration or of the possibility that some sectors may benefit mightily from the arrival of newcomers and others may pay a hefty price for their presence. Put differently, the NRC panel had no idea, or chose not to delve into the American class structure and the different ways in which mass immigration may affect different social classes. The result is an unpersuasive report since it is obvious that the consequences of immigration are not exhausted by what migrants put into state coffers and what they take from them.

Whenever an analysis of major social processes neglects the underlying class structure, results are bound to be limited, if not trivial. This applies to other broadly encompassing phenomena such as crime and incarceration, educational achievement, or patterns of consumption. The classless fallacy consists of assuming that the incidence and effects of major processes in society occur evenly across the population with variations being affected by individual, family, or at best community characteristics. The resulting accounts are quite limited because they ignore differences in the incidence of such phenomena, patterned by major cleavages of power. Crime rates and especially incarceration are not evenly distributed, but shift abruptly across classes distinguished by different levels of economic and social resources. Attendance at Ivy League schools and rates of graduation from them are similarly conditioned by family class position. Consumption patterns shift widely among the masses, limited to purchases for survival, and those able to consume conspicuously, signaling a position of privilege.[11]

Additional examples will be examined in detail later on. For the moment, it suffices to note that enduring accounts of major social processes always contain a map of the class structure to which reference is made in order to clarify the differential and sometimes contradictory effects of particular forces. It is not necessary that the analyst provides an explicit account of his or her understanding of class differences or that the latter be identical in every case. It suffices that the narrative indicates an awareness of the role that these broad aggregates play in the process in question and the differential ways in which they are affected by it. Saskia Sassen's well-known account of the rise of global cities emphasizes the dynamics of global capitalism and the need to concentrate command and control functions in certain metropolitan areas. Yet her analysis would have been incomplete without a detailed account of the class structure and the redefined roles of its components in the global city.[12]

Sociology has emphasized since its origins the existence of sharp cleavages in political and economic power and their influence on manifold social phenomena. When Charles Tilly, to take another example, gives us his account of four hundred years of political struggles in France, his implicit social map does not feature groups positioned in a continuous distribution of income or social rank, but rather sharply defined aggregates marked by ownership of land, entitlement to rents from the peasantry, or the lack of any such entitlement.[13] Similarly, when Pierre Bourdieu analyzes the consumption of high art as a sign of possession of cultural capital and a symbolic demarcation of class differences, he does not have in mind a finely grained ladder of art forms associated with differential levels of education. Instead, he bases his analysis on the sharp and discontinuous cleavages separating power elites from the middle salaried groups and working masses.[14]

For economic sociology, the incorporation of class as an explanatory ideal type is fundamental to avoid the classless fallacy and, hence, the criticism, reviewed in the prior chapter, that it envisions economic exchange as taking place in a level playing field. To the contrary, power as a meta-assumption and its embodiment in the class structure allows the addition of a political economy perspective to those suggested by other assumptions. It bears repeating that the imputation of causal effects to class cleavages need not coincide with the actual definition of the situation by actors. Individuals may proceed blissfully unaware of the underlying forces giving rise to their behavior, but serious sociological analysis cannot limit itself to this surface level. Table 5.1 fleshes out the different levels of causal significance described in chapter 4 by considering how different analytic perspectives bear on two important social phenomena mentioned previously—crime and incarceration and immigration.

TABLE 5.1
Social Phenomena from Different Analytic Perspectives

Perspective	Immigration	Crime and Incarceration
Classless: Society as a level playing field	Prompted by individual motivations for economic mobility. Cost or benefit to society depends on migrants' tax contributions and their demand on educational, health, and welfare services.	Reflects weakening of normative controls and individual cost-benefit calculations of risks *vs.* potential benefits of deviant behavior.
Gradational: Society as a system of finely grained status hierarchies	Expands the low-education, low-income population requiring additional services. Upward mobility as an equilibrium-restoring mechanism.	Negatively correlated with income and education. Declines with reductions in unemployment and with the size of the police.
Class: Society as structured by sharp inequalities of power	Promoted by organized political efforts by employers. Opposed by unions and native workers. Weakens working-class solidarity through ethnic cleavages.	Prompted by major gaps in access to legitimate means to fulfill material aspirations. Likelihood of incarceration for a given offense is disproportionately higher for the subordinate classes.

The Reification Fallacy

In his extraordinary history of the origins of the capitalist economy, British historian Maurice Dobb cites Marx several dozen times. Not one of these references over the 393 pages of his *Studies in the Development of Capitalism* is critical or negative. It would seem that Marx had foreseen every event, examined every contingency, and unfailingly diagnosed the contradictions produced by capitalism and its inevitable demise.[15] The tendency is even more evident in the distinguished French historian Ernest Mandel's *Late Capitalism*, whose goal is precisely to explain modern economic history on the basis of the "laws of motion" of capital discovered by Marx.[16] To the present, a great deal of class writings from this tradition has focused on debates about how to fit an increasingly diverse population into the mappings of class structure inherited from Marx's nineteenth-century analysis.

Curiously, Marx proved considerably more flexible in his own writings than his disciples. His accounts of the cleavages produced by different modes of production changed with the context, producing multiple versions of the capitalist class structure. Thus the classes identified in the final, interrupted chapter of the third volume of *Capital* are only a subset of those underlying his historical accounts of the *Eighteenth Brumaire* or of French class struggles in the mid-nineteenth century.[17] The otherwise moving deference to the founder, shown by many Marxist scholars, weakens the power and scope of class analysis because it forces into a relatively static framework changing economic and political realities. Intellectual contortions are required to fit increasingly diversified economic positions into a nineteenth-century typology, and to reconcile the expectation of conscious, class-for-itself mobilizations with the reality of relatively inert social aggregates.

Grusky and Sørensen are right that occupationally based associations are far more active politically and produce greater closure than those based on classic Marxist definitions of class. However, calling occupations "classes" leaves no baby after the bath water. To retain the power of class analysis and extend its application to the wide variety of phenomena encompassed by economic sociology, it is necessary to leave the founders to their well-deserved rest. The following propositions offer a counter to the reification fallacy:

- Basic cleavages of political and economic power change over time, giving rise to different class configurations.
- Classes are *midrange theoretical constructs* devised for the structural interpretation of social phenomena and the prediction of major long-term trends.

From these assumptions, two logical corollaries follow:

- The number, composition, and patterns of interaction of social classes will vary over time.
- Particular "maps" of the class structure used for the explanation of different social phenomena may vary, without rendering such variations necessarily invalid.

Much of the existing post-Marx class literature resists these assumptions. It implicitly or explicitly asserts that the "real" class structure must first be identified in order to apply it afterward to the analysis of various phenomena. As it happens in every instance when theorists confuse ideal types with reality itself, a great deal of debate follows as authors vie with one another to identify what this "real" structure is. The nominalist perspective proposed here leaves these debates behind by setting the value of a particular definition of class structure on its explanatory power in relation to a particular set of phenomena. The question then becomes to what extent a specific definition of the class structure yields the most theoretically insightful account of these processes.

For the analysis of certain problems, a two-class model suffices; others may require three or four. To return to an earlier point, Marx shifted with remarkable nimbleness between alternative models of the class structure as he sought to explain various aspects of the societies of his time. In the *Manifesto*, the two-class confrontation between bourgeoisie and proletariat holds center stage, but in the *Eighteenth Brumaire*, the peasantry and the lumpen play key roles.

Richard Sennett and Jonathan Cobb's classic book, *The Hidden Injuries of Class*, relies on a simple two-class model of American society—those privileged to have economic means and education and those who must do manual work for a living.[18] The merit of the book does not hinge on the accuracy or completeness of this simple distinction, but on how well it serves the authors to account for their topic: the malaise, insecurity, and self-doubt felt by blue-collar workers in a large American city. Nor does the analysis depend on the workers' being fully aware of their plight; indeed, the injuries are "hidden" precisely because the victims cannot fully comprehend the set of social forces leading to their condition and trapping them in it.

BASIC ASSUMPTIONS OF CLASS ANALYSIS

Having reviewed the various pitfalls bedeviling class analysis—from its wholesale rejection to its reification—I seek next to identify the core insights captured by the concept that make it durable and relevant. These insights may be summarized in four statements:

- Social phenomena are not explainable by their surface manifestations. There is "deep structure," defined by durable inequalities, among large social aggregates.
- Classes are defined by their relationships to one another and not simply by a set of "gradational" positions along some hierarchy. In this sense, status rankings are a manifestation, not a defining feature of class.
- Classes are defined by differential access to power within a given social system.
- Class position is transmissible across generations.

These four elements flesh out the meta-assumption of power and provide criteria both for constructing suitable "maps" of the class structure and using them for the analysis of concrete economic and social phenomena. The first three of these elements have already been seen in chapter 4 in connection with the proper placement of the concept of institutions and the determinants of social change. It is worth focusing here on the fourth element, namely transmissibility.

Control over power resources that define a position of dominance in society is transmissible across generations. This element is important because it removes, as a criterion of class, power that depends exclusively on office-holding. Class position may translate into eligibility to occupy certain offices and the latter may, in turn, confer durable resources on occupants, but the bureaucratic authority derived from an office is not, by itself, class defining. In the absence of other resources, the officeholder suddenly deprived of his or her position is utterly powerless. On the contrary, a third-generation heir of a great family fortune can shift from job to job or even choose not to work at all without this altering her privileged class position.

Class-defining power has to do with the regular and autonomous control of the means of violence or the means of acquisition, that is, money capital. This is in general agreement with the usage of the term *class* by Marx, although he emphasized control of the means of production as a source of both repressive capacity and wealth.[19] In advanced societies, regular control of the means of violence has been largely removed from individuals, leaving wealth as the principal power-conferring resource. As Bourdieu has pointed out, other resources are also associated with class position, such as the possession of technical or cultural skills—sometimes called human capital—or membership in particular social networks, which he labels social capital. Bourdieu makes the point, however, that these resources are power conferring insofar as they are ultimately translatable into the money form.[20]

The typology of the American class structure presented in the next section follows Bourdieu's lead by assuming that expertise or connections that do not "pay" do nothing to improve the class position of individual actors. While undoubtedly a number of other social and cultural dimensions are associated with class position, it is possible to construct a useful typology of the modern American class system on the basis of a key defining criterion. Wealth and wealth-conferring resources recommend themselves for this task because of their simplicity and obvious connection to power, as defined previously.[21] Class position, defined by differential possession of wealth, provides the broad framework of social inequality within which economic phenomena take place and where interactions among economic actors transcur on a regular basis.

THE CLASS STRUCTURE OF THE ADVANCED SOCIETIES

The following map of the American class structure seeks to give concrete expression to the four elements discussed in the prior section and to demonstrate the utility of the concept for the analysis of specific phenomena. As said previously, the typology is nominalist in the sense that it does not seek to capture the "real" or "true" essence of the class system, but only to construct a useful approximation to it for several specific applications. Accordingly, the following sections should be read as a "demonstration project" of what class analysis can achieve rather than a final statement either about the class structure itself or the phenomena to which the typology is applied.

The Dominant Classes

Wealth represents a fundamental divide in modern capitalist society with possessors and nonpossessors expected to behave differently and line up systematically on opposite sides of many political issues. This statement, by itself, is a truism and needs to be refined by identifying subsidiary cleavages within each of these broad social aggregates. Owners of wealth are, of course, not equal and their relative control of this resource can be used to categorize them.

First, we find individuals whose wealth liberates them from the need to sell their labor time for a living. For purposes of class analysis, it does not matter whether they exercise this option or not. It suffices that they have it within their power to withdraw themselves at any time from their position in the labor market. Hence, two persons working side by side may occupy different class positions depending on their relative possession of wealth— one doing so voluntarily and the other because of economic need. This first class of wealth possessors may be termed *rentiers* for two reasons: first, their capital is too small to reproduce itself actively in independent enterprise and must do so as passive investment in the economic activities of others; second, their political contributions and influence are too minute to alter the economic rules of the game in their personal favor.

Rentiers differ from the second class of wealth possessors whose fortune is of sufficient size to require active management. Whether the proprietor is directly involved in these activities or not is immaterial, for the very size of the capital drives the need to hire others. Wealth of this kind acquires its own dynamic, actively seeking new opportunities for reproduction and expansion. People in this category are commonly prominent in their places of residence, carrying considerable weight with local authorities and making gifts that fund local cultural and philanthropic initiatives.[22]

Members of this class generally lack the power to swing single-handedly major economic policies in their favor but, in association with others, they can fund powerful lobbies able to accomplish this goal. In contrast with rentiers, the political contributions and activities of this class of people are not anonymous, for they are of an order of magnitude sufficiently large to gain the attention of elected officials and directly affect their actions. The *sugar lobby*, the *growers' lobby*, various *builders' associations* are familiar terms that designate these collective interests as they impinge on official rules governing various markets. *Capitalists* is a proper term for this class of proprietors since they fit, in every respect, the known profile of the propertied elites under classic competitive capitalism. Marxist and non-Marxist writers alike have dwelt on the personal identification of these people with their wealth and their collective power to impose their interests on society.[23]

Above regular capitalists, there is a numerically minute but socially decisive class composed of individuals whose extraordinary wealth puts them in a position to influence decisions at the national level and to impose their will on vast sectors of the economy, either directly through the corporations they control or indirectly through the political process. These are individuals whose names are linked to fortunes in the hundreds of millions of dollars and the control of vast financial and industrial empires. When they turn their attention to philanthropy, they are able to fund private organizations that commonly match or exceed the resources of state agencies. Ford, Mellon, Rockefeller, Carnegie, and, these days, Soros and Gates are so many names, familiar to scholars and other lucky recipients of their private largesse.

In Marxist theory, this class is usually labeled *monopoly capitalists* to differentiate it from the more common variety.[24] However, it is not the case that the achievement and reproduction of such fortunes necessarily require monopoly. The latter is difficult to sustain under conditions of state regulation in modern economies so that wealth of this kind is associated with the discovery and temporary occupation of uniquely profitable economic niches. *Grand capitalists* is a suitable label for members of this class. Their difference from regular capitalists is more than the simple size of their holdings. While regular capitalists need to associate with their fellows in order to gain privileges and influence major economic decisions, their superiors can do so on their own by dint of their control of vast monetary and organizational resources.

In addition, the economic interests of grand capitalists are global in scope and, hence, do not always coincide and may actually come into conflict with those of smaller, locally minded proprietors. Hence, to cite but a familiar example, the desire of grand capital for free trade in order to gain access to other countries' markets and labor comes regularly into conflict with the need of local capitalists for protection against foreign competition in order to maintain their firms' profit levels.[25]

Common to the three classes of wealth possessors is that individuals need not be born into them, but can access them through extraordinary skill and luck. The "self-made millionaire" and multiple "rags to riches" stories are the basis of the myth of an open society, where positions of privilege are readily accessible to all. These stories are, of course, highly exceptional. Far more common is the transmission of class position across generations. Thus, lucky descendants who, through no merit of their own are born into wealth, can enjoy similar or higher levels of power and prestige than their dynasty's founder. In America, people speak of the Kennedys, the Rockefellers, the Vanderbilts, or the Dukes— clans of individuals whose own capacities and achievements may be quite ordinary, but who are the direct beneficiaries of this fundamental criterion of class—its heritability. At a less exalted level, children of ordinary capitalists and rentiers do likewise.

Occupations and their holders lack this key criterion of class. The daughter of a brilliant neurosurgeon does not necessarily become one herself, anymore than the son of a cabinet minister will be entitled to a similar position. It is only by translating the advantages of particular occupational roles into wealth, that talented individuals can improve their class position and, more importantly, transmit its privileges to their descendants. Power associated with a dominant class position is manifested in the personal autonomy it confers on occupants and their capacity to direct the actions of others, either directly through economic means or indirectly through the political process.

The Subordinate Classes

Marxist and Marxist-inspired writers never tire of repeating that, despite the myth of an open society, the size of the wealth-owning classes is tiny, both in absolute terms and in relation to the rest of the population. Numerous statistics can be cited in support of that assertion. Individuals able to live off their wealth, whether acquired or inherited, represent no more than 2 percent of the American working-age population.[26]

The vast majority must work for a living, and this common trait makes its members share a basic subordinate position. This does not mean, of course, that all belong to the same class but that, despite internal differences, the majority of the population finds itself on the same side of the fundamental divide in capitalist societies. Endless debates have ensued at this point concerning the best way to categorize this vast population. The preoccupation of Marxist scholars to make contemporary realities fit into a predefined framework have led to such implausible solutions as lumping into the "proletariat" corporate managers and highly paid consultants along with wage workers, or declaring the entire nonmanual work force to be part of the "new petty bourgeoisie."[27]

From the nominalist standpoint adopted here, it is possible to derive classificatory criteria from the same dimension used previously, namely power as the basic source of class cleavage and the possession of wealth or wealth-conferring resources as its principal indicator in modern capitalist societies. If a prime criterion for membership in the dominant classes is heritability, a prime consideration for those who must live from their work is the demand for what they have to offer. Both neo-Marxist and functionalist analysts of stratification have emphasized the significance of scarcity of skills.[28] However, scarcity is nothing if the vaunted skills are not in demand. A juggler may be very good at tossing and picking things, but this ability will hardly suffice to improve his class position. On the contrary, the inventor of a new and popular computer game has gold in her hands and may be well on her way to joining the class of rentiers. The key question is, of course, demand from whom. In capitalist societies, the answer is evident: for those able to pay for the needed skills. In other words, individual abilities are important as a class-conferring attribute to the extent that they are needed or wanted by members of the dominant classes and the institutions they control.[29]

Powerless individuals may thus improve their class position through the selective marketing of rare and desirable skills. Any skill that, for any reason, is in high demand becomes relevant as a class-conferring resource. It can be the surgical ability of a physician, the legal acumen of a lawyer, the sensibility and originality of a painter, or the batting prowess of a baseball player. From our nominalist perspective, it does not matter whether these workers are "productive" or not in the traditional Marxist sense. All that matters is that skills are of such a kind that they hold the potential to lift their possessors across the fundamental class divide in capitalist society.

Elite workers is a suitable label for this class, distinguished from the rest of the labor force precisely because they are poised to cross this basic divide. The manager who becomes eligible to purchase stock options in his company, the lawyer who makes partner in a famous firm, and the player who just signed a multi-million-dollar contract are all on the way to a higher class position. Commonly, this mobility only goes as far as the class of rentiers, but, in exceptional cases, it can reach into the ranks of true capitalists. The software engineer or computer science professor who leaves paid work to start his own company in Silicon Valley or Route 128 stands as an example of this economic journey, aimed at the very heights of the class structure.[30]

Nor is it important from this analytic perspective whether elite workers are salaried or independent. Another large batch of debates has focused on whether independent workers are part of the proletariat or belong to the petty bourgeoisie.[31] While these debates go on, capital nimbly sidesteps the issue by hiring desirable individuals as regular employees, consultants, or independent contractors depending on the interests of the firm and, often, the convenience of the worker. The legal form of the remuneration is secondary; what is important is the ability of the individual to negotiate compensation of such a magnitude as to put him or her on the road to economic autonomy and even entry into the true capitalist class.

By contrast, *common workers* form that class whose skills are sufficiently in demand to earn a living, but insufficient to access wealth. The defining feature of membership in this class is dependence on a paycheck or its equivalent for life. Unlike rentiers, common workers do not have the luxury of simply quitting work while maintaining the same lifestyle; unlike elite workers, they do not have the opportunity of striking extraordinary "deals" with their employers. This class comprises the vast majority of the working population, and its size and diversity leads to the temptation of further subdividing it according to such criteria as manual/nonmanual labor, educational criteria, or cultural orientations. This temptation is especially strong when there is the expectation that a more narrowly defined working class will become, at some point, conscious of its position and able to mobilize on that basis.

It is well nigh impossible to imagine high school teachers and garment cutters, corporate clerks and restaurant waiters getting together to act politically in unison. But, as seen in the previous discussion of the real-ist fallacy, this class-for-itself expectation is not desirable analytically because it introduces a needless teleological dimension. Common workers may not rise together against the capitalist system, but they possess three important characteristics in common: first, their powerlessness and dependence on the existing institutional order; second, their dependence on associative forms—unions, guilds, or professional organizations—for defense of their common economic interests. Unlike capitalist lobbies whose goal is to insure profitability of investments, associations of workers seek, first of all, security of job tenure and then wage improvements on a predictable basis.[32] Third, this is the class where occupational "closure" is commonly practiced in order to restrict competition. Neither rentiers nor elite workers seek closure because the very nature of their class-conferring attributes—extraordinary wealth or skills—suffices as a barrier to entry. Common workers are not in this position since the more ordinary character of their skills puts them in danger of replacement. For this reason, they seek to erect barriers to entry in the form of lengthy apprenticeships, licensing requirements, and restrictions to immigration, among others.[33] The practice of erecting such barriers and, more generally, of seeking associative defenses against possible redundancy is common to all members of this class—whether teachers, clerks, carpenters, or truckers—and is what defines them as occupants of a common social position.[34]

Unlike their elite counterparts, mode of remuneration is important for common workers. This is the case because the ability to countermand individual powerlessness through associative strategies varies with the form of the employment contract. Regular salaried and waged workers are in a much better position to come together in defense of their interests than isolated home workers and those paid on a piece rate basis. Mutual visibility and awareness of a common position among regular workers facilitate their association and the search for occupational closure. This is also the reason why corporate managers have energetically pursued employment *flexibility* in recent years—a codeword for breaking the power of employee associations through fragmentation of the labor process and the use of manifold subcontracting arrangements.[35] The success of this strategy has pushed a number of common workers into one of the two remaining classes.

Common workers who find they are without regular waged employment have two options. One is to go into business for themselves, hoping to earn a living through the provision of some good or service; the second is to join the ranks of the permanently unemployed. The two options define the character of the remaining class positions. The small and often informal enterprises that displaced workers start cannot be equated with those established by members of the dominant classes because the latter are driven by the logic of capital accumulation, while petty enterprise is just a means for survival. Petty entrepreneurs commonly start their businesses in the absence of other options. The displaced factory technician who sets himself up as an appliance repairman, the laid off steel worker who starts driving a cab, or the redundant middle manager who begins a "consulting" business provide familiar examples.[36]

As with common workers, there is, of course, a wide range of variation among petty entrepreneurs. Small salesmen have always harbored grand visions of business success. Some actually do, accumulating capital, being able to hire others, and achieving a measure of financial independence. For the most part, however, it is a struggle just to keep small businesses alive, which explains the high rate of bankruptcies and disappearances among such firms.[37] In general, petty enterprise, or *self-employment* as it is labeled in the official statistics, runs parallel to regular wage and salaried work, offering an alternative for people who must labor for a living. That alternative ranges from bare survival to the seldom-fulfilled prospect of building successful businesses that place their owners into the ranks of the dominant classes.

This diversity of outcomes, added to the isolation of their workplaces, renders the probability of joint political action by petty entrepreneurs remote. The atomized character of petty enterprise is not divorced, of course, from its resurgence in recent years and its articulation with the flexible specialization strategies of large corporate firms. We will return to this topic below as one of the principal illustrations of the explanatory potential of this class typology.

Recent Marxist and neo-Marxist discussions of the class structure generally conclude with the proletariat. This is a logical consequence of classificatory criteria where a "minus" sign is assigned to wage workers in all power-conferring resources. In Erik Wright's scheme, for example, the proletariat is the class that lacks control over the means of production and control over the labor of others; in Nicos Poulantzas's analysis, it is the class that lacks control of the means of production and ideological/political hegemony over others.[38] This classificatory outcome is also linked to Marx's own writings in which only the reserve army of labor and the lumpen rank below the proletariat. The reserve army is a theoretical construct that, when given concrete form, amounts essentially to proletarians-in-waiting.[39] The lumpen is a derogatory concept, frequently invoked by Marx in his historical writings, but never dealt with in a systematic fashion.

Not surprisingly, the Marxist maps of the class structure end at this point, omitting what is perhaps the most significant position among the subordinate classes. This consists of a class of people who have been systematically expelled from regular employment without having the means to establish themselves as independent entrepreneurs. Past successes of proletarian organization and mobilization had the consequence of creating a protected work force eventually deemed too costly by their corporate employers. As large firms in the United States and Western Europe became increasingly exposed to global competition, they confronted their own secure and well-paid workers as a key obstacle to competitiveness.[40]

Through a variety of strategic ploys, described at length in the specialized literature, the dominant classes succeeded in imposing the logic of globalization on their unionized work forces, converting a significant portion into "redundant workers."[41] The same ruthless logic led smaller employers to avail themselves of the least expensive and most vulnerable sources of labor, avoiding those touched by past experiences of class mobilization. This practice added to the redundant labor force entire categories of people typified by employers as somehow undesirable:[42]

> Employers exhibit a strong preference for just about any immigrant workers, whether Mexican, Eastern European, or Oriental. Perhaps most resounding of all in terms of employer "tastes" is the widespread concern with the quality of particular categories of black workers . . . black job applicants, unlike their white counterparts, must indicate to employers that the stereotypes do not apply to them. Inner city workers were seen as undesirable, and black applicants had to signal to employers that they did not fall into those categories.[43]

Redundant workers, whether expelled by large firms or barred from work by small and medium ones, do not readily fit into the conceptual categories inherited from classic Marxism. They are not a "reserve army" because no one intends to hire them, unless compelled to do so. Indeed, their situation is commonly due to their prior condition as conscious and organized workers and their subsequent displacement by more vulnerable laborers.[44]

Nor are redundant workers part of the lumpen, if by that concept is meant a class of petty criminals. While they may engage in informal and illegal economic activities, these are commonly a *consequence* of their class position rather than its defining feature. Unemployed factory workers may start doing home repairs without a license or smuggling cigarettes across state lines; jobless minority youths may start selling drugs on street corners, but these ventures follow from a common situation of redundancy instead of causing it.[45]

The prime characteristic of this class, aside from its complete lack of economic power, is the involuntary nature of its members' situation. It represents, in a sense, the living sequel of the defeat of past efforts by organized segments of the working class to impose their will or, at least, negotiate terms with capital. Successful past mobilizations had the unexpected consequence of turning secure and protected workers into principal adversaries of many corporate firms in the new globalized economy. Managers' efforts to redress this situation expelled tens of thousands of common workers into the petty bourgeoisie or into straight redundancy.

Table 5.2 summarizes this typology by listing the main features of each class and empirical indicators of its potential size. This map of the class structure is intended as a counter to the three fallacies listed previously by showing the significance of class position and presenting an alternative way of conceptualizing it. With this conceptual spadework done, it is now possible to place this typology into motion for explanation of specific processes relevant to economic sociology.

GLOBALIZATION AND FLEXIBLE SPECIALIZATION

Change always frightens people. And today the world's economy is going through two great changes. . . . The first change is that a lot of industrial production is moving from the United States, Western Europe, and Japan to developing countries in Latin America, Southeast Asia, and Eastern Europe. . . . The second change is that, in rich countries, the balance of economic activity is shifting from manufacturing to services. . . . These trends have caused an agonized debate about the "deindustrialization of the West." . . . By the mid-1980s, a lot of Americans had come to believe that their country's industry was being "hollowed out." . . . A sudden cancer had gripped the entrails of American industry.[46]

This is just one of the numerous accounts of capitalism's new era ushered by the onset of global competition and strategies to successfully cope with it. The tone of these accounts is decidedly contradictory, with Marxist and neo-Marxist versions being uniformly critical and neoliberal ones being consistently celebratory. The changes that led to these contradictory evaluations featured the gradual abandonment of Keynesian economic policy—the reigning orthodoxy since the Great Depression—and

TABLE 5.2
A Typology of the American Class Structure

Classes	Economic Characteristics	Political Characteristics	Empirical Indicators
Dominant:			
Grand Capitalists	Ownership or control of businesses of international scope. Capital in the hundreds of millions of dollars	National political influence based on individual resources and contacts	Annual incomes in the tens of millions or higher; named philanthropies and control of institutions of national and international reach
Capitalists	Ownership or control of businesses of regional or national scope. Capital in the tens of millions	Local political influence based on individual resources. National influence through "lobbies"	Annual incomes in the millions; named philanthropies and control of institutions of local reach
Rentiers	Diversified financial/business investments in the millions. No direct control of large firms	Collective influence through contributions to business associations representing large numbers	Annual incomes in the hundreds of thousands; paid work optional. Modest social or philanthropic recognition, but no independent institutional presence
Subordinate:			
Elite Workers	Possession of exceptional skills in demand by major economic organizations. Rapid accumulation of wealth from paid work	Individual influence based on personal fame and occupational distinction	Annual salaries in the hundreds of thousands. Awards and honors based on career achievements

TABLE 5.2 (*continued*)

Common Workers	Possession of standard occupational skills in demand by employers. Little or no wealth accumulation	Collective influence based on membership in unions and other occupationally-based organizations. No personal political influence	Annual salaries in the tens of thousands; home ownership as the principal form of investment. Little or no occupational recognition
Petty Entrepreneurs	Self-employment in small businesses requiring owner's labor. Provision of goods and services to the public or under subcontract to larger firms	No individual influence and little collective solidarity because of isolated work conditions	Fluctuating annual incomes in the tens of thousands; higher incomes in exceptional cases. No occupational security or recognition
Redundant Workers	Excluded from labor market because of dated skills or work attitudes. Dependence on government assistance and casual work	No organized mobilization and primary focus on day-to-day survival. Isolated explosions of discontent	Fluctuating annual incomes in the thousands. Personal survival through government assistance, informal work and, in some cases, petty criminal activities

the resurrection of neoclassical free markets as the dominant economic paradigm. This shift was accompanied by a momentous reallocation of employment from industry to services in the advanced countries and by a change in preexisting labor practices.[47] For the most part, the story of industrial restructuring has been told with an emphasis on global competition, pioneered by Japan, and on the new industrial practices introduced by Japanese firms—such as quality circles and just-in-time sourcing. It is possible, however, to reinterpret the process in terms of class analysis and, in particular, to place it in the framework provided by the preceding typology.

During the post–World War II period, American corporate capital forged a pact with organized labor that permitted gradual improvement

in the incomes and life standards of common workers and the incorporation of women and minorities into this class. Both self-employment and
unemployment declined during the 1950s and 1960s, while the growth
of a giant mass of salaried workers created the requisite market for industrial production.[48] Although strikes and other forms of labor conflict
continued, the fundamental situation was one of a symbiotic alliance
between the interests of capitalist firms and that of common workers,
insofar as wage and salary improvements for the latter expanded the
market for mass production.[49]

The rise of Japanese competition in autos and durable goods, followed
by the surge of other newly industrialized countries, broke the oligopo-
listic control exercised by American companies over domestic and global
markets. It made less and less sense to expand the mass of protected
workers when their demand for big-ticket items was increasingly met
from abroad. Instead, American capitalists confronted the challenge of
global competition by discarding the social pact with organized labor
and promoting flexibility and entrepreneurship. The latter included the
use of an increasing number of subcontractors—individuals and small
firms—to whom tasks previously performed by protected workers were
rechanneled. Thus, the class of petty entrepreneurs, formerly a declining
segment of the working population, rebounded under the impact of the
new strategy of productive decentralization and the simultaneous waves
of corporate downsizing.

The rate of self-employment ceased to decline in the 1970s and then
picked up while the proportion of unionized workers diminished rapidly.[50]
Flexibility also meant a rush to relocate industrial activities to cheaper
areas, including foreign countries. Along with managerial downsizing, this
policy displaced a sizable mass of salaried employees and wageworkers,
not all of whom could transform themselves into petty entrepreneurs. The
Reagan era brought in a wave of mergers and acquisitions and the rise of
the idea of "shareholder value." When faced with strong foreign competition, American conglomerates simply divested themselves of assets rather
than seeking to produce better products or competed on price based on
relocation abroad of production facilities. In search of bottom-line profits, acquisitions experts bought up undervalued industrial companies and
broke them up for their assets, throwing thousands out of work in the process.[51] This, in turn, ushered the era of unbridled financial capitalism that
was to lead the world to its worst global crisis in half a century in 2008.

In a few years, the American industrial belt became the rustbelt, leaving in its wake a mass of redundant labor. Industrial employment plummeted from over one-third of the labor force in 1950 to less than 15 percent in 1996. A large number of displaced line workers, supervisors, and middle managers not only became unemployed, but also unemployable because of dated skills, seniority, or association with past trade union activities. The story of formerly stable working-class communities ravaged by plant closings and downsizing have been told in poignant terms by a number of authors.[52]

With deindustrialization and industrial restructuring, the American labor market ceased to resemble a pyramid, with opportunities for gradual economic mobility for common workers distributed evenly from the bottom up, to resemble an "hourglass," with employment growth concentrated at the bottom (in low-paid service jobs) and at the top (in positions requiring advanced educational credentials). Elite workers and selected petty entrepreneurs, fostered by this economic transformation, fared well on the basis of novel and advanced skills demanded by the new service economy. These were the classes that buttressed the impression, by the late 1990s, that "everybody is getting rich," as their own improved earnings were reinforced by investments in a booming high technology sector.[53]

But this impression was faulty. While the median American household net worth climbed 10 percent in the 1990s to about $80,000, almost half of all households (43.8 percent) did not reach $25,000 and exactly a third (33.0 percent) had annual incomes below this figure. Ten percent of families achieved incomes over $100,000 by 1998, allowing them to invest substantial amounts in stocks and other wealth-creating instruments, but more than half (57 percent) of Americans did not own any equities and fell ever further behind in terms of economic power.[54] The high-tech investment bubble and the notion of "shareholder value" took hold during the 1990s, further benefiting owners and investors. Clearly, flexibility and restructuring were not a universal good, but produced instead a bifurcation of the social structure where the spectacular success of some classes concealed the growing marginalization and relative impoverishment of others.

For common workers displaced by the process and unable to transform themselves into petty entrepreneurs, the situation became bleak as they were forced to compete, often in conditions of disadvantage, for the low-wage service jobs at the bottom of the labor market. In the new competitive economy brought about by global restructuring, employers of this kind of labor have opted consistently for the most vulnerable sources, including recent immigrants. The shriveled industrial towns surrounding closed plants, the block after block of boarded up urban housing where the families of industrial workers used to live, and the clusters of idle men on street corners stand as silent testimony of the underside of the postindustrial economy. This redundant population, not the proletariat of old, represents the true bottom of the modern class structure.[55]

The dominant classes were the principal beneficiaries of the processes of industrial restructuring and flexible specialization, albeit with variants and exceptions. Grand capital reaffirmed its global vocation, becoming increasingly able to profit from investments at home and abroad. Under the aegis of free trade policies, foisted on all countries—large and small— by international finance organizations, global corporations became increasingly able to access all consumers and all types of labor.[56] As the destruction of the old unionized industrial proletariat at home increased flexibility, global corporations became able to reorganize production, benefiting from de facto competition between domestic and foreign workers.

The success of these strategies directly strengthened the power of those atop the class structure, and also enriched rentiers who invested in their firms. The miraculous climb in American stock prizes during the 1990s was fueled, in part, by a growing confidence among members of the rentier class in the ability of American corporations to confront the challenges of international competition. The consolidation of "shareholder value" as the dominant philosophy of American conglomerates was a further boon for members of this class.[57] Smaller firms producing for the domestic market and unable to access the global strategy of the majors suffered, however. This is especially true of industries using older technologies, replicable in countries with cheaper labor. The American textile, garment, and footwear industries offer poignant examples of the wholesale disappearance of firms ravaged by the new economic order. The losers were not only the workers, but the owners of these firms.[58]

The process leading to the signing of the North American Free Trade Agreement (NAFTA) in 1994 offers a good example of the divergent interest of the propertied classes. Although supported by global banks and large corporations (i.e., grand capital), NAFTA was fiercely opposed by local capitalists, including small industrialists and growers, threatened by a flood of cheap Mexican imports. Sectors of the Republican Party and the Reform Party, which emerged at the time, gave political expression to the interests of this class. Simultaneously, a strategic alliance was built between national unions and this sector of capital, an alliance that, though ultimately unsuccessful, served to highlight the disjuncture of interests within the dominant classes and the costs to the old social order of the process of globalization.[59]

These processes led to the relentless rise of economic inequality which, as Douglas Massey, Richard Freeman, and others have noted, has brought the United States to a level of economic disparity resembling that of a third world country.[60] This alarming rise in inequality has been documented in a number of official and academic reports, but its underlying causes have not been accounted for satisfactorily. Class analysis brings light to this process by showing that it is not a gradational or smooth change in the distribution of income, but one characterized by sharp "bumps" corresponding to different class positions. While capitalists, rentiers, and some elite workers gained mightily in wealth and power, common workers lost out, their organizations became feebler, and many went on to engross the ranks of the struggling petty bourgeoisie and of redundant labor. The next systemic crisis of the global system, brought about by an unbridled financial bubble, was not only to impoverish further the subordinate classes but also to seriously weaken the class of rentiers. The way in which this downturn, which finally brought to an end the era of neoliberalism, happened is discussed in the concluding chapter.

IMMIGRATION

Flexible specialization and the movement of capital abroad have been accompanied by the rise of labor migration into the advanced countries. The same period that witnessed the demise of large segments of the protected industrial working-class in the United States and the successful efforts of the International Monetary Fund and corporate conglomerates to open up foreign markets also saw the resurgence of international migration on a mass scale. Today, close to 14 percent of the American population is foreign born, and the number of immigrants has been rising six times faster than the native-born population during the last decade. In cities like Los Angeles and New York, immigrants already constitute one-third of the respective metropolitan populations. In Miami and border cities, they are an absolute majority.[61] The twin processes of capitalist globalization and labor immigration are, of course, not unrelated but, for our purposes, the key point of interest is the relationship of the class structure to this mass foreign inflow and its subsequent effects. As seen previously, unskilled and semiskilled immigrants have contributed heavily to the supply of low-wage labor, competing with native workers displaced by industrial restructuring. That competition has been most marked in services and in the remnants of labor-intensive industry.[62]

At the other end of the spectrum, highly trained foreign scientists, engineers, and professionals have contributed to enlarge the class of elite workers and technologically savvy entrepreneurs. During the 1990s, over 100,000 persons classified as professionals, executives, and managers entered the United States on an annual basis. Foreigners represent approximately one-third of the faculties in engineering schools; in 1993, they were awarded 44 percent of all U.S. doctorates in science and engineering.[63] The H-1B program, created by the 1990 Immigration Act, allowed the mass hiring of foreign professionals and technicians on a temporary basis. By 2002, the number of H-1B immigrants exceeded 200,000, most coming from India and China. By 2006, they exceeded 400,000.[64] Immigrant scientists and professionals from such countries as India, the Philippines, and Taiwan have annual incomes that significantly surpass those of the native white population. Immigrant nationalities are also overrepresented among petty entrepreneurs, with rates of self-employment as high as 15 percent for the Chinese, 18.2 percent for Cubans, and 34.2 percent for Koreans, as compared with a national average of 9.7 percent in the 1990s.[65]

Thus, unlike the situation at the beginning of the twentieth century in which immigrants entered mostly at the bottom of the American class structure, at present they add to all the subordinate classes, including elite workers and petty entrepreneurs. The presence of this new and diversified source of labor has benefited *all* dominant classes during the transition to a postindustrial economy, albeit for somewhat different reasons. Mass immigration is compatible with the strategy of global flexibilization of production promoted by grand capital, but has also contributed to the survival of smaller firms threatened with extinction. Today, local capitalists in all sectors—agriculture, services, and industry—regularly avail themselves of immigrant labor as a means to increase flexibility and lower production costs.[66]

The contemporary situation is one in which grand capital benefits directly from third world labor reserves by moving production facilities abroad or by recruiting foreign professionals and scientists; local capital benefits from the ready presence of foreign manual labor, much of it in an unauthorized status.[67] This is the reason why efforts to stop the foreign labor flow or regularize the status of its manual component have been actively resisted by lobbyists in the service of these classes.

The only class negatively affected by immigration is common workers, but, as seen previously, it lacks the internal cohesiveness and political power to effectively oppose the flow. In areas of high immigrant concentration, native workers are commonly confronted with the options of turning themselves into petty entrepreneurs (and possibly hiring immigrants themselves), migrating to other parts of the country, or joining the class of

TABLE 5.3
Immigration and the Class Structure

Type of Immigration	Class	Effects
Dominant:		
—	Grand Capitalists	+: Increases labor supply and flexibility for firms. Facilitates global organization of production.
—	Capitalists	+: Increases competitiveness with imported goods; lowers labor costs.
—	Rentiers	+: Increases profitability of investments in restructured firms; adds to the supply of domestic and personal service workers
Subordinate:		
Scientists, professionals, artists	Elite Workers	+: Increases quality and diversity of workers in high demand in various sectors of the economy. Foreigners supplement, but do not replace native elite workers
Semiskilled and unskilled laborers	Common Workers	−: Weakens labor organization and occupational closure; replaces native common workers in several sectors
Foreigners with some capital and business expertise	Petty Entrepreneurs	−: Increases supply of goods and services for the market; facilitates subcontracting by large and medium firms. Foreigners supplement but do not replace native entrepreneurs
—	Redundant Workers	−: Contributes to expansion of this class by rendering former common workers uncompetitive

redundant workers. Sectors employing mostly native workers are those requiring specialized expertise, U.S. citizenship, and fluent English. All others
have become open to foreign competition.[68] Table 5.3 outlines the relationship between labor immigration and the American class structure. Based
on the balance of class forces analyzed here, it becomes clear that U.S.-
bound labor migration can be expected to continue indefinitely into the
future. Although the massive economic crisis, brought about by the end of
the financial bubble in 2008, has significantly slowed down the flow, it can
be expected to return to prior levels once conditions return to normal.[69]

REPRISE

We can return now to the critique of the three fallacies at the start of the
chapter and see how the analysis just completed bears on it. Class analysis would not be a useful approach to the phenomena of industrial restructuring and mass immigration if we restricted the term to consciously
mobilized social aggregates. To accept the realist fallacy—the postulate
that only a class-for-itself is real—would mean doing away with such
heuristic categories as elite workers and petty entrepreneurs since the
social aggregates to which they refer seldom act in unison or define
themselves as part of the same unit. For the same reason, the class of
"redundant workers" would disappear since, unlike the industrial proletariat, marginalized workers seldom coalesce in defense of common interests. In brief, by anticipating what should be examined, the realist fallacy unduly narrows class analysis, depriving it of flexibility and scope.

Since classes-for-themselves are scarce these days, a logical conclusion
of the realist approach is that class analysis must be abandoned. This
would lead us directly into the classless fallacy and into the arms of those
for whom society is just an aggregate of individuals or a seamless web
of networks. The previous analyses of industrial restructuring and labor
migration are intended to show that a class perspective represents an indispensable tool for understanding these social processes. As seen earlier,
the classless fallacy leads to an analysis of immigration in terms as super-
ficial as how much immigrants put into state coffers and how much they
take out of them. The same view of capitalist societies as a level playing
field would lead to an interpretation of the momentous changes wrought
by industrial restructuring as a result of supply and demand and market
competition. The specific effects of such changes on the various subordinate classes would disappear from view.

Lastly, the use of a class framework to interpret contemporary processes of change is severely restricted if we have to depend on nineteenth-century typologies. The capitalist class was not as differentiated in Marx's time as it is today, nor did the subordinate classes feature the same profile as they do at present. Recent attempts to save Marx's scheme through the introduction of ad hoc criteria do not prove very helpful either. These attempts are more preoccupied with achieving formal theoretical consistency than with any specific practical application. Similarly, various attempts to conflate elite workers, common workers, and the displaced into a single modern "proletariat" obscure rather than clarify major effects of contemporary capitalist restructuring.

These modified schemes may prove useful in other contexts, and a nominalist perspective would readily grant their validity, if shown applicable for other purposes. The reification fallacy deprives class analysts of this flexibility by insisting on the primacy of the original Marxist typology or its approved successors, even when it means forcing reality into rigid and awkward molds. For class analysis to achieve its theoretical potential, it is imperative to leave such efforts behind in favor of an approach as agile as the social processes that it is called upon to explain.

CONCLUSION

Class analysis has largely disappeared from view in modern economic sociology. This may be what Richard Swedberg had in mind when he called for the reintroduction of the concept of "interests" in the field's theoretical framework.[70] Reasons for this abandonment have to do with the self-defeating character of the realist fallacy and the intellectual contortions needed to fit contemporary capitalist society into a nineteenth-century framework. An emergent and reenergized field like economic sociology appropriately views such exercises as useless baggage. Class analysis freed from these rigidities has a useful, even necessary role in modern economic sociology. It does so for at least three reasons:

First, by highlighting a major element of the social context in which economic phenomena are "embedded." Without a class perspective, sociological analyses of the economy are limited to social networks, social interactions, and their immediate effects. While valuable, these analyses are incomplete because they neglect the broader framework created by stable differentials in interests and power. We would thus be back into the classless fallacy that, in economic sociology, takes the form of a focus

on interactional patterns among individual actors and their crystalliza-
tion into microstructures, oblivious of the macrostructures within which
such interactions take place.

Second, by situating and hence clarifying the scope of sociological
analyses of the economy. As Neil Fligstein has noted, in a related context:
"There are many sociological analyses that do not situate market structures in larger institutional contexts. Network analyses often ignore factors not associated with conventional network measures in their analyses
of firms and markets."[71] Eonomic sociology has gained much purchase
by studying interactional patterns among actors situated at the "heights"
of the class structure: government decision-makers and corporate managers; central bank governors; firms bent on monopoly and entrepreneurial
challengers; determinants of firm creation, consolidation, and failure.[72]
While this is an exciting literature, its common neglect of a class perspective obscures the socioeconomic level at which the studied interactions
are situated and their potential effects on others. For it is not the case that
corporate managers' decision to focus on "shareholder value" or government policies favoring some sectors of the economy to the neglect of
others are self-contained. They have major consequences that filter down
from the heights of the class structure to the majority of the population,
grouped in the subordinate classes.

Third, class is a concept that has "legs" and can travel. It is not a meta-
theoretical assumption, but a measurable reality and, as such, amenable
to incorporation into testable propositions. Freed from the fallacies of
the past, class represents a midrange ideal type that can be flexibly defined, integrating part of an indispensable tool kit for the sociological
analysis of the economy. Put differently, class systems are not only a key
component of the macrosocial context in which economic processes are
embedded, but they are themselves objects of study as determinants and
consequences of such processes. How the capitalist class has evolved over
time, what led to the demise or reduction of the industrial proletariat,
and what accounts for the rise of an informal working class are examples
of such questions. The next chapter illustrates this form of inquiry in an
altogether different setting.

CHAPTER SIX

Social Class (Continued)

THIS CHAPTER EXTENDS the preceding analysis of social class with an empirical application. Its purpose is to show how definitions of classes can vary with the social context and how, despite this variation, it continues to be central for analyzing concrete processes of economic and social change.[1] The context in question is Latin America in the late years of the twentieth century, and the problem at hand is the impact on society of radical economic adjustment programs in the region, inspired by the neoclassical school of economics and supported by influential organizations such as the U.S. Treasury and the International Monetary Fund.

During the last decade of the twentieth century, Latin America experienced a momentous change as country after country abandoned the autonomous industrialization path advocated by its own intellectuals of an earlier period and embraced a new model of development based on open economies and global competition. *Neoliberalism*, as this model is dubbed, is actually a throwback to an earlier era when Latin American countries participated in the world economy on the basis of their differential advantages as producers of primary goods while importing manufacturers and technology from the industrialized world.

The policies advocated by the resurrected liberal orthodoxy and the "Washington consensus" that gave it ideological momentum have been described at length in the contemporary social science literature.[2] Less studied have been the effects of this profound reorientation of Latin American countries on their social structures and, in particular, their long-term patterns of social stratification. As seen in the case of the Mexican privatization program, described in chapter 4, neoliberal reforms were imposed from the heights of the power structure of these countries without consensus and often against active opposition from below. As an explanatory mechanism, social class helps us better understand what factors led to the implementation of these policies and what effects they had in these societies. This analytic lens is absent in conventional reports on the region by international agencies, affected by the classless fallacy.[3]

CLASS STRUCTURES IN CENTER AND PERIPHERY

As seen in the prior chapter, the concept of social class refers to discrete and durable categories of the population characterized by differential access to power-conferring resources and related life chances. In advanced capitalist societies, such class-defining resources are explicitly tied to markets and the ability of individuals to compete effectively in them.[4] The common advantage of class analysis, both classic and contemporary, is its focus on the *causes* of inequality and poverty and not just its surface manifestations, as commonly done in standard official publications. In exploring the class structure of particular societies, the analyst seeks to uncover not only those key social aggregates defined by common life chances, but also the ways in which some groups consciously attempt to stabilize the social order in defense of their privileged situation and in which other groups seek to subvert it to improve their lot.[5]

Systematic analyses of the class structure of the advanced societies have been based on the criteria of control over the means of production, control over the labor of others, and control over scarce intellectual assets. Based on these criteria, such authors as Erik Wright, John Goldthorpe, and Terry Clark and Seymour Lipset have sought to map the basic configuration of classes in the United States, the United Kingdom, and other European countries.[6] The analysis presented in the prior chapter is an alternative to these exercises, although based on comparable criteria. Latin America, however, is different in that a significant proportion of the population is not incorporated into fully commodified, regulated labor relations, but survives at their margin in a variety of subsistence and semiclandestine activities.

In Marxist terms, the difference between the global economic centers and peripheries, such as Latin America, lies in the imperfect development of modern capitalist relations in the latter and, hence, the coexistence of different modes of production—modern, petty entrepreneurial, and subsistence. For a number of authors in this tradition, the articulation among these various modes of production provides the key for understanding the dynamics of peripheral capitalism and the emergence of unequal exchange between colonies and semicolonies and the global capitalist centers.[7]

Regardless of whether this or another theoretical framework is employed, the fact remains that social classes such as the proletariat can be defined as relatively homogenous entities in the advanced societies while, in the periphery, they are segmented by their limited incorporation into fully monetized, legally regulated economic relations. Immanuel Wallerstein referred to workers only partially incorporated into modern capitalist relations as the semiproletariat, although small entrepreneurs can also be found on both sides of this structural divide.[8]

Juxtaposing class-defining criteria in the advanced societies with the structural conditions found under peripheral capitalism yields the array of assets presented in the top row of table 6.1. By noting whether individuals have access (+) or not (–) to each of these assets, we can arrive at a typology of the class structure of Latin American societies. This typology follows a Guttman-like logic in which each successively inferior class is defined by the lack of one or more of the resources available to its predecessors. Comparing this map with that of the American class structure in the prior chapter, it becomes clear that while the latter required a more refined differentiation of the dominant classes, the present analysis shifts emphasis to the bottom classes whose characteristics are distinct. These are described next.

LATIN AMERICAN CLASSES DURING THE NEOLIBERAL ERA

As in the advanced countries, dominant classes in Latin America are defined by control of key power-conferring resources in the capitalist market. Owners of large-scale means of production sit atop the class structure. This group, labeled *capitalists*, is operationally defined as large and medium-sized employers in private firms. Estimates based on household surveys representing three-fourths or more of the total Latin American population indicate that the size of this first class fluctuates between 1 and 2 percent of the economically active population (EAP) in every country.[9]

Senior executives are top-level administrators of large and medium private or public firms and state institutions. While lacking direct ownership of capital, senior executives run sizable organizations controlling large, bureaucratically organized labor forces. Next to employers, they commonly receive the highest average incomes. The available estimates put the size of this class as between 1 and 5 percent of the EAP in different Latin American countries.

The next echelon is occupied by professionals, defined as university-trained elite workers employed by private firms and public institutions to

TABLE 6.1
The Latin American Class Structure

Class	Membership	Defining Criteria					Mode of remuneration	% of labor force[1]
		Control of capital and means of production	Control of impersonal, bureaucratically-organized labor force	Control of scarce, highly-valued skills	Control of subsidiary, technical-administrative skills	Protected and regulated under the law		
I. Capitalists	Proprietors and managing partners of large/medium firms	+	+	+	+	+	Profits	1.8
II. Executives	Managers and administrators of large/medium firms and public institutions	-	+	+	+	+	Salaries and bonuses tied to profits	1.6
III. Elite workers	University-trained salaried professionals in public service and large/medium private firms	-	-	+	+	+	Salaries tied to scarce knowledge	2.8
IV. Petty bourgeoisie	Own-account professionals and technicians, and micro entrepreneurs with personally supervised staff	+	-	+/-	+	+/-	Profits	8.5

TABLE 6.1 (continued)

		Defining Criteria						
Class	Membership	Control of capital and means of production	Control of impersonal, bureaucratically-organized labor force	Control of scarce, highly-valued skills	Control of subsidiary, technical-administrative skills	Protected and regulated under the law	Mode of remuneration	% of labor force[1]
Va. Nonmanual formal proletariat	Vocationally trained salaried technicians and white-collar employees	–	–	–	+	+	Salaries subject to legal regulation	12.4
Vb. Manual formal proletariat	Skilled and unskilled waged workers with labor contracts	–	–	–	–	+	Wages subject to legal regulation	23.4
VI. Informal Proletariat	Noncontractual waged workers, casual vendors, and unpaid family workers	–	–	–	–	–	Unregulated wages, irregular profits, nonmonetary compensation	45.9

[1]Weighted average of data from eight Latin American countries that jointly comprise three-fourths of the regional economically active population. These countries are presented in table 6.2. Figures do not add to 100% because 3.6% of workers were reported as "unclassified."

staff positions of high responsibility. They neither control large amounts of capital nor command large numbers of workers, but derive their position from scarce expertise required by corporations and government agencies. This class is akin to that of elite workers in the United States, as described previously, except that, in this case, they are identified less by extraordinary abilities than by university credentials. Estimates of the relative presence of professionals in their countries' respective population go as high as 10 percent but, for the region as a whole they represent no more than 5 percent of the EAP according to most recent surveys.[10]

Jointly, large and medium employers, senior executives, and professionals comprise the dominant classes in all Latin American countries (with the exception of Cuba). As we will see, their remunerations far exceed the average in their respective nations although they come in different forms: capitalists receive profits, executives earn salaries and bonuses tied to profits of the organizations they lead, and professionals receive salaries commensurate with the value and scarcity of the expertise they command. While the relative presence of these classes fluctuates among specific countries, for Latin America as a whole they represent approximately 10 percent of the EAP. This decile can be confidently expected to be at the top of the regional and national income distributions.

The next social class corresponds to the classic Marxist description of the petty bourgeoisie except that, in peripheral societies, it assumes a distinct form. This is dictated by the superimposition of modern capitalist and various informal modes of economic organization. The principal characteristics of this group—commonly labeled *microentrepreneurs*—is the possession of some monetary resources; some professional, technical, or artisanal skills; and the employment of a small number of workers supervised on a direct, face-to-face basis.

This class is quite similar to that of petty entrepreneurs in the United States and its members engage in these tasks for similar reasons, namely lack of opportunities in salaried employment. However, the social position and economic function of this class is distinct. In Latin America, microentrepreneurs have traditionally performed the role of linking the modern capitalist economy, led by the dominant classes, with the mass of informal workers at the bottom of society. Microentrepreneurs organize this labor to produce low-cost goods and services for consumers and low-cost inputs subcontracted by the large firms. Several authors have argued that this role is fundamental both for the survival of the poor and the continuation of the capital accumulation process, as it takes place in these economies.[11]

During the 1990s, the petty bourgeoisie acquired a new function in Latin America as a place of refuge for public servants, salaried professionals, and other workers displaced by neoliberal adjustment policies. Public sector employment, which constituted the backbone of the urban middle class in many countries, declined significantly during this decade. This loss was not compensated by growth in private employment, forcing displaced employees to create their own economic solutions in petty enterprise. As a result, petty entrepreneurship became *the* major source of employment creation in the region. Between 1990 and 1998, of every one hundred new urban jobs, thirty were created in small enterprises and another twenty-nine in self-employment, proportions vastly larger than those registered during previous decades.[12]

Consequences of the application of the neoliberal model in Latin America ran parallel to those of industrial restructuring in the United States. In both instances, labor market flexibilization led to rises in self-employment, as those displaced from protected jobs in private industry and public service had to invent new forms of employment. As in the United States, benefits of "market opening" and "flexibilization" concentrated disproportionately in the dominant classes, a trend to be demonstrated below.

The formal proletariat corresponds to workers in industry, services, and agriculture who are protected by labor laws and covered by legally mandated systems of health care, disability, and retirement. This class can be divided, in turn, into an upper echelon of salaried white-collar workers and technicians and a lower one of blue-collar industrial and service workers and rural laborers in modern agricultural enterprises. Jointly, this class represented approximately 35 percent of the Latin American regional EAP in 2000 although, as will be shown, the figure varies widely among countries.

During the post–World War II era and up to the 1980s, formal waged employment grew steadily, although it never succeeded in absorbing all of the Latin American labor force. Between 1950 and 1980, 60 percent of all new employment was created in the formal sector, with government being responsible for 15 percent and modern large and medium enterprises for the remaining 45 percent.[13] During the 1990s, however, the situation changed dramatically, with the modern private sector reducing its share of employment creation to 20 percent and the government actually shrinking. As a result, the class of formal workers did not continue to expand, but remained stagnant or actually declined in many countries.[14]

Most accounts of the class structure of the advanced societies end with the formal proletariat, defined as the class that lacks access to the means of production and has only its own labor to sell. As seen in the previous chapter, only the class of "redundant workers" can be identified in the United States as below the proletariat. In Latin America, as in other peripheral regions, this account would be incomplete because of the existence of a large mass of workers excluded from the modern capitalist sector who must procure a living through unregulated employment or direct subsistence activities. In the 1960s, these workers were labeled the *marginal mass* to denote their exclusion from the modern economy. Subsequent research documented their links with the modern economy and the manifold ways in which their activities contribute to capitalist accumulation.[15]

One of these ways is furnishing labor for firms organized by petty entrepreneurs who, in turn, supply low-cost goods and services to consumers and cheap inputs to large enterprises.[16] For this reason, this class is best labeled the *informal proletariat*. Operationally, it is defined as the sum total of own account workers (minus professionals and technicians), unpaid family workers, domestic servants, and waged workers without social security and other legal protections in industry, services, and agriculture. The vast majority of labor in microenterprises is informal, but there are also informal workers in large and medium firms. These are mostly temporary workers hired off the books and without contracts.

The evolution of the informal proletariat in Latin America represents the exact obverse of the formal working class. The proportion of informal workers shrank, slowly but steadily, during the post–World War II decades, corresponding to the period of application of import substitution policies. The modern sector created the majority of new employment during this period, slowly contracting the informal proletariat. That trend reversed during the neoliberal era as the modern industrial sector was ravaged by cheap imports under the new "open markets" doctrine. As a result, the informal proletariat did not continue its decline, but actually grew during the 1990s.

According to the International Labour Organization (ILO), informal employment amounted to 44.4 percent of the Latin American urban EAP in 1990 and 47.9 percent in 1998.[17] The rise of the informal proletariat is reproduced in almost every country of the region and is interpretable as the popular counterpart to the rise of petty entrepreneurship among former salaried government employees and private sector professionals and technicians. A sizable proportion of the informal working class is formed by own account workers—vendors and other low-skilled personnel forced to survive through the least remunerative forms of enterprise. From this overview, it is evident that neoliberal policies during the 1980s and 1990s quantitatively weakened the class that could most effectively challenge the power of elites—the organized formal proletariat. It sent vast swathes of its members into the informal sector; by the very character of their situation, informal workers and entrepreneurs appeared least able to mount effective resistance to the established order. This was, at least, the expectation of architects of the new model. As we shall see below, the course of history did not follow that expectation, taking instead an unanticipated turn.

MEASURING THE LATIN AMERICAN CLASS STRUCTURE

Official statistics neither use the term *social class*, nor report figures based on it. For this reason, it is not possible to arrive at precise estimates of the size and evolution of the different classes on the basis of census figures. In recent years, various international agencies have been conducting studies of the informal sector in Latin American countries that produced useful approximations to the informal working class. More importantly, the Economic Commission for Latin America and the Caribbean (ECLAC) has carried out a detailed study of occupational and income stratification in eight Latin American countries that jointly contain 73.5 percent of the region's population. The detailed occupational tabulations produced by this study form the basis for the regional estimates presented in table 6.1 and also allow fairly close approximations to the size of each of the social classes described in the prior section. These estimates are presented in table 6.2.

The capitalist class is operationally defined as owners of firms of more than five workers. These figures are an overestimate since small employers, owners of firms employing between five and twenty persons, are probably closer to the category of microentrepreneurs than that of true capitalists. Even taking this overestimate into account, the proportion of the EAP represented by the capitalist class is minimal in all countries. If small entrepreneurs are excluded, these already low estimates would be cut by 50 percent or more.

The next two classes are defined empirically as executives and administrators in public agencies and private firms employed more than five

TABLE 6.2
The Class Structure of Selected Latin American Countries, 2000*

	Brazil %	Chile %	Colombia %	Costa Rica %	El Salvador %	Mexico %	Panama %	Venezuela %
I. Capitalists	2.0	1.5	2.2	1.7	1.2	1.6	0.8	1.4
II. Executives	1.8	1.1	0.8	2.4	1.5	1.3	5.2	2.5
III. Professionals	1.4	6.9	7.7	3.2	2.3	2.8	5.2	10.0
Dominant Classes:	5.2	9.5	10.7	7.3	5.0	5.7	11.2	13.9
IV. Petty Bourgeoisie	7.4	9.4	9.3	10.8	11.8	9.4	8.3	11.2
Va. Nonmanual Formal Proletariat	12.7	16.2	7.9	14.1	10.5	13.7	16.3	9.2
Vb. Manual Formal Proletariat: (I)	25.3	33.7	31.9	32.8	27.5	30.9	23.8	33.6
(II)	20.7	29.0	27.1	28.2	22.5	25.4	20.9	27.2
VI. Informal Proletariat: (I)	43.5	30.2	40.1	34.3	45.0	40.2	40.1	31.6
(II)	48.1	34.9	44.9	38.9	50.0	45.7	43.0	38.0
Unclassified	5.9	1.0	0.1	0.7	0.2	0.1	0.3	0.5
Totals	100.0	100.0	100.0	100.0	100.0	100.0	100.0	100.0

* Percentages of the national working population aged 15 or over.
Sources: Economic Commission for Latin America and the Caribbean, Panorama Social, table 11; International Labour Organization/Lima, Panorama Laboral, table 8-P.

workers (Class II) and as salaried professionals employing by the same agencies or firms (Class III). Again these are overestimates for the same reasons given previously but, even after taking this bias into account, the sum total of the three dominant classes barely reaches 10 percent of the population, falling below that figure in most countries and exceeding it by a small margin in only three.

The available data do not allow us to distinguish between formal and informal microentrepreneurs. Detailed studies in particular cities indicate that a large proportion of microenterprises are entirely informal and that others operate in a twilight zone, complying with some regulations, but escaping others. Emilio Klein and Victor Tokman report that, in 1998, between 65 and 80 percent of workers in these firms did not have medical insurance or social security.[18] Owners of such firms, employing up to five workers, plus own account professionals and technicians, comprise the petty bourgeoisie. It represents another 10 percent of the Latin American EAP. Despite its internal heterogeneity, the relative size of this class is remarkably consistent across the eight countries studied.

These figures imply that the subordinate classes, broadly defined, comprise approximately 80 percent of the Latin American population. These classes are not homogenous, however, and must be disaggregated further for a proper understanding of the dynamics at play. The nonmanual formal working class, composed of salaried technicians and subordinate white-collar employees, accounts for another 15 percent of the regional EAP, although the figure fluctuates between a low of 8 percent and a high of 16 percent across countries.

Table 6.2 presents two estimates of the manual formal proletariat. The first is the sum total of waged workers in small, medium, and large urban firms plus agricultural workers in medium and large modern enterprises. These figures assume that *all* such workers are covered by labor contracts and existing legal regulations. This assumption yields an overestimate because some workers in formal enterprises are paid off the books and lack legal protection. The ECLAC study provides no data to adjust these series. However, a second set of tabulations by the International Labour Organization presents the proportion of workers in the formal sector (defined as government employees and workers in small, medium, and large private firms) who do not contribute to the national social security system.

Social security coverage can be used as a reasonable proxy for formal employment. The average coverage for workers in formal sector firms is 80 percent, and the figure is remarkably consistent across years and across countries. This statistic suggests that approximately one-fifth of the labor force in the presumably formal sector of the economy is composed of unprotected workers. I use national figures on social security coverage to adjust the initial estimates and present results in the next row of table 6.2. Based on these figures, the manual formal proletariat fluctuates between 20 and 30 percent of the adult working population, and it does not exceed one-third of the EAP in any country.

Estimates of the proportions of the working population represented by the informal proletariat are the obverse of these series. The table presents two estimates. The first represents the sum total of own account workers, minus professionals and technicians, plus workers in urban micro-enterprises, small rural enterprises, domestic servants, and unpaid family laborers. These figures underestimate the informal proletariat for the same reasons given previously, namely the exclusion of unprotected workers in larger firms. The second series adjust for this undercount with the same figures used to reestimate the formal working class. Based on these calculations, the informal proletariat fluctuates between one-third and one-half of the employed population, the figure being no lower than one-third in any country. This makes informal workers *the largest class everywhere*. Put differently, the numerically most important segment of the employed population in Latin America is the one excluded from modern capitalist relations and which must survive through unregulated work. As seen previously, the era of neoliberal adjustment saw an increase in the size of this class, reversing the progress achieved in the prior decades.

OCCUPATIONAL INCOMES AND THE CLASS STRUCTURE

It is well known that Latin America as a whole features the most unequal distribution of wealth and income in the world.[19] A look at this situation from a class perspective clarifies how particular sectors of the population are positioned in this distribution and how their condition has evolved over time. Income inequality during the decade of neoliberalism increased significantly for the region and, with exceptions, for each individual country. By 1998, the regional Gini index of inequality had inched up to reach the same value that it had in 1970 (0.52). This means that the top 5 percent of the population received incomes that were twice those of the comparable group in the Organization for Economic Co-Operation and Development (OECD) countries, while the bottom 30 percent survived on 7.5 percent of the total income or only 60 percent of the respective proportion in the advanced nations. However, if the Gini index is computed on the *bottom* 90 percent of the Latin American population, its value would only be 0.36, which is similar to that of the United States.

Since the three dominant classes comprise about one decile of the population, this finding is interpretable as indicating that *all* the excess income inequality of the region is attributable to the combined share of income received by these classes. Simultaneously, this produces a situation in which 75 percent of the employed population, corresponding approximately to the sum of the formal and informal proletariats, does not generate enough income from their jobs to surpass the poverty level.[20] This implies that with few national exceptions, to be a worker in Latin America means to be poor.

The same study of eight Latin American countries cited previously divides the national EAP into four useful categories that correspond to distinct positions in the class structure. The three dominant classes (employers, executives/managers, university professionals) comprise 9.4 percent of the work force in these countries and receive average earnings of 13.7 times the per capita poverty line. The intermediate classes—petty entrepreneurs and nonmanual formal workers (technicians, lower-educated professionals, administrative employees) account for 13.9 percent of the workforce and receive earnings of five times the poverty line.

The manual proletariat (formal and informal) earns incomes of less than four times the poverty line, a level too low to lift the average family out of poverty.[21] This category is subdivided by the ECLAC study into two subgroups: (a) urban workers in commerce and blue-collar workers and artisans (comprising a mix of formal and informal proletarians) represent 38.7 percent of all employed persons with average incomes of 3.5 times the poverty line; (b) service workers and agricultural laborers (overwhelmingly informal) account for 34.5 percent of the labor force and receive incomes of just twice the poverty line.

It is possible, on the basis of these figures, to compute average incomes reflecting major divisions in the class structure of individual countries. We do this and report the results in table 6.3. Two facts become immediately obvious. First, the enormous disparities in incomes between the dominant classes, especially capitalists, and the rest of the population. Second, the wide variation across countries. Average income levels of the dominant classes are underestimated because they include owners and managers of microenterprises who are part of the petty bourgeoisie and who receive much lower incomes. Even after rolling microentrepreneurs

TABLE 6.3
Average Incomes by Social Class in Eight Latin American Nations, 1997[1]

Classes	Brazil	Chile	Colombia	Costa Rica	El Salvador	Mexico	Panama	Venezuela
Dominant:								
Employers	18.4	34.6	9.4	8.8	8.1	14.0	15.6	11.4
Executives	12.3	16.2	9.0	12.1	11.3	11.0	10.2	6.6
Professionals	20.5	15.4	6.8	11.3	8.8	7.8	13.0	4.9
Intermediate:[2]								
Nonmanual workers (technicians and white-collar employees)	5.7	7.0	4.1	7.0	5.0	4.1	5.7	2.4[3]
Subordinate:[2]								
Quasi-formal proletariat (blue collar workers and artisans/workers in commerce)	4.1	4.8	2.9	4.9	2.8	2.6	4.5	3.4
Informal Proletariat:								
(Service workers and agricultural laborers)	1.7	3.4	2.4	3.8	1.9	2.2	3.6	2.9
Total:	4.5	7.4	3.5	5.7	3.3	3.4	5.2	3.7

[1]In multiples of the national poverty line.
[2]Weighted averages.
[3]Includes administrative employees only.
Source: Economic Commission for Latin America and the Caribbean, *Panorama Social*, table 4.

into the employer class, the income ratio of this group as a whole to that of informal workers is 6 to 1 in Mexico, 10 to 1 in Chile, and 11 to 1 in Brazil.

Within this general picture, these are significant variations. The most egalitarian nation is obviously Costa Rica, where both formal and informal workers receive the highest relative incomes and where the ratio of this figure to the average for the dominant classes is less than 3 to 1. At the other extreme, we find Brazil and Chile with the important difference that, in Brazil, the average income of informal workers is less than twice the poverty level, while in Chile it is almost four times that figure. Chile has the highest absolute incomes of all the countries considered, which leads to the paradoxical situation in which extreme inequality coexists with the gradual reduction of poverty among the subordinate classes.[22] Such is not the case in Brazil or even in Mexico where those at the bottom must subsist on wages that, in the absence of other sources of income, condemn them to poverty.

The available data also allow a glimpse of the evolution of income inequality within the class structure during the last two decades. While the series are available for a larger number of countries, they contain several limitations that reduce their utility. First, figures are limited to urban areas and, in the cases of Argentina and Paraguay, to the capital city. Second, they are reported for different years, depending on the timing of the national census or household surveys. Third, they are based on categories that obscure the relative income levels accruing to the different classes. In particular, the category "employers" includes owners of firms of all sizes. Microentrepreneurs, who are far more numerous than medium and large employers, swamp these figures, leading to significant underestimates of the actual incomes of the capitalist class.

More useful are the figures for total average incomes and for microentrepreneurs, formal sector workers, and the different components of the informal proletariat. These categories are defined consistently across years and between countries. The available series are presented in table 6.4. They indicate that, for most Latin American countries, average urban incomes either stagnated or declined during the period of neoliberal adjustment. In Brazil and Mexico, they declined fractionally—from 5.6 and 4.8 multiples of the per capita poverty line in the early 1980s, to 5.0 and 4.1 in the late 1990s. In Uruguay and Venezuela, however, the decline was much more dramatic, reducing average incomes by one-third in Uruguay and by more than 50 percent in Venezuela.

TABLE 6.4
Evolution of Average Occupational Incomes by Social Classes in Latin America[1]

Country	Year	Total	Employers[2]	Professionals/ Technicians	Micro-entrepreneurs[3]	Formal Workers[4]	Informal Workers		
							Waged Laborers[5]	Own Account	Domestic Servants
Argentina[6]	1980	6.9	19.3	15.6	18.4	6.6	5.1	5.2	3.1
	1990	6.4	20.6	9.4	18.4	4.5	3.6	7.2	3.5
	1997	7.2	24.2	–	23.1	–	–	–	2.6
Bolivia	1989	4.2	16.2	7.7	11.8	3.6	2.7	3.8	1.6
	1994	3.5	10.3	7.3	8.1	2.7	2.0	2.2	1.0
	1997	3.6	10.1	8.8	7.1	3.2	2.2	2.3	1.1
Brazil	1979	5.6	21.8	9.4	16.6	4.8	2.5	5.2	1.1
	1990	4.7	16.1	8.2	11.3[7]	3.8	2.6	3.4	1.0
	1996	5.0	19.1	10.7	14.0	3.9	2.5	3.7	1.5
Chile	1990	4.7	24.8	7.4	19.0	3.5	2.4	5.0	1.4
	1994	6.2	33.7	9.6	18.0	4.0	2.9	6.3	2.0
	1998	7.4	33.8	11.7	24.5	4.3	3.0	8.6	2.2

[1]Urban areas only. Figures are in multiples of the per capita poverty line for each country/year.
[2]All employers, including microentrepreneurs.
[3]Owners of firms employing up to 5 workers.
[4]Workers in firms employing 5 or more workers.
[5]Workers in microenterprises with less than 5 workers.
[6]Buenos Aires metropolitan area.
[7]Figure is for 1993.

TABLE 6.4 (continued[1])

Country	Year	Total	Employers[2]	Professionals/ Technicians	Micro- entrepreneurs[3]	Formal Workers[4]	Informal Workers		
							Waged Laborers[5]	Own Account	Domestic Servants
Colombia	1980	4.0	17.1	8.3	--	2.2	--	3.7	2.1
	1994	3.8	13.1	7.9	--	2.6	--	3.0	1.7
	1997	3.8	10.9	6.9	--	2.7	--	2.9	1.6
Costa Rica	1981	6.6	13.1	11.4	12.9	4.8	3.5	6.9	1.8
	1994	5.2	10.8	8.4	9.2	4.4	3.6	4.0	1.6
	1997	5.6	8.4	9.0	7.4	4.8	3.2	3.6	1.8
Ecuador	1990	2.8	4.8	6.0	4.0	2.9	2.3	1.9	0.8
	1994	2.9	6.6	5.2	6.1	2.6	1.9	2.0	0.9
	1997	3.0	6.6	5.7	6.5	2.9	1.8	2.1	0.9
Mexico	1984	4.8	14.8	8.8	13.3	4.4	--	1.7	4.1
	1994	4.4	18.3	9.5	13.8	3.0	1.7	1.2	3.3
	1998	4.1	18.2	6.9	11.7	3.1	1.9	1.3	2.6
Panama	1979	5.6	6.5	13.6	--	5.0	--	2.9	1.4
	1991	5.0	11.8	9.4	7.7	4.1	2.6	2.3	1.3
	1997	5.6	15.4	10.0	11.5	4.1	2.6	3.4	1.4

[1]Urban areas only. Figures are in multiples of the per capita poverty line for each country/year.
[2]All employers, including microentrepreneurs.
[3]Owners of firms employing up to 5 workers.
[4]Workers in firms employing 5 or more workers.
[5]Workers in microenterprises with less than 5 workers.

(continued on next page)

TABLE 6.4 (*continued*[1])

Country	Year	Total	Employers[2]	Professionals/ Technicians	Micro- entrepreneurs[3]	Formal Workers[4]	Informal Workers		
							Waged Laborers[5]	Own Account	Domestic Servants
Paraguay[6]	1986	3.1	9.0	6.9	7.6	2.6	1.7	2.2	0.7
	1990	3.4	10.3	4.7	8.2	2.6	1.8	3.8	0.8
	1996	3.6	10.6	6.5	7.2	3.1	2.3	2.8	1.2
Uruguay	1981	6.8	23.6	10.0	19.9	4.1	3.0	1.8	8.1
	1990	4.3	12.0	7.6	8.9	3.7	2.5	1.5	5.1
	1997	4.9	11.5	9.8	9.8	4.6	3.0	1.8	3.5
Venezuela	1981	7.6	11.6	14.9	11.0	6.9	6.7	4.9	4.1
	1990	4.5	11.9	6.6	9.5	3.6	2.5	4.3	2.1
	1997	3.6	11.2	5.8	9.4	2.4	1.7	3.9	1.4

[1]Urban areas only. Figures are in multiples of the per capita poverty line for each country/year.
[2]All employers, including microentrepreneurs.
[3]Owners of firms employing up to 5 workers.
[4]Workers in firms employing 5 or more workers.
[5]Workers in microenterprises with less than 5 workers.
[6]Asunción only.
Source: Economic Commission for Latin America and the Caribbean, *Panorama Social*, tables 6, 11.

The clear exception to this pattern is Chile where incomes increased by 57 percent during the 1990s. Reflecting this favorable scenario, the incomes of *all* classes rose in agreement with the conventional economic expectation that a "rising tide lifts all boats."[23] However, the "lifting" was unequal. Employers as a group increased their share from twenty-five times the poverty line to thirty-four times, while formal sector workers only rose from 3.5 to 4.3. As a result, the income gap between the two groups rose from a ratio of 7 to 1 to 8 to 1. Microentrepreneurs and the self-employed did better in this expanding economy than waged workers (formal or informal). As a consequence the relative incomes of microentrepreneurs increased fractionally from 7.9 times those of informal workers to 8.2 times.

With this exception, the evolution of the incomes of microentrepreneurs and of the different sectors composing the informal proletariat reflected the overall performance of the urban economies of the region: in almost every case, the incomes of these classes either stagnated or declined during the last decades. The same is true for the formal proletariat, again defined as employees in firms employing five or more workers. In Brazil, the incomes of the formal proletariat declined from 4.8 to 3.9 the poverty line; in Mexico, from 4.4 to 3.1; and in Venezuela, from 6.9 to 2.4. In all these countries, the incomes of informal workers followed a parallel negative trend.

Rising Gini indexes of income inequality and related measures indicate that incomes of the capitalist class followed the opposite course. By 1997, the detailed ECLAC analysis of eight countries showed that while average occupational incomes of all employers represented 15.8 times the poverty line, those of large and medium employers had reached thirty times this figure.[24] As a result, the income ratio between the true capitalist class and the formal proletariat in these countries was 10 to 1; the corresponding ratio between the top and bottom of the class structure (informal workers) was of 15 to 1.

Klein and Tokman analyzed the evolution of income inequality in nine Latin American countries on the basis of changes in the ratio of income accruing to the top 20 percent of the population and that received by the bottom 40 percent. Their results are summarized in table 6.5. They show that in every country, with the exception of Panama, the incomes of the top quintile of the population grew faster (or declined less) than those of the bottom two quintiles. As a consequence, the coefficient of inequality between the two groups increased significantly in eight of the nine countries.

TABLE 6.5
Income Growth and Distribution in Nine Latin American Countries
during the 1990s

	Annual Income Growth Rates[1] (1990–1996)		Coefficient of Inequality[2]	
	Bottom 40 percent	Top 20 percent	1990	1996
Argentina	3.5	6.4	7.0	8.0
Brazil	1.3	1.5	19.2	21.5
Chile	4.1	5.9	9.4	10.4
Colombia	2.5	3.9	4.3	4.6
Costa Rica	−0.6	2.7	3.0	3.4
Mexico	−3.8	0.2	6.0	7.1
Panama	2.6	2.2	4.7	4.7
Peru	2.7	3.0	7.9	8.5
Venezuela	−11.5	−9.1	4.7	7.6

[1] Income growth rates in constant prices for each country.
[2] Ratio of nominal average income of the top quintile of the population to the bottom two quintiles.
Source: Klein and Tokman, "La estratificación social bajo tensión," tables 5 and 6.

The figures reported by Klein and Tokman are an underestimate of the growing economic disparity between the elites and the formal and informal proletariat. This is so because the top quintile of the population is approximately twice the size of the three dominant classes combined. Since, as seen previously, the incomes of *all* the other classes, including petty entrepreneurs, declined or stagnated during this period, the advantage of the top quintile of the population must be due exclusively to the gains accruing to those at the very top. On the assumption that the incomes of the next-to-highest decile remained stagnant during the 1990s (an assumption rendered plausible by results in table 6.4), the rate of income growth of the dominant classes should be approximately double the figures reported by these authors.

In synthesis, results of this analysis show that: (a) with the exception of Chile, the average incomes of the Latin American urban workforce stagnated or declined in real terms during the period of neoliberal adjustment; (b) the average incomes of all the subordinate classes, including the urban petty bourgeoisie, declined as well; (c) the incomes of the dominant classes increased faster than average in all countries, with the exception of Panama, but including Chile; (d) as a result, the ratio of income received by these classes relative to the various proletarian classes increased during this period, exacerbating what already was a gulf in the economic condition and life chances of the wealthy and the poor. More than ever, the fact was reaffirmed that, in Latin America, it is not necessary to be unemployed in order to be poor. The vast majority of the *working* population receives wages that condemn it to poverty, in part because of the generalized underdevelopment of their national economies, but also because of the highly skewed distribution of the economic pie.

CRIME AND INSECURITY

From the preceding results, it appears evident that while the Washington consensus advocated neoliberal adjustment policies as the means for salvation of countries as a whole, it had a clear class subtext. The elites who implemented and defended these policies also benefited mightily from them, while the subordinate classes paid the price in terms of growing inequality and, in most countries, absolute immiseration. In normal times, one would have expected organizations of the working class to forcefully resist these policies; these were not normal times, however, as one of the principal consequences of the new model was the severe weakening of the unionized proletariat by the wholesale expulsion of their members from formal employment. It is always easier to confront working-class mobilization with plant closures than with police, and this is, in effect, what happened throughout the region.[25]

The evaporation of employment opportunities and chances for economic mobility for the formal and informal working classes took place against a backdrop in which the prosperity of the elites led to novel forms of conspicuous consumption.[26] From this social context, one can infer that not only absolute but also relative deprivation would rise, as informal workers and petty entrepreneurs contrasted their lot with that of those above them. The unfolding of the neoliberal experiment produced a social landscape resembling that portrayed by Robert Merton in his classic essay, "Social Structure and Anomie": Desirable standards of modern consumption were broadcasted for all to see and want, while the means to attain them were available to only a few.[27] Merton's prediction was that such a situation would lead to a series of unorthodox outcomes, including rising property crime. This is indeed what took place. In the new free-for-all market promoted by neoliberal ideology, it is not surprising that some of the most disadvantaged members of society would seek redress by ignoring the existing normative framework. Perceptions of crime and civil insecurity have risen as a result in most Latin American major cities. As an ECLAC report on the topic concludes: "Latin America and the Caribbean have experienced an increase in crime and violence. The situation is such that the mortality rate associated with violent deeds has begun to affect the general mortality rate. Delinquency has increased in all Latin American cities and is identified as a rising problem in all public opinion surveys."[28] A different Inter-American Development Bank report on the same subject concludes: "Crime has become a staple feature of many cities in Latin America. Muggings, burglaries, car jackings, and even homicides occur with alarming frequency and disarming impunity in many urban centers throughout the region."[29]

In support of these assertions, the latter report presents figures on the evolution of the homicide rate per 100,000, which are reproduced in table 6.6. They show a generalized rise in homicides for the region as a whole, albeit with significant national differences. The regional homicide rate stood at 20 per 100,000 in 1995, which made Latin America the most violent region of the world. The regional figure is significantly affected by extraordinary rates in Colombia and El Salvador. The countries of the Southern Cone plus Costa Rica still have low rates, but homicides have been on the rise in the Andean region countries, particularly in Venezuela and Brazil.

The evolution of property crime in two Latin American countries and their capital cities are graphically portrayed in figures 6.1 and 6.2. More than homicides, thefts and other forms of property crime are relevant here since they directly reflect attempts to appropriate wealth by unorthodox means. In Argentina, formerly a relatively tranquil country, the rate of property crimes increased 113 percent during the 1990s; in metropolitan Buenos Aires, the rate tripled. The evolution of Argentine crime rates shows two significant trends: First, property crimes grew everywhere, but where the situation reached truly critical levels was in the capital city, Buenos Aires. This trend is portrayed in figure 6.1. Second, as the figure also shows, crime rates actually declined during the early 1990s. It was during the second half of the decade, coinciding with the crisis of the neoliberal model, when property crimes virtually exploded.

TABLE 6.6
Homicide Rates per 100,000 Inhabitants: Selected Countries

Country	ca. 1980	ca. 1990	ca. 1995
El Salvador	—	138.2	117.0
Colombia	20.5	89.5	65.0
Brazil	11.5	19.7	30.1
Venezuela	11.7	15.2	22.0
Mexico	18.2	17.8	19.5
Peru	2.4	11.5	10.3
Panama	2.1	10.9	
Ecuador	6.4	10.3	
Argentina	3.9	4.8	
Costa Rica	5.7	4.1	
Uruguay	2.6	4.0	
Chile	2.6	3.0	

Sources: Ayres, "Crime and Violence as Development Issues," table 1; Arriagada and Godoy, "Prevention or Repression?" table 2.

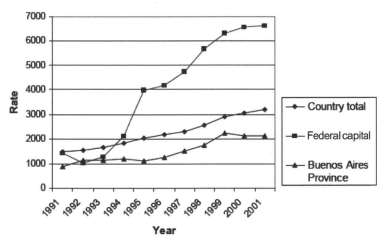

Figure 6.1 Argentina: Total Crime Rates (per 100,000 inhabitants)
Source: Cerrutti (2003) based on official crime statistics.

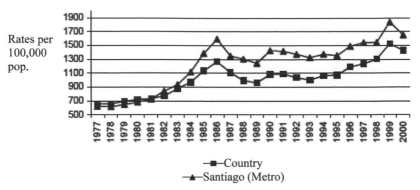

Figure 6.2 Property Crime in Chile, 1977–2000
Source: Wormald et al. (2003) based on annual police reports.

It is not surprising that the new crime wave was greater in the large cities because it is there where the dominant classes concentrate and where the disparities between their lifestyles and those of the proletariat are most apparent. A parallel trend was seen in Chile where property crimes doubled between 1977 and 2000, and those involving personal violence tripled. As shown in figure 6.2, the situation was even worse in the capital city, Santiago, where property crimes increased from 600 per 100,000 in 1977 to 1,650 per 100,000 in 2000. Hence, in the Latin American country held to be the "model" of neoliberal success, the situation was not much better than in the rest of the region. Chilean adjustment policies did reduce poverty significantly, but kept inequality at record levels. As seen previously, inequality is the factor leading directly to relative deprivation and, hence, unorthodox wealth appropriation.

The available quantitative figures on crime pale by comparison with the reactions of the citizenry, which, in survey after survey, highlights crime and insecurity as its major concern.[30] A study based on the *Latin Barometer* surveys of the mid-1990s report staggering victimization rates. As shown in figure 6.3, more than 40 percent of urban households in five countries (Ecuador, Guatemala, Mexico, Venezuela, and El Salvador) had at least one member victimized during the previous year. In Guatemala, the victimization rate exceeded 50 percent of urban households. For Latin America as a whole, the rate stood at 38 percent or more than twice the reported figure for Spain and seven times that for the United States.[31]

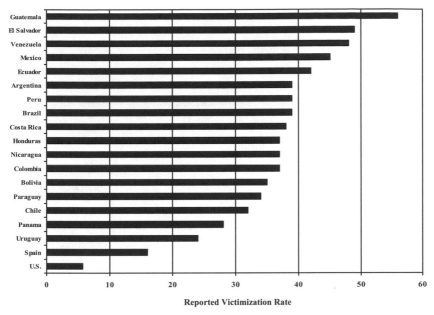

Figure 6.3 Victimization Rates by Country
Source: *Latin Barometer* 96–98 in Gaviria and Pages, "Patterns of Crime Victimization in Latin America." U.S. Bureau of the Census (2000b: Table 240).

Rising crime and insecurity throughout the region in the 1990s and 2000s stood as the not-so-unexpected counterpart of an ideology that preached individualism and self-reliance to all, while removing subsidies and other protective measures for the poor and failing to generate employment opportunities, save in the informal sector. Subsequent studies in Buenos Aires, Santiago, Mexico City, and elsewhere in the region showed that property crimes—thefts and robberies—were not limited to working-class settlements but extended increasingly to central city areas and the enclaves of the wealthy.[32] Thus, the wave of property crime affecting the region was not simply a matter of the poor preying on the poor, but exhibited a certain entrepreneurial logic in which some of the dispossessed went to areas where wealth concentrates to appropriate resources otherwise denied to them. The rising sense of insecurity reported in one study after another reflects the fact that muggings and robberies now occur through entire cities, not being limited, as before, to "dangerous" areas.

The reaction of the dominant classes to this situation has been swift. There has been a rapid growth of fortresslike gated communities where the wealthy isolate themselves from the rest of the urban population in Mexico City, Rio de Janeiro, São Paulo, and Buenos Aires. Similarly, there has been an explosive growth of private security services, especially in Colombia, but also in the other Andean countries, Brazil, and Mexico. In São Paulo, there are three times as many private security guards as policemen; in Guatemala, total private expenditure in security is estimated to exceed by 20 percent the public security budget.[33]

While the tiny segment of the population belonging to the dominant classes barricades itself in gated communities and hires private guards, all existing studies coincide in noting that the bulk of the perpetrators and often victims of urban crime are young males from impoverished families, themselves unemployed or informally employed. In Chile in 1996, 94 percent of those identified as responsible for armed robbery were young men, 60 percent were between fifteen and twenty-four years of age, and seventy-five were either jobless or manual workers. Among those captured for homicide in the same country, 87 percent were men, 46 percent below age twenty-five, and 77 percent jobless or informally employed.[34]

In agreement with Merton's hypothesis and, more generally, with sociological theories of property crime as a direct outgrowth of relative deprivation, there is consensus that the wave of crime engulfing Latin American cities is most prevalent in the more inegalitarian countries. Despite all the private security purchased by the wealthy, reported victimization rates—especially theft and other property crimes—are highest among the top income quintile of the population.[35] As seen previously, property crime is also highest in the largest cities, where members of the dominant classes generally live, and where the contrast between their lifestyles and the struggle for subsistence of the working classes becomes most glaring.

Urban crime should not be seen as a functional equivalent to the proletarian political mobilizations of the past because, despite rising rates, it is still remarkable how *few* members of the informal working class have taken that route. The actual political consequences of neoliberal policies took a different turn, as we shall see next. Nevertheless, the remarkable temporal coincidence between implementation of these policies and the crime wave throughout the region clearly points to one of the major social consequences of the model. As Argentine sociologist Marcela Cerrutti succinctly put it: "The causal association between the deterioration of labor market conditions—particularly, the rapid rise of open unemployment—with the rise in the crime rates is indisputable."[36]

CONCLUSION

This and the preceding chapter have presented two typologies of social classes and applied them to the analysis of major contemporary economic processes—industrial restructuring and immigration in the United States and neoliberal adjustment in Latin America. The difference between the two typologies illustrates their nominalist character. They do not seek to fit these processes into nineteenth-century molds, but are constructed as heuristic tools adapted to the respective contexts. As an explanatory tool, the concept of class serves, first and foremost, to clarify who gains and who loses from specific economic processes and policies and with what consequences. An analytic lens that views society as a level playing field obscures these differences, and even the concept of "inequality" does not provide sufficient analytic purchase because it does not fully clarify among whom inequality occurs and what are its basic structural causes and effects.[37]

In all three macroprocesses examined in this and the preceding chapter, it is clear that the principal beneficiaries were the dominant classes, including proprietors and elite professionals, while the main victims were the subordinate masses and, in particular, the formal proletariat. This was true both in North and South America. It is not the case, however, that all class struggles follow the same course or that elites invariably prevail. As an illustration of this final point, we may consider what has happened in Latin America in the aftermath of the neoliberal adjustment period.

If the experiment was successful in weakening the unions and the parties of the left, it also set the stage for a series of subsequent mobilizations unforeseen by its architects. The Washington consensus strongly supported liberal democracy as the political counterpart of economic "free markets," assuming that sustained growth and the elites' hold on the levers of power would guarantee that "safe" politicians and parties would be elected to office. However, rapidly rising inequality and widespread popular discontent gave an opening to ambitious populist leaders. These were not commonly affiliated with traditional parties of the left, but created their own vehicles of electoral mobilization.

In one country after another, new social movements emerged to protest the social debacles brought about by neoliberalism and challenge the parties and elected officials associated with it. Although the social atomization of the informal petty bourgeoisie and, especially, the vast informal proletariat prevented them from organizing their own class parties, it did not prevent them from joining populist mobilizations organized by new charismatic leaders. Unlike the organizations of the traditional working class, which were employment based, the new populist movements are residentially based. The informal proletariat may not have in common places of work, but it shares places of residence in decaying inner-city neighborhoods and in the vast suburban belt of poor irregular settlements.[38] To these areas went the newly minted nationalist and populist leaders in search of popular support for their programs.

The Argentine economic debacle of 2000 brought about by the most orthodox application of neoliberal policies in the region forced the resignation of a conservative president and created a golden opportunity for a resurgent nationalist leftist Peronism. The new leaders defied the International Monetary Fund and the U.S. Treasury by devaluing the currency, freezing the rates charged by foreign-owned utilities, protecting domestic industry, and creating a vast emergency employment program. This unorthodox program reduced poverty by more than half, brought down unemployment to the single digits, and produced sustained economic growth for several years. These achievements were so popular that they enabled Peronist president Nestor Kirchner to have his wife elected to the presidency by a wide margin.[39]

In Brazil and Uruguay, populist leaders displaced traditional parties, being elected to office with a clear mandate to do away with neoliberal adjustment. Although presidents Lula da Silva and Tabaré Vazquez subsequently adopted more moderate policies than in Argentina, their orientation and goals were the same. In Chile, two socialist presidents were elected in succession, charged by the citizenry to reduce economic inequalities and do away with the social depredations of neoliberal policies under the Pinochet dictatorship.

Arguably the most radical rejection of the Washington consensus and the politicians associated with it took place in Venezuela. Overwhelming popular support for nationalist leader Hugo Chávez and his successive elections to the presidency effectively destroyed the traditional party structure of Venezuela and severely undermined the power of its dominant classes. Chávez went on to spearhead a new hemispheric anti-imperialist alliance by establishing close ties with Cuba and supporting like-minded leaders in other countries. In rapid succession, election of populist leaders to the presidencies of Bolivia, Ecuador, and Nicaragua effectively completed the transformation of the balance of power throughout the region.[40]

While the wave of property crime that engulfed the region in the 1990s may be interpreted as an individualistic response to rising inequality and relative deprivation, the massive political mobilizations of the 2000s revealed hitherto unsuspected sources of solidarity among the dispossessed. These mobilizations certainly took local elites and their North American sponsors by surprise, as they effectively challenged established power arrangements and produced consequences that were exactly the opposite of what neoliberal planners had anticipated.

Thus we end our review of the transformation of Latin American class structures on a very different note from that with which we started it. Recent events exemplify the importance of three economic sociology assumptions and concepts examined in prior chapters: first, the unexpected consequences of seemingly rational policies; second, the role of bounded solidarity among the subordinate classes in challenging elite power under certain conditions; third, the danger of policies imposed from the heights of the power structure without sufficient legitimacy in the value system.

The framers of the Washington consensus dreamed of an endless era of free markets for Latin America, with economic power secure in the hands of domestic, and especially global, capital and with docile parties playing a restricted and predictable democratic game. These dreams came crashing down out of failure to take into account the warnings implicit in the preceding three assumptions and concepts. Policies implemented from above by orthodox economists and their political allies without regard for popular sentiment brought about the very consequences that they had sought to prevent. In the process, neoliberalism succeeded in achieving a feat that political theorists had thought nearly impossible in the past—the effective mobilization of the informal proletariat and its success in imposing the power of its numbers over entrenched privilege. As a consequence, the "map" of the Latin American class structure is changing and may be expected to change further in the coming years.

CHAPTER SEVEN

The Informal Economy

HAVING EXAMINED a set of three midrange ideal types that function as explanatory tools for economic sociology, this chapter introduces the first of strategic field sites for research mentioned in chapter 2.[1] Each of them is the subject of an extensive literature in which the meta-assumptions of the field, as well as its explanatory mechanisms, figure prominently. They are by no means exhaustive of all such subjects but serve to illustrate, with clarity, the ways in which sociological concepts can be used for the study of economic phenomena.

The phenomenon of the informal economy is deceivingly simple and extraordinarily complex, trivial in its everyday manifestations and capable of subverting the economic and political order of nations. We encounter it in our daily life in such simple activities as buying a cheap watch or a book from a street vendor, arranging for a handyman to do repair work at our home for cash, or hiring an immigrant woman to care for the children and clean the house while we are away. Such apparently trivial encounters may be dismissed as unworthy of attention until we realize that, in the aggregate, they cumulate into the billions of dollars of unreported income and that the humble vendor or cleaning woman represents the end point of complex subcontracting, labor recruitment, and labor transportation chains.

We do not commonly realize either that the clothing we wear, the restaurant meals we eat, and even the laptop computer we regularly use may have anything to do with the informal economy. In fact they do, and the intricate ways in which informal labor and goods enter into production and distribution chains underlie both the lower cost of the final products and their ready availability. To take the mystery away from these assertions, we will simply mention the facts underlying them: (a) The garment industry that produces the clothing items we buy and use is commonly anchored, at the other end of the production chain, by unregulated or poorly regulated sweatshops and home workers sewing, stitching, and packing for a piece rate and with no social benefits;[2] (b) the "back of the house" staff that does much of the cleaning and food preparation work in many restaurants is composed of immigrants, frequently recently arrived and undocumented, who are paid in cash and are not covered by labor contracts;[3] (c) the computer industry that produces the laptops we use is known for subcontracting assembly of circuit boards and other components to small, often unregulated shops and even home workers; these subcontractors are paid a piece rate in an updated version of the "putting out" system. Beverly Lozano, who studied these practices in Silicon Valley, concludes:

> [T]he computer industry requires a reliable supply of basic components that can be delivered quickly. Many small and medium-sized firms compete effectively as subcontract vendors with operations overseas. One of my respondents works for such a subcontractor out of her garage, putting together the most labor intensive portion of an assembly. . . . Rush jobs, custom work, confidential projects—managers describe them as rare events. . . . But when all these rare events are aggregated, we find that every day another "entrepreneur" . . . joins the ranks of the self-employed.[4]

The examples could be multiplied. However, the purpose of this chapter is not to describe the vast range of informal enterprises covered in the literature, but to explore how these activities interact with existing social structures and the policies and enforcement practices of national states. It is in these interactions that the character of the informal economy emerges clearly and where its lessons for both economic and sociological theories of market behavior are shown most compellingly. After examining alternative definitions and measurement approaches, the analysis will focus on these dynamics centered on four paradoxes: the social underpinnings of the informal economy, its ambiguous relationships with state regulation, its elusiveness, and its functionality for the economic and political institutions that it supposedly undermines. The known dynamics of the informal economy reflect well the meta-assumptions of economic sociology. As the following sections will show, informal economic activities depend on social embeddedness; they represent the unexpected consequences of seemingly rational policies and lead, in turn, to unanticipated effects. As seen in the prior chapter, informal entrepreneurs and workers are integral components of the class structure of certain societies and, under specific circumstances, can effectively challenge existing power arrangements. Informality is the obverse of regulated, predictable economic behavior and, for this reason, it is intrinsically subversive, challenging many expectations about how such behavior occurs in reality.

DEFINITIONS

Origins of the Concept

The concept of *informal economy* was born in the third world, out of a series of studies on urban labor markets in Africa. Keith Hart, the economic anthropologist who coined the term, saw it as a way of giving expression to "the gap between my experience there and anything my English education had taught me before." In his view, the empirical observations about popular entrepreneurship in Accra and other African capitals were clearly at odds with received wisdom from "the western discourse on economic development."[5]

In his report to the International Labour Organization (ILO), Hart postulated a dualist model of income opportunities of the urban labor force, based largely on the distinction between wage employment and self-employment. The concept of informality was applied to the self-employed. Hart emphasized the notable dynamics and diversity of these activities that, in his view, went well beyond "shoeshine boys and sellers of matches."[6] This dynamic characterization of the informal sector was subsequently lost as the concept became institutionalized within the ILO bureaucracy, which essentially redefined informality as synonymous with poverty. The informal economy was taken to refer to an "urban way of doing things" characterized by: (1) low entry barriers in terms of skill, capital, and organization; (2) family ownership of enterprises; (3) small scale of operation; (4) labor intensive production with outdated technology; and (5) unregulated and competitive markets.[7]

Additional characteristics derived from this definition included low levels of productivity and a low capacity for accumulation. In later publications of the ILO's Regional Employment Programme for Latin America (PREALC), employment in the informal sector was consistently termed *underemployment* and assumed to affect workers who could not gain entry into the modern economy. This characterization of informality as an excluded sector in less developed economies has been enshrined in numerous ILO, PREALC, and World Bank studies of urban poverty and labor markets.[8]

That negative definition of the informal sector was challenged by other students of the subject who saw it in the opposite light. From that alternative stance, informal activities were regarded as a sign of the popular entrepreneurial dynamism, described by Hart as "people taking back in their own hands some of the economic power that centralized agents sought to deny them."[9] The Peruvian economist Hernando de Soto reformulated Hart's original theme and gave it renewed impulse. In his book, *The Other Path*, De Soto defined informality as the popular response to the rigid "mercantilist" states dominant in Peru and other Latin American countries that survive by granting the privilege of legal participation in the economy to a small elite. Hence, unlike its portrayal by ILO and PREALC as a survival mechanism in response to insufficient modern job creation, informal enterprise represents, from this alternative perspective, the irruption of real market forces in an economy straitjacketed by state regulation.[10]

Contemporary Definitions

The strong normative component attached to these competing analyses of the informal sector in the third world is not entirely absent in the industrialized countries, but research there has attempted to arrive at a more precise and less tendentious definition. There appears to be growing consensus among researchers in the advanced world that the proper scope of the term *informal sector* encompasses "those actions of economic agents that fail to adhere to the established institutional rules or are denied their protection."[11] Or, alternatively, it includes "all income-earning activities that are not regulated by the state in social environments where similar activities are regulated."[12]

These definitions do not advance an a priori judgment of whether such activities are good or bad, leaving the matter to empirical inquiry. In this sense, they are superior to those described previously, which anticipate from the start the conclusions to be reached. However, even neutral definitions are hampered by the very breadth of the subject matter they try to encompass. Writing from the perspective of the New Institutional Economics, Edgar Feige proposes a useful taxonomy as a way of specifying the relevant universe further. His classification is based on the institutional rules that go unobserved by a particular economic activity. Under the umbrella term *underground economy*, he distinguishes four subtypes:

1. The *illegal* economy encompasses the production and distribution of legally prohibited goods and services. This includes such activities as drug trafficking, prostitution, and illegal gambling.
2. The *unreported* economy consists of actions that "circumvent or evade established fiscal rules as codified in the tax code."[13] The amount of income that should be reported to the tax authorities but is not represents a summary measure of this form.

3. The *unrecorded* economy encompasses activities that circumvent reporting requirements of government statistical agencies. Its summary measure is the amount of income that should be recorded in national accounting systems but is not.
4. The *informal* economy comprises economic actions that bypass the costs and are excluded from the protection of laws and administrative rules covering "property relationships, commercial licensing, labor contracts, torts, financial credit, and social security systems."[14]

Of course, there is much overlap between these various forms since activities termed informal are also, for the most part, unrecorded and unreported. The most important conceptual distinction is that between informal and illegal activities since each possesses distinct characteristics that set them apart from the other. Sociologists recognize that legal and criminal, like normal or abnormal, are socially defined categories subject to change. However, illegal enterprise involves the production and commercialization of goods that are defined in a particular place and time as illicit, while informal enterprise deals, for the most part, with licit goods.

Manuel Castells and I attempted to clarify this distinction in the diagram reproduced as figure 7.1. The basic difference between formal and informal does not hinge on the character of the final product, but on the manner in which it is produced and/or exchanged. Thus, articles of clothing, restaurant food, or computer circuit boards—all perfectly licit goods—may have their origins in legally regulated production arrangements or in those that bypass official rules. By explicitly distinguishing among these three categories—formal, informal, and illegal activities—it is possible to explore their mutual relationships systematically, a task that becomes difficult when illegal and informal are confused.[15]

A Functional Typology

This distinction plus a number of past studies have given rise to a functional classification of informal activities according to their goals. Such activities—always defined as those taking place outside the pale of state regulation may aim, first, at the survival of the individual or household through direct subsistence production or through the simple sale of goods and services. Second, they may be oriented toward increasing managerial flexibility and decreasing labor costs of formal sector firms through off-the-books hiring and subcontracting of informal entrepreneurs. Third, they may be organized for capital accumulation by small firms through

I. Definitions:

+ = Licit
− = Illicit

Process of Production and Distribution	Final Product	Economic Type
+	+	Formal
−	+	Informal
−	−	Criminal

II. Relationships:

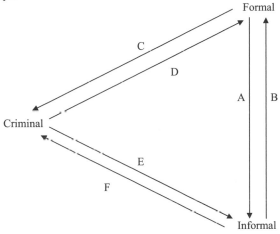

A. State interference, competition from large firms, sources of capital and technology.
B. Cheaper consumer goods and industrial inputs, flexible reserves of labor.
C. State interference and disruption, supplies of certain controlled goods.
D. Corruption, "gatekeeper's rents" for selected state officials.
E. Capital, demand for goods, new income-earning opportunities.
F. Cheaper goods, flexible reserves of labor.

Figure 7.1 Types of Economic Activities and Their Interrelationships
Source: Castells and Portes, "World Underneath," p. 14.

mobilization of their bonds of solidarity, greater flexibility, and lower costs. The three types are labeled respectively informal economies of *survival*, *dependent exploitation*, and *growth*.[16] The self-construction of shelter and the proliferation of street vending in cities of the third world are commonly cited as examples of the first type. The relationships among underground subcontractors, jobbers, and large firms in the U.S. apparel industry provide an example of the second. The highly successful networks of artisan microproducers in central Italy (cited in chapter 2 and described at greater length below) represent an instance of the third.[17]

In practice, the three types are not mutually exclusive, either in terms of their coexistence in the same urban settings or the intentions of participants. Thus, the same work that represents "survival" for an informal laborer may be appropriated as "flexibility" by the formal firm that hires her. Similarly, informal subcontractors linked in subordinate relations with larger firms may amass sufficient capital and cooperative ties to launch themselves into an autonomous path of growth. The three types are distinguished less by the motivation of actors than by the successively more complex levels of social organization that they require. Hence, while survival strategies of informal vendors in third world cities are by no means simple, they are in a different plane altogether than the complex coordination required by an entire community of producers to achieve sustained growth.[18]

The Dynamics of Informality

The Paradox of Social Embeddedness

Because of the absence of state regulation, informal transactions are commonly portrayed as the reign of pure market forces. Indeed, celebratory accounts of the informal economy often define it as the irruption of the "true market" in an otherwise straitjacketed economy, stifled by state regulation. Based on his African experience, Hart called it the "untamed market" and declared that such liberating practices are becoming global in scope.[19] The substantive problem is, however, that the absence of regulation in informal economic exchange opens the door for violations of normative expectations and widespread fraud. The question arises: in the absence of supervisory agents, who is to control unscrupulous producers, purveyors of adulterated goods, and defaulters on loans? Isolated arms-length transactions may still occur among strangers, such as the quick sale of a contraband good, but activities that require greater resources and a longer-time perspective are subject to every kind of uncertainty and peril.

The problem manifests itself even at the level of short-term face-to-face transactions. The immigrant laborers who are commonly seen standing on street corners waiting for work in New York, Miami, Los Angeles, and other cities exemplify the dilemma. They are commonly picked up by contractors who hire them for days or even weeks only to defraud them at the end by paying them lower wages than originally promised. In the absence of a contract and a secure legal status in the country, how are these laborers to seek redress?[20]

It is worth noticing the significant difference in this respect between practices defined as illegal and as informal. Illegal enterprise that provides illicit goods or services on a recurrent basis is always accompanied by some means of enforcing agreements, usually by force. This is the role played by the pimp in prostitution, the bouncer in underground nightspots, and the professional enforcer in Sicilian crime families. Here the illegal economy is closer to the formal in the sense that both possess established systems of redress and enforcement, be they through the police and the courts or through specialized enforcement personnel. In contrast, many of the practices defined as informal are devoid of such protection. The garment subcontractor who delivers one hundred shirts to an informal middleman on the promise of future payment is entirely at the mercy of that promise. Similarly, the immigrant worker who is hired informally by a labor contractor has no means of enforcing his claim to the stipulated wage.

The first paradox of the informal economy is that the more it approaches the model of the "true market," the more it is dependent on social ties for its effective functioning. The dynamics of social embeddedness is nowhere clearer than in transactions where the only recourse against malfeasance is mutual trust by virtue of common membership in some social structure.[21] Trust in informal exchanges is generated by shared identities and feelings and by the expectation that fraudulent actions will be penalized by the exclusion of the violator from key social networks and from future transactions. This is the source of social capital identified in chapter 3 as "enforceable trust." To the extent that economic resources flow through such transactions, the socially enforced penalty of exclusion can become more threatening, and hence more effective, than legal sanctions.

The Central Italian Informal Economy

Examples of this paradox abound in the literature. The famed Italian industrial district in the central region of Emilia-Romagna, referred to in chapter 1, is the best-known instance of an informal economy of growth. The trust necessary to sustain relationships of cooperation and complicity among small firms and between proprietors and employees is anchored in a common history and political culture. The artisanal tradition in

Emilia-Romagna dates back to the Middle Ages, while starting in the twentieth century political solidarity was strengthened by a fierce struggle against fascism and, subsequently, against the attempts of the Christian Democratic government in Rome to impose a capitalist model based on large firms in Milan and other northern cities.[22]

To these attempts, Emilian artisan-entrepreneurs opposed a social capital stemming from bounded solidarity and reinforced by the regional government in the hands of the Communist Party. In a very practical turn, the Italian Communist Party (PCI) abandoned its proletarian ideology to support cooperative small-firm capitalism through technical training and marketing assistance. It also protected fledgling informal enterprises from the central government's regulatory and taxing apparatus. This protection and the common front presented by the producers themselves allowed such firms to grow and find a niche in the networks of local cooperative economic activity.[23] The success of each individual firm depended on the unique social context in which it was embedded so that enforceable trust underlay complex credit and production exchanges within the community.

According to Sebastiano Brusco, Vittorio Cappechi, and other students of the Emilian system, its central feature was the absence of vertical relationships between large firms and their subcontractors. Instead, complex products, including motorcycles and machine tools, were put together by a network of small firms of which the final assembler was not necessarily the largest.[24] Social capital grounded on bounded solidarity and enforceable trust, local government support, and technological know-how enabled a band of small producers, who elsewhere would have been fragmented by market competition, to create an industrial district that for decades functioned as one of the principal engines of economic growth in Italy.

Informality under Socialist Regimes

By definition, informal economic activities bypass existing laws and the regulatory agencies of the state. It follows that the more pervasive the enforcement of state rules and the greater the penalties for violation, the more socially embedded informal transactions must be. This is so because their success in highly repressive situations depends not only on preventing malfeasance by partners but also on avoiding detection by the authorities. Secrecy in these situations demands a high level of mutual trust, and the only way trust can be created is through the existence of tight social networks.

The operation of the Jewish informal economy in the former Soviet Republic of Georgia, also described in chapter 2, represents a good example of this type of situation. While Soviet authorities defined these activities as criminal and penalized them accordingly, they represented an instance of an informal economy of growth since they focused on the clandestine production of consumer goods. The high levels of trust necessary for the operation of this economy were cemented on strong ethnic/religious bonds and a common opposition to the Soviet regime. Furthermore, participants in these activities were fully aware of the dearth of economic opportunities outside of what they were doing.[25]

High levels of mutual support in the face of great risks were reinforced by periodic rites of solidarity that included lavish feasts in which other network members were entertained, often at great expense. Bounded solidarity among network members, symbolized and strengthened by these rites, represented an added element supporting clandestine transactions and preventing breaches of secrecy. Nevertheless, it was not spontaneous feelings of solidarity, but the enforcement capacity of the community that constituted the ultimate guarantee against such violations.[26] Enforceable trust lay at the heart of this unique informal economy of growth.

Reports from Cuba—the last formally socialist regime in the West—confirm these results. Despite the threat of heavy fines and prison terms, the Cuban informal economy has flourished, comprising, according to some estimates, up to 40 percent of the national domestic product in 2000. There are clandestine factories making and repairing motors for water pumps and refrigerators, manufacturing soft drinks and beer, and producing cigars for export. Home construction and, especially, home repairs are increasingly informalized. In all instances, inputs for production, construction, and repairs come from thefts of state property.[27]

While short-term transactions involving black market goods do not require any particular social bond, entire clandestine factories and marketing enterprises are invariably undergirded by family and other ties among implicated state personnel, middlemen or *bisneros* (from "businessman"), and final consumers. As in Soviet Georgia, those bonds are indispensable for generating enforceable trust, which, in turn, makes possible extensive and sustained informal enterprise:

> Legally, it is impossible to own a small enterprise in Cuba. Yet there is a great variety of clandestine enterprises with a notable capacity of innovation and accumulation. . . . When one enters the exclusive zone of Miramar in Havana, vendors call in a low voice "microwave," "air conditioner," "bedroom set," "parabolic antenna" . . . a great variety of products forbidden to Cubans.

Where do they get them? Without doubt from state supplies, but there are also clandestine networks departing from the special export processing zones. Here we find everything: theft, corruption, speculation, delivery of products by foreign firms to their Cuban workers for sale in the black markets.[28]

THE ROLE OF THE STATE

The Paradox of State Control

As an example of what he calls the "predatory state" in the third world, Peter Evans describes the case of Zaire (today's Congo). Under the long regime of Mobutu Sese Seko, the Zairian state degenerated into a collection of fiefdoms—offices freely bought and sold—that thrived on the collection of "gatekeepers' rents" from firms and from the population at large. For Evans the situation is one in which state officials squeeze resources from civil society "without any more regard for the welfare of the citizenry than a predator has for the welfare of its prey."[29] He notes that this is an extreme example, buttressing the critique by public choice theorists about the nefarious consequence of state interference in the economy. For public choice advocates, all states sooner or later become predatory.[30]

The logical corollary of this position, and more broadly that advanced by neoutilitarian theorists, is the complete removal of state interference from the market as inimical to its development. This position finds an enthusiastic third world echo in the critique of the mercantilist state advanced by De Soto and his followers. The neoliberal experiment in Latin America, described in chapter 6, was largely anchored by the same theoretical rationale. There is, however, another perspective from which the behavior of rapacious state officials may be described. More than predators, these officials can be defined as de facto employees of outside entrepreneurs who hire their services in order to obtain privileged access to scarce government resources, be they contracts or the nonobservance of regulations. The more state officials are willing to bend the rules for a price, the more the situation approaches that of a free market in which goods and services—in this case those purveyed by the state—are sold to the highest bidder.

This marketization of the state does not so much represent the triumph of the informal economy as the elimination of the distinction between the two sectors. In a situation where the state does not regulate anything because it is at the mercy of market forces, there is no formal economy.

Hence, the formal/informal distinction loses meaning since all economic activities approach the character of those labeled informal. This triumph of the "invisible hand" does not lead to capitalist development, as would be anticipated from public choice theory and from De Soto's critique; the opposite is actually the case. In the absence of a stable legal framework and credible enforcement of contracts, long-term productive investment becomes impossible. Under these conditions, entrepreneurship consists of the opportunistic appropriation of rents through purchase of state privileges rather than of any long-term planning for profit. Since there is no outside arbiter of market competition, the rules become uncertain, frustrating systematic capitalist planning and the development of a modern business class. This is precisely what happened to Zaire, which descended from a relatively prosperous colony under Belgian rule to become one of the poorest nations in the world.[31]

The human propensity to "truck, barter, and exchange one thing for another," the Smithian dictum so dear to neoclassical theorists, does not in fact furnish a basis for economic development on a national scale. Someone must stand outside the competitive fray, making sure that property rules are enforced and contracts observed.[32] There is, however, a flip side to this situation well captured by Richard Adams's epigram that "the more we organize society, the more resistant it becomes to our ability to organize it."[33] A naive evolutionary view of the informal economy would depict it as dominant during an early era of weak regulation, while gradually becoming marginal and even insignificant as all facets of economic activity fall under state control. In fact, largely the opposite is the case. Since informal activities are defined precisely by their bypassing and escaping such controls, it follows that the greater the scope and reach of attempted state regulations, the more varied the opportunities to bypass them.

Larissa Lomnitz makes the point succinctly: "Order creates disorder. The formal economy creates its own informality."[34] The paradox of state control is that official efforts to obliterate unregulated activities through the proliferation of rules and controls often expand the very conditions that give rise to these activities. The point is graphically portrayed in figure 7.2. Under conditions of limited state control, most economic activity is self-regulated but not informal since it does not contravene any official rule. As rules expand, opportunities to bypass them increase concomitantly until, at the limit, the entire economy is subject to the possibility of rule violation for profit. To illustrate the point with a case familiar to most readers, tax havens and tax-avoiding schemes would not

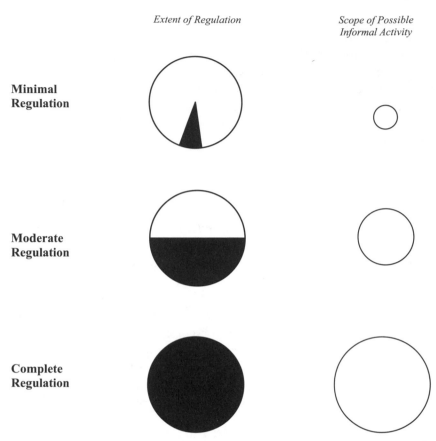

Extent of Regulation

*Scope of Possible
Informal Activity*

**Minimal
Regulation**

**Moderate
Regulation**

**Complete
Regulation**

Figure 7.2 The Paradox of State Control: Regulation and the Informal Economy

exist if there were no taxation system, the more intrusive the latter, the greater the incentive and the broader the opportunities to seek redress through concealment and through various transfer ploys. The paradox of state control is, in essence, a specific manifestation of unexpected consequences since attempts at controlling the economy can end up producing the very opposite effect.

State Capacities and Intent

The complex relationship between the state and the informal economy does not end there, however. Figure 7.2 makes clear that state regulation can create informality or, put differently, that the informal economy would not exist without a universe of formal, controlled activities. Yet, empirical evidence indicates that the scope and extent of the informal economy varies greatly among states with comparable formal regulations and, within nation-states, among different regions and localities. For example, the economies of northern European nations are highly regulated, but this has not produced a parallel bourgeoning informal sector, as would be predicted from figure 7.2. Similarly, rising unemployment in the old industrial cities of the U.S. northeast did not lead to a massive informal economy organized by members of the old displaced working class. While these workers commonly engaged in casual income-earning and self-provisioning activities, the construction of complex chains of informal industrial subcontracting was beyond their reach. In the United States, these chains remained confined, for the most part, to immigrant enclaves.

In the light of this and other evidence, Adams's and Lomnitz's hypothesis can be reformulated as predicting that the expansion of state regulation enhances the opportunities for engaging in irregular activities, but does not determine their actual size or form. The implementation of these opportunities depends on two other factors: (a) the state's regulatory capacity, and (b) the social structure and cultural resources of the population subject to these regulations. It is obvious that the capacity of official agencies to enforce the rules they promulgate affects the extent to which informal opportunities can be implemented and the forms they can take. It is less obvious that state strength is, in principle, independent of the set of rules it seeks to enforce. Put differently, states with comparable regulatory capacities may assign to themselves very different "loads" of attempted control of private economic activity. The point is highlighted in table 7.1, which distinguishes among several ideal-typical situations.

States with little enforcement capacity may be conscious of that fact and leave civil society to its own devices. This leads to a "frontier" economy where observance of commitments and regulation of economic exchanges depend on private force or traditional normative structures. Alternatively, a weak state may seek to transform this frontier economy into a more law-abiding one by promulgating a limited set of rules. This would lead naturally to a partition between an "enclave" of formal capitalism and legal enforcement of contracts and a largely self-regulated economy on the outside. This situation is typical of many third world nations where the formal enclave is usually limited to the capital city and its environs.[35]

TABLE 7.1
State Types According to Regulatory Intent and Capacity

		Regulatory Intent		
		Minimal	Limited	Total
State Strength	Weak	The Frontier State	The Enclave State	The Mercantilist State
	Strong	The Liberal State	The Social Democratic Welfare State	The Totalitarian State

Zaire under Mobutu (as described by Evans) or the Peruvian mercantilist state (as portrayed by De Soto) can be regarded as instances of a third situation in which extensive paper regulations of the economy coexist with an inept and weak state. This is the situation that favors the rise of a predatory pattern where only a small elite benefits from state protection and resources.[36]

Strong states oscillate, in turn, between a circumspect approach to regulation of the private economy and an attempt to supplant or control its every aspect. The first type represents the laissez faire state so dear to liberal theorists: markets operate with limited, but reliable supervision and the state orients its resources toward other pursuits. The opposite extreme devolves into totalitarianism, as exemplified by the nations of the defunct Soviet bloc. In these situations, the state seeks to subsume civil society, provoking both widespread resistance to the rules and multiple opportunities for their violation. In between are those governments that seek an activist, but partial regulatory role for the sake of a more equitable wealth distribution. The welfare states of Western Europe fall into this type. Thus, the political context in which economic exchange is embedded produces a "variable geometry" leading to alternative levels and forms of informality.

The Role of Civil Society

Variations in the scope of official regulations and states' differential capacity to police them interact with the characteristics of the population subject to these rules. It stands to reason that societies also vary in their receptivity or resistance to official regulation and in their ability to organize underground forms of enterprise. A population that is socialized into regular waged employment as the normal form of work, that channels demands through unions and other formal associations, and that weathers economic downturns through state-provided welfare and unemployment benefits is unlikely to organize an underground economy and is far more inclined to denounce those who engage in such activities.

This is the case of Germany, which offers the most generous unemployment benefits in Western Europe, but has also legislated tough sentences for those engaging in off-the-books economic activities while receiving those benefits. The policy is reported to receive strong support from public opinion, which regards such "side" employment as free-riding on law-abiding and tax-paying citizens. The British working class during the period of Thatcherist economic adjustment in the 1980s offers a parallel example. Despite double-digit rates of unemployment, declining wages, and widespread dissatisfaction with state policies, widespread informalization failed to emerge in Britain. Instead, those displaced from full-time formal work turned to part-time legal employment and to self-provisioning.[37]

In his study of working-class and middle-class households in the island of Sheppey, Raymond Pahl found, for example, that 55 percent engaged in self-provisioning for a variety of goods and services but only 4 percent performed the same tasks for informal wages outside the home.[38] Roberts argues that the failure of a large informal economy to materialize in Britain despite increasingly precarious employment conditions was due to the individualistic character of the welfare system, which fragments community solidarity, and to a working-class tradition that supports state control of the economy. In this context, independent efforts at informal entrepreneurship are more likely to be denounced as violations of the law than supported by neighbors and fellow workers.[39]

At the opposite end, networked communities accustomed to relying on their own devices for survival and suspicious of official intervention are more likely to view the organization of informal enterprise as a normal part of life and involvement in the underground economy as a justifiable form of resistance. Possessing sufficient social capital, undergirded by solidarity and enforceable trust, such communities are capable of sustaining regular economic transactions in "frontier" situations where little official regulations exists. This is the case of stateless or nearly stateless nations where tribal and clan solidarities come to occupy the place of official regulation. Somalia, a near-stateless country with a functioning private economy offers a case in point. Self-reliant communities confront state efforts to expand and strengthen the formal sector with an awesome adversary: no matter how strong the state apparatus is, a densely networked civil society is capable of derailing and resisting official authority at every turn. The Emilian story of resistance to the dictates of the central Italian state offers an example, in an altogether different context, of the potential effects of such networks.

It is thus necessary to complement the typology of political embeddedness in table 7.1 with one that incorporates the characteristics of society itself. This modified typology is presented in table 7.2. The resulting sixfold classification serves to highlight the point that an individualistic, atomized society "works" well only in tandem with states able to enforce limited regulation of market activity and to respond effectively to economic downturns through universalistic welfare programs. The democracies of Western Europe approximate this type. In the limiting case of little state control over an atomized population, the situation would reverse to a theoretical Hobbesian war since neither the state nor society would enforce sufficient restraint on self-seeking behavior. At the opposite extreme of complete atomization coupled with a powerful state, we would have the basis for totalitarianism, as society lies defenseless before governmental power. The Soviet Union in the heyday of Stalinism approximated this type.

It is difficult, however, to identify empirical instances of either extreme type because, in the absence of effective state regulation, civil society self-organizes on the basis of whatever grounds for solidarity and normative control can be found. In "frontier" situations, Hobbesian wars are prevented by the emergence of social hierarchies grounded on tradition and

TABLE 7.2
Civil Society and State Regulation of the Economy

		Extent of Intended Regulation		
		Minimal	Limited	Total
Character of Civil Society	Atomized	Hobbesian War	Universalistic State Enforcement of Rules (Western Democracies)	Totalitarian Planning
	Networked	Informal Enforcement of Rules	Competing Formal/Informal Enforcement of Rules	Widespread Anti-Statist Resistance

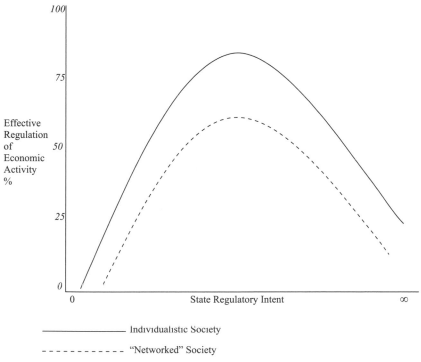

Figure 7.3 State Regulatory Power and the Extent of Regulation

able to enforce a minimum of predictability and order. In the totalitarian case, the initially unchecked government power becomes increasingly contested by sectors of civil society that find grounds for solidarity and ways to bypass omnipresent state rules. The end stage of this confrontation commonly features a state economy weakened, in multiple ways, by its inability to stamp out popular initiatives and simultaneously be dependent on them. This is what happened in the former Soviet Union and its East European satellites where the "second" economy succeeded in undermining and eventually replacing the state as the true pivot of economic activity.[40]

A logical corollary of this analysis is that the high point of formal regulation of the economy and ability to neutralize recalcitrant informal sectors is achieved in the midpoint of limited oversight by a competent state apparatus. Attempts to go beyond this limit inevitably trigger resistance, reducing the very scope of control that state rules seek to achieve. Figure 7.3

highlights the complementary point that densely networked communities are more difficult to subdue at any level of state regulation. This helps explain why organized informal subcontracting and other forms of informal enterprise in Western democracies are commonly rooted in tight-knit ethnic enclaves. It also explains why the most effective challenges to Soviet totalitarianism were mounted by groups who, like the Georgian Jews, could rely on solidaristic networks and a cultural basis for high social capital.[41]

To summarize, the basic paradox of state control is that increased official regulation of economic activity does not necessarily reduce the informal economy, but may expand it as it creates opportunities for profitable violation of the rules. However, the extent to which these opportunities are used varies with the scope of official control, the effectiveness of the state apparatus, and the countervailing power of society to resist or bypass official rules. The dual embeddedness of the economy in political and social contexts thus determines the geometry that formal-informal relations take. The discussion also makes clear that power is not a one-way street. Efforts by strong states to stamp out all traces of nonregulated economic activity seldom achieve this goal, as they consistently activate latent sources of solidarity among the population, leading to consequences that are frequently the opposite of those intended.

Measuring the Unmeasurable

The Labor Market Approach

By definition, informal activities violate the law, and thus participants seek to conceal them. This makes it impossible to arrive at precise and reliable estimates of the extent of these activities or the number of people involved in them. The capacity of society to confront the state is nowhere clearer than in its ability to mislead taxmen, inspectors, and statisticians as to what is really taking place. This capacity gives rise to a third paradox described later in this section.

In the absence of precise measures of the informal economy, a variety of approximations have been devised. They fall into four main categories: (a) the labor market approach, (b) the small firm approach, (c) the household consumption approach, (d) the macroeconomic discrepancy approach. Labor market approximations seek to estimate the percentage of the total or economically active population (EAP) that works informally on the basis of specific employment categories identified in censuses or nationally representative surveys. The assumption is that certain categories of people are more prone to conceal all or some of their income-earning activities from taxing and recording authorities. The self-employed are foremost among these groups.

Presumably, as Barry Molefsky points out, "the self-employed have greater opportunities to hide income and participate in the underground economy than other workers."[42] Indeed, a study by the U.S. Internal Revenue Service, cited by this author, found that 47 percent of workers classified as independent contractors did not report any of their earnings for tax purposes. A similar rationale has led the International Labour Organization (ILO) and its regional affiliates, such as the Regional Employment Program for Latin America (PREALC) to categorize the self-employed, minus professionals and technicians, as part of the informal sector.

A second suspect category is the unemployed because of the possibility that they may be working "on the side" while receiving benefits. This rationale is not plausible in third world countries where unemployment benefits are nonexistent, but it is quite applicable in advanced countries. For the United States, economist Peter Gutmann states flatly that "the U.S. unemployment rate, on which so much government policy depends, is substantially overstated."[43] In Gutmann's view, reinforced by later authors, about one in five of the officially unemployed is really a disguised informal worker or entrepreneur.

In a field study in Cleveland, R. MacDonald found that working while claiming benefits was "a way of life" among the poor, justified as a necessary strategy to make ends meet. Informal employment was provided by subcontractors who paid low wages for irregular work.[44] A similar pattern has been uncovered in a number of European countries. In Italy, the national statistical agency, ISTAT, estimated an irregular labor force in the construction industry numbering half a million workers in the early 1990s. These workers combined spells of unemployment, funded by state benefits, with periods of formal or informal employment. A common pattern is for construction firms to hire workers on the books for the minimum number of weeks legally required for benefits and then to dismiss them and rehire them informally through subcontractors. Similar findings have been reported in Greece and Ireland.[45]

A fourth category is the occupationally inactive. The rationale is that those not working and not looking for work are more likely to engage in underground activities, at least on a part-time basis. Gutmann used the recorded decline in male labor force participation between 1951 and 1976 and again between 1970 and 1990 to hypothesize that many of these drop-outs had actually moved to the underground economy.[46] This hypothesis is open to challenge on a number of counts, including the fact that the largest and only significant declines took place among male workers aged fifty-five or older. Clearly, other factors such as ill health, disability, or retirement can play a major role in accounting for these figures. In other age categories, male labor force participation rates fluctuated erratically while, among females, they increased consistently and sizably for all age groups, except the oldest.[47] These inconsistencies have led to the dismissal of labor force nonparticipation as a reliable indicator of informality.

The ILO adds other occupational categories to the informal sector based primarily on data from less developed countries but with applications to wealthier nations as well. Domestic servants and unpaid family workers are thus classified as informal. So are workers in microenterprises that employ up to five workers on the rationale that these enterprises are either off the books or, if registered, commonly fail to observe legal rules in their hiring practices. Based on these employment categories, as recorded in national household surveys, UN agencies can provide estimates of the informal labor force for most countries. Table 7.3 presents recent estimates for selected Latin American countries. These estimates reproduce those for the informal proletariat in the same countries, reported in the prior chapter. For comparative purposes, figures for the United States and three major states are also presented.

The U.S. figures are much lower than for Latin America, representing less than 10 percent of the adult civilian population. Even this small proportion declined marginally during the last decades. To see if there were significant regional variations in these estimates, we examined the series for California, Florida, and New York—states where rising informal activities associated with mass immigration have been reported. As shown in table 7.3, the state-level series follow closely the national pattern and provide no evidence of a significant rise in informal employment anywhere. According to these figures, informal employment represents a phenomenon of limited significance in the United States involving less than one decile of its labor force.

The Small Firm and Household Consumption Approaches

A second, related method is based on the evolution of the number and proportion of "very small enterprises" (VSEs) as an indicator of change in informal activities. VSEs are defined as those employing fewer than

TABLE 7.3

Estimates of the Informal Economy Based on Selected Employment Categories, 1980–1998

		Employment Category			
Country[1]	Year	Workers in Micro-enterprises[3] %	Own Account Workers[4]	Domestic Servants	Total %[2]
Argentina	1998	15.7	19.6	4.8	40.1
Brazil	1997	9.7	25.8	8.6	44.1
Costa Rica	1998	10.6	15.4	4.8	30.8
Mexico	1998	14.9	20.5	4.1	39.5
Panama	1979				
	1998	6.4	18.2	6.6	31.2
Uruguay	1981				
	1998	10.6	19.9	7.2	37.7
Venezuela	1981				
	1994	9.2	27.4	4.0	40.6
United States	1980	4.0	4.5	0.9	9.4
	2000	3.6	4.0	0.5	8.1
California	1980	4.0	4.5	0.8	9.3
	2000	3.3	4.3	1.0	8.6
Florida	1980	4.5	4.5	0.6	9.6
	2000	4.0	3.5	0.5	8.0
New York	1980	3.9	2.5	0.9	7.3
	2000	4.0	2.9	0.7	7.6

[1] For all Latin American countries, estimates are available only for the urban economically active population.

[2] As percent of the civilian economically active population aged fifteen to sixty-four.

[3] Salaried and unpaid family workers in firms employing fewer than five workers.

[4] Self-employed individuals minus professionals and technicians.

Sources: Economic Commission for Latin America and the Caribbean, Panorama 2000, tables 6, 11. U.S. Bureau of the Census, Current Population Surveys, 1980, 2000; U.S. Bureau of the Census, Statistical Abstract, 2000.

ten workers. This approach has been applied in the United States in lieu of labor market data. The assumption is that, in advanced countries, most activities defined as informal occur in smaller enterprises because of their lesser visibility, greater flexibility, and greater opportunities to escape state controls. Larger firms are assumed to be more subject to state regulation and more risk-averse to potential penalties. Hence, they are less likely to engage in informal activities directly, although they can subcontract work to smaller firms that do.

The idea for this approach came from interviews with officials of the Wage and Hour Division of the U.S. Department of Labor, the agency charged with enforcing minimum wage, overtime, and other protective codes for American workers. The interviews indicated widespread violations of labor codes among garment, electronics, and construction subcontractors as well as in all kinds of personal and household services, especially in large metropolitan areas. Most of the enterprises involved were small, employing fewer than ten workers.[48] A separate study by the General Accounting Office identified the restaurant, apparel, and meat processing industries—all sectors where small firms predominate—as having the greatest incidence of "sweatshop practices." Included in this category were failure to keep records of wages and work hours, wages below the legal minimum or without overtime pay, employment of minors, fire hazards, and other unsafe work conditions.[49]

As an indicator of the extent of informality, the evolution of VSEs is subject to two contrary biases. First, not all small firms engage in informal practices, which leads to an overestimate; second, fully informal VSEs escape all government record keeping, which leads to underestimation. The extent to which these biases neutralize each other is not known. In this situation, the statistical series are best interpreted as a rough estimate of the evolution of the informal sector on the basis of those recorded firms that most closely approximate it.

About three-fourths of U.S. establishments counted by the Census were VSEs in 1965, and they absorbed approximately one-seventh of the economically active population. By 1985, the figures were almost exactly the same, although the variations along the way are instructive. Between 1965 and 1970, there was a 6 percent decline in the proportion of VSEs and a 2 percent drop in the proportion of the labor force employed by them. The reversal of this trend between 1970 and 1975 is an artifact of the small-size class of establishment reported by the Census—from fewer than eight to fewer than ten employees. Thereafter and until 1980, there was again a gradual decline, but, in that year, the trend reversed once more with the proportion of VSEs in 1985, reaching the same level as in 1965. After 1985, there has been a new slow decline in the relative number of VSEs and the proportion of the labor force employed by them.[50]

By 2005, figures were not much different from what they had been forty years earlier. This stability in the relative number of VSEs and the proportion of the labor force employed by them, is in line with results from the labor market approach above, indicating little variation over time in those sectors or employment categories that come closest to the definition of informality. These results also support the stability of the class of petty entrepreneurs, as described in chapter 5.

A third approach, the household consumption method, is based on the recognition that direct survey measures of informal employment are difficult to obtain in developed countries. For this reason, James Smith and his associates developed an ingenious method based on the consumption of informally provided goods and services by American households. The studies were based on national probability surveys conducted by the Survey Research Center of the University of Michigan. Informal activity was defined as market transactions that should be recorded or taxed but were not. Respondents were asked to report the amounts spent over the preceding year on goods and services acquired off the books or on the side. On that basis, the authors estimated that U.S. households spent a maximum of $72.4 billion in informal purchases, representing 14.6 percent of all expenditures (formal and informal) in the late 1980s. The study also reported that fully 83 percent of all American households made use of at least one type of informal supplier. Home repairs and improvements topped the list in terms of dollars spent, followed by food purchases, child care, other personal and domestic services, and auto repairs.[51]

This method has the merit of relying on statistically representative survey measures and, hence, yielding authoritative estimates of household consumption. As an indicator of the scope of informality in the national economy, it suffers the fatal flaw of neglecting informally produced inputs for larger firms and irregular labor practices within them. In other words, the entire universe of informal subcontracting in the apparel, electronics, furniture, construction, and many other industries as well as off-the-books employment by formal enterprises is excluded by a measurement approach focused exclusively on final household consumption. The method shares with the VSEs approach the assumption that informality is found predominantly in the smallest economic units; however, in both cases, there is considerable slippage between what actually happens on the ground and what these numbers can tell us. Both approaches are best characterized as partial and tentative approximations to the real underlying phenomenon.

Macroeconomic Estimates

The fourth strategy, the macroeconomic discrepancy method, attempts to measure the magnitude of the total underground economy as a proportion of the gross national product (GNP). This method is based on the existence of at least two different, but comparable, measures of some aspect of a national economy. Discrepancies between these measurements are then attributed to underground activities. For example, gaps in the income and expenditure side of national accounts can be used to estimate the size of unreported income to the extent that individuals can be assumed to be less likely to misrepresent their expenditures than their incomes. These methods have been more popular in the advanced countries where government record keeping and national accounts are better developed and where the probability of obtaining valid reports on participation in underground activities through survey questions is low. The more elaborate of these methods, based on the ratio of currency in circulation to demand deposits, were pioneered by Gutmann and subsequently modified by Feige and Vito Tanzi. This "currency ratio" approach is based on the assumption that informal transactions are conducted mostly in cash in order to avoid detection by the authorities.[52]

The approach consists of building an estimate of the currency in circulation required by the operation of legal activities and subtracting this figure from the actual monetary mass. The difference, multiplied by the velocity of money, provides an estimate of the magnitude of the underground economy. The ratio of that figure to observed GNP then gives the proportion of the national economy represented by subterranean activities. The method depends on the identification of a base period in which the underground economy was assumed to be insignificant. The ratio of currency in circulation to the reference figures (demand deposits for Gutmann; GNP for Feige; M2 for Tanzi) is established for this period and then extrapolated to the present. The difference between this estimate and the actual ratio provides the basis for calculating the magnitude of underground activities. Using this approach, Feige reported that the U.S. underground economy as a proportion of total reported adjusted gross income (AGI) rose from 0 in 1940 (the base year) to 20 percent in 1945, declined subsequently to about 6 percent in 1960, increased rapidly to reach 24 percent in 1983, and then declined again to about 18 percent in 1986.[53]

More recently, Feige noted that earlier calculations had been grossly distorted by the failure to take into account currency that left the United States to serve as a deposit of value or a means of exchange in other countries. According to his calculations, up to 80 percent of U.S. currency is unaccounted for, and much of it is held abroad. After a series of complex calculations, Feige concluded that unreported income in the United States was approximately $700 billion in 1991 and not the over $1 trillion estimated with unadjusted models. Even after this adjustment, the size of the unreported economy reached 25 percent of reported AGI in 1990-91.[54]

Macroeconomic methods for estimating the size of the underground economy through unreported income have been increasingly used by economists in other countries. In Canada, for example, various researchers utilizing these methods arrived at figures ranging from 2.8 percent of GDP in 1981 (reported by Statistics Canada) to 14.1 percent (reported by Mirus using Tanzi's approach). A decade later, Guttman's method, as applied by Vladimir Karoleff and his colleagues yielded an estimate of 21.6 percent of GDP, but the figure from Statistics Canada remained at 2.7 percent.[55]

The macroeconomic procedures have serious weaknesses that have been noted by a number of analysts. First, the assumption that informal transactions take place mostly in cash is questionable in settings where bank checks and other instruments can be used with little fear of detection by the authorities. Second, the assumption that informal activities did not exist in some arbitrarily designated period is also subject to question. Third, and most important, these estimates do not differentiate between criminal and informal activities. As seen above, informal activities involve goods and services that are otherwise licit, but whose production or distribution bypass official channels. Hence, the huge estimates of the subterranean economy sometimes reached through these methods can be due to the presence of a large criminal underground whose operation and character are quite different from those of the informal economy proper.[56]

Estimates based on macroeconomic methods also vary widely according to the assumptions and figures employed. Richard Porter and Amanda Bayer replicated the methods used by Guttman, Feige, and Tanzi to obtain estimates of the absolute and relative size of the U.S. underground economy. Their results are reproduced in table 7.4. The three

TABLE 7.4
Estimates of the U.S. Underground Economy According to Macroeconomic
Discrepancy Methods

	Guttmann		Tanzi		Feige	
Year	Billions $	% of GNP	Billions $	% of GNP	Billions $	% of GNP
1950	15.9	5.6	14.5	5.1	27.6	9.6
1955	14.7	3.7	12.8	3.2	1.7	0.4
1960	17.3	3.4	20.7	4.1	−3.4	−0.7
1965	31.6	4.6	26.3	3.8	9.6	1.4
1970	62.4	6.3	45.6	4.6	101.0	10.2
1975	150.8	9.7	77.0	5.0	467.3	30.2
1979	317.8	13.1	130.7	5.4	628.4	26.0
1980	372.8	14.2	159.9	6.1	1,095.6	41.6

Source: Porter and Bayer, "A Monetary Perspective," p. 178.

sets of estimates vary widely. In 1980, for example, Guttman's method (as applied by Porter and Bayer) yielded an estimate of the underground economy of 14 percent of the GNP; Tanzi's approach reduced the figure to 6 percent, while Feige's method increased it to 42 percent. Similar discrepancies have been found in later estimates for other countries, such as Canada, Great Britain, Germany, and Mexico.[57]

The Measurement Paradox

The limitations of all existing methods of measurement stem from the nature of the phenomenon they attempt to gauge, which is elusive by definition. However, the extent to which informal activities are concealed is not uniform. There are levels of concealment depending on the character of state regulation and the effectiveness of its enforcement. In settings where the informal economy is widespread and semiopen, as in many third world countries, it is possible to arrive at reliable estimates of its size on the basis of direct surveys. Lax enforcement and the generalized character of these activities make informal owners and workers less apprehensive about answering questions about their work. In Latin America, survey methods applied during the last three decades have produced acceptable estimates of the size of the labor force employed informally in most countries.

When state regulation is both highly effective and extensive, as in many industrialized nations, the situation changes. In these instances, informal activities are better concealed and, as we have seen, embedded in tighter social networks. Hence, no matter how well organized the official record-keeping apparatus is, it is likely to miss a significant amount of informal activity. In the United States, for instance, analysts have long discounted the possibility of measuring the informal or underground economy through direct survey questions and hence are forced to rely on the approximate methods described earlier. The measurement alternatives, from household consumption patterns to macroeconomic discrepancy ratios, have yielded estimates too feeble to guide either theory or policy.

The third paradox of the informal economy is that the more credible the state enforcement apparatus is, the more likely its record-keeping mechanisms will miss the actual extent of the informal economy and, hence, the feebler the basis for developing policies to address it. If Feige's estimates are taken at face value, an entire quarter of all economic activity in the United States took place outside the pale of state regulation in the 1990s. Since the government knows little about the character and scope of these practices, it proceeds as if, in effect, they did not exist. The assumption can lead to serious policy distortions: "To the extent that national accounting systems are based on data sources primarily collected from the formal sector, a large and growing informal economy will play havoc with perceptions of development based on official statistics, and consequently with policy decisions based exclusively on information provided by official sources."[58]

This statement must be qualified, however, by the previous discussion concerning the extent of state enforcement and the character of the civil society subject to it. As described in figures 7.4 and 7.5, the informal economy is likely to be weakest when limited regulation of economic activity by a competent state apparatus is coupled with a population accustomed to regular waged employment and to legal welfare programs. In these situations, working "on the side" or "off the books" is likely to meet with public disapproval, leading to a situation in which civil society itself and not only the state enforces legal rules. Informal enterprise in these social contexts is limited to marginal activities and sectors, and the bulk of the "unreported economy" is probably accounted for by criminal, not informal, activities. In these contexts, the altruistic sources of social capital described in chapter 3—value introjection and bounded solidarity—tend to work for the state rather than against it.

At the other extreme, the capacity of civil society to resist complete absorption by a totalitarian state is nowhere clearer than in its withdrawal of information from state record-keeping agencies. The best example of this third paradox is provided by the now-defunct Eastern European command economies. In these contexts, state policies aimed at controlling every aspect of economic activity required vast amounts of information in order to function properly. However, the same policies gave rise to a vast underground economy whose existence depended precisely on escaping official detection. The result was that the information on which state managers had to rely became progressively illusory and the subsequent policies unrealistic.[59] Firms and state agencies in the "first" economy became trapped in a make-believe world, feeding one another's misperceptions and operating at an ever-growing distance from the real world. The outcome is well known.

CONCLUSION: THE CHANGING BOUNDARIES OF INFORMALITY

Reprise

This chapter has reviewed various definitions of the informal economy, distinguished it from criminal activities, and explored some of its peculiar characteristics. From the definition of the phenomenon used in the analysis, it is clear that the elements composing the informal sector will vary across countries and over time. The relationship between the state and civil society defines the character of informality, and this relationship is in constant flux. The changing geometry of formal/informal economic activities follows the contours delineated by past history and the nature of state authority. There is thus no great mystery in the diversity of formal-informal interactions reported in the literature. Every concrete situation has in common the existence of economic practices that violate or bypass state regulation, but what these are varies according to state-society relations. Hence, what is informal and persecuted in one setting may be perfectly legal in another; the same activity may shift its location across the formal-informal divide over time. The economic sociology assumption of social embeddedness finds few clearer expressions than in the informal economy.

Informality may be characterized as a constructed response by civil society to unwanted state interference. The universal character of the phenomenon reflects the considerable capacity of resistance in most societies to the exercise of state power. An activity can be officially declared illegal without disappearing at all; entire economic sectors may be legislated out of existence and still flourish underground. The universality of the informal economy is confirmed by a bourgeoning research literature that describes its characteristics and consequences in settings as diverse as Canada, the Netherlands, Mexico, Jordan, and South Africa.[60]

This literature also illustrates the diverse functionality of informal activities for the actors involved. While a good portion of this literature, coming from economics, views the phenomenon as tax evasion, sociological and social anthropological studies provide a more nuanced view. It is obvious that informal enterprise is "functional" for those so employed, since they create a means for survival. It is equally obvious that large firms that subcontract production and marketing to informal entrepreneurs or who hire workers off the books also benefit from higher flexibility and lower labor costs. It is less evident, however, that the informal economy can also have positive consequences for the very actor whose existence and logic it challenges.

A Final Paradox

The fourth paradox of the informal economy is that it can have positive consequences for the state, the very institution charged with its suppression. This paradox also adopts different forms depending on national context. In less developed countries, where protective labor legislation runs ahead of the capacity of the formal economy to provide full employment, informal enterprise has a double function. First, it employs and provides incomes to a large segment of the population that otherwise would be deprived of any means of subsistence. The "cushion" provided by the informal economy can make all the difference between relative peace and sustained political upheavals in these settings.[61] Second, the goods and services provided by informal producers lower the costs of consumption for formal workers and the costs of production and distribution for larger firms, thus contributing to their viability. The low wages received by formal sector employees in third world nations are thus partially compensated by the greater acquisitive power of these wages through informally produced goods and services. In turn, large firms can compensate for costly tax and labor codes by restricting the size of their formally employed labor force and subcontracting the rest to informal entrepreneurs. Through these mechanisms, the informal economy contributes to the political stability and economic viability of poorer nations.[62]

In the advanced countries, the cushioning function of informality is also present, especially in relation to marginal segments of the population. When for political or economic reasons, unemployment and other state-provided benefits are meager, recipients compensate by finding additional sources of income, commonly through informal employment. This gives rise to the situation reported by MacDonald, where combining welfare with off-the-books casual jobs becomes a "way of life" for minority workers in the American inner city.[63] While such arrangements are regularly condemned by the media and by government officials, it is conveniently forgotten that these casual jobs make possible the perpetuation of a social welfare system bearing little relation to the actual cost of living.

Informality can also provide a protective environment for fledgling but innovative forms of entrepreneurship. The Emilian case again offers a good example. Although the government in Rome took a dim view of what was taking place in Emilia-Romagna, the informal networks of cooperation and solidarity among Emilian artisans eventually gave rise to an industrial district that became a world model. This is not the sole example of this "incubator" function, as the experiences of Silicon Valley firms started in owners' garages and basements attest.[64] For fledgling but viable entrepreneurial ventures, the informal economy can operate as a protective and flexible cushion sparing them from burdensome and costly regulations that can prematurely sink them. As firms mature, they enter the formal economy, contributing to its growth. This is what happened in central Italy, in Silicon Valley, and elsewhere.[65]

The unheralded positive effects of the informal economy may help explain why governments in advanced and less developed countries commonly adopt an ambiguous attitude toward these activities, tolerating their existence, at least on a temporary basis. Too much tolerance would compromise the credibility of the rule of law and the willingness of formal firms and taxpayers to continue shouldering their obligations. Too repressive a stance would do away with the "cushion" provided by informal activities or, what is worse, may drive them further underground, depriving authorities of any information about them. As seen in chapter 6, the free market approach toward economic adjustment in Latin America used the informal economy to absorb those displaced from regular employment on the tacit premise that casual workers cannot organize politically.

The complex relationships between the state and the informal economy, and the multiple forms adopted by informal activities, rule out an approach to the phenomenon based on a simple tax-evasion perspective.

The analytic stance to study these phenomena must be as nuanced and flexible as the informal economy has proven to be, combining the use of aggregate statistics and large surveys with careful firsthand investigation. By the same token, these activities will continue to be a privileged site for examining the social underpinnings of economic action. While a naive approach may see this universe as the reign of the "free market," it is in reality the realm where the embeddedness of economic action in social networks and the unanticipated consequences of purposive official action emerge most clearly.

CHAPTER EIGHT

Ethnic Enclaves and Middleman Minorities

THIS PAIR OF CONCEPTS, ethnic enclaves and middleman minorities, has served well to analyze the economic behavior of nonmainstream groups and the internal dynamics that have made their enterprises viable and sustainable over time.[1] Although these phenomena appear marginal in comparison with large corporations and other major economic institutions, they represent a strategic site for economic sociology for two reasons: First, they help explain how apparently poor and resourceless minorities have managed to move ahead and create enterprises that compete effectively with larger mainstream firms. Second, they illustrate the embeddedness of economic action with singular clarity, revealing facets of these dynamics that are unexpected and do not exists in other contexts.

Enclaves are assemblages of enterprises owned and operated by members of the same cultural/linguistic groups that concentrate in an identifiable geographic area, maintain intense relations with one another, and hire significant numbers of their coethnics. Enclave entrepreneurs may or may not live in the enclave area, but the siting of their firm in it is a precondition for their viability and success. Middleman minorities are groups from the same cultural/linguistic background who specialize in operating commercial activities in downtrodden urban areas, profiting from a quasi-monopolistic position given the absence of competitive firms in them.

Minorities who become middlemen or enclave entrepreneurs rely on unique mechanisms of solidarity based on a common cultural experience, not only to make their firms sustainable but also to accumulate sufficient capital to propel their offspring into the professions. For this reason, these economic formations tend to be short-lived unless the original entrepreneurial generation is reinforced by new migrants from the same origin or replaced by others from a different ethnic background. These ethnic phenomena bring into play, in singular ways, the operation of several concepts analyzed in previous chapters, in particular:

- Social capital
- Social classes and the class structure
- The informal economy

Enclaves and middleman minorities represent specific instances of these more fundamental concepts, but they also possess heuristic value of their own given the singular ways in which basic forces interweave and manifest themselves within these formations.

ETHNIC ENCLAVES

Basic Characteristics

Near downtown Los Angeles there is an area approximately a mile long where all commercial signs suddenly change from English to strange pictorial characters. Koreatown, as the area is known, contains the predictable number of ethnic restaurants and grocery shops; it also contains a number of banks, import-export houses, industries, and real estate offices. Signs of "English spoken here" assure visitors that their links with the outside world have not been totally severed. In Los Angeles, the propensity for self-employment is three times greater among Koreans than among the population as a whole. Grocery stores, restaurants, gas stations, liquor stores, and real estate offices are typical Korean businesses. They also tend to remain within the community because the more successful immigrants sell their earlier businesses to new arrivals.[2]

A similar urban landscape is found near downtown Miami. Little Havana extends in a narrow strip for about five miles, eventually merging with the southwest suburbs of the city. Cuban-owned firms increased from 919 in 1967 to 8,000 in 1976 and approximately 28,000 in 1990. Most are small, averaging 8.1 employees at the latest count, but they also include factories employing hundreds of workers. Cuban firms are found in light and heavy manufacturing, construction, commerce, finance, and insurance. An estimated 60 percent of all residential construction in the metropolitan area is now done by these firms; gross annual receipts of Cuban manufacturing industries increased 1,067 percent during a recent ten-year period.[3]

These areas of concentrated immigrant entrepreneurship are known as ethnic enclaves. Their emergence has depended on three conditions: first, the presence of a number of immigrants with substantial business expertise acquired in their home countries; second, access to sources of capital; third, access to labor. The requisite labor is not too difficult to obtain because it can be initially drawn from family members and then from more recent immigrant arrivals. Sources of capital are often not a major obstacle either, because the sums required initially are small. When immigrants do not bring them from abroad, they can accumulate them through individual savings or obtain them from pooled resources in the community. In some instances, would-be entrepreneurs have access to financial institutions owned or managed by conationals. Thus, the first requisite is the critical one. The presence of a number of immigrants skilled in what sociologist Franklin Frazier called "the art of buying and selling" can usually overcome other obstacles to entrepreneurship. Conversely, their absence tends to confine an immigrant group to wage work even when enough savings and labor are available.[4]

Entrepreneurial minorities have been the exception in both turn-of-the-century and contemporary immigrations. Their significance is that they create an avenue for economic mobility unavailable to other groups. This avenue is open not only to the original entrepreneurs, but to later arrivals as well. The reason is that relations between immigrant employers and their coethnic employees often go beyond a purely contractual bond. When immigrant enterprises expand, they tend to hire their own for supervisory positions. Today Koreans hire and promote Koreans in New York and Los Angeles, and Cubans do the same for other Cubans in Miami, just as eighty years ago the Jews of Manhattan's Lower East Side and the Japanese of San Francisco and Los Angeles hired and supported those from their own communities.[5] I review next the histories of these earlier groups as background for analysis of the specific social traits underlying these formations.

Historical Examples

Two immigrant groups arriving during the 1890–1914 period differed markedly from other minorities both in the way their labor was utilized and in their mode of adaptation. The similarity between these two groups after their arrival in the United States could not have been anticipated on the basis of their background, for it is difficult to imagine more different national origins. One of these groups came to the United States to escape the brutal persecutions of their own country's government; the other came as part of an officially sponsored and monitored flow. One came to fill industrial and service jobs in an urban economy; the other came to meet labor demands in agriculture. One was committed from the start to permanent settlement in the country; the other viewed its sojourn as a temporary stay until debts could be settled or land bought in the mother country.

Both groups were non-Christian, but they were different in religion, language, and race. They disembarked at opposite ends of the continent and never met in sizable numbers at any point. Yet, Jews and Japanese developed patterns of economic and social adaptation that were remarkably similar. What both groups had in common was their collective resistance to serving as a mere source of labor power. From the start, their economic conduct was oriented toward two goals: (1) the acquisition of property, and (2) the search for entrepreneurial opportunities that would given them an "edge" in the American market.

In coastal cities at both ends of the land, Jews and Japanese created tight-knit communities that in appearance resembled the ethnic neighborhoods of many other immigrant groups but differed from these neighborhoods in their social and economic organization. These communities were not exclusively residential—places where an immigrant working class could find comfort and sociability. They were instead economic hubs where a substantial proportion of immigrants were engaged in business activities and where a still larger proportion worked in firms owned by other immigrants.[6]

To overcome the lack of capital, the absence of connections in the general economy, and the patent hostility surrounding them, Jewish and Japanese entrepreneurs made use of the resources available in their own communities. For the entrepreneurially inclined, ethnic solidarity had clear economic potential. The community was (1) a source of labor, which could be made to work at lower wages; (2) a controlled market; and (3) a source of capital, through rotating credit associations and similar institutions.

Starting from very humble beginnings, many immigrant enterprises reached a modicum of success, and some expanded into major firms. Characteristically, these immigrant groups experienced significant economic mobility in the first generation, and this process frequently preceded, not followed, acculturation. There were immigrant millionaires who spoke broken English and whose cultural allegiance was still to the home country. This pattern contradicted the typical assimilation saga, whereby economic advancement was supposed to involve a long and difficult acculturation process.[7]

The combination of cultural distinctness and economic success provoked in both cases a number of racist campaigns. Quotas were established for keeping Jewish students out of the best universities. Increasing in frequency and intensity, anti-Semitic campaigns forced the creation

of the Jewish Anti-Defamation League and other ethnic defense organizations. On the West Coast, continuous attacks against the Japanese
culminated in confiscation of their property and their mass internment in
camps during World War II.

THE JEWISH ENCLAVE

The first major wave of Jewish immigration took place roughly between
1840 and 1870, when about 50,000 Jews of German origin arrived in
the United States. These immigrants engaged almost exclusively in commerce. Starting as street peddlers and small merchants, they managed to
reach significant economic prosperity in the course of a single generation.
By 1890, the German Jewish community in the United States was better
off economically than the average native population. Merchants specializing in the sale of "dry and fancy goods" pioneered in the creation of the
modern department store, laying the basis for such firms as Macy's and
Sears Roebuck. In banking, Jewish companies such as Kuhn and Loeb,
Speyer, and the Seligmans reached significant size. In 1870, about 10 percent of Jewish firms were capitalized at or above $100,000; in 1890,
almost 25 percent reported a minimum capital of $125,000.[8]

Starting in 1870, a new wave of Jewish immigration overtook the
original one. Between 1870 and 1914, more than 2 million Jews abandoned Russia, where the Jewish population had been confined to the
"Pale of Settlement," a belt of land extending from the Baltic to the Black
Sea. After the onset of industrialization, the Russian government pursued
a policy of systematic discrimination destined to keep ownership out of
Jewish hands. In addition to economic and geographic restrictions, Jews
suffered increasing political persecution. After the assassination of Tsar
Alexander II in 1881, a wave of major pogroms against the Jewish population occurred with the connivance of the government. Major pogroms
took place in 1881, 1882, 1903, and 1906.[9]

To escape such conditions, Eastern European Jews moved en masse to
the United States. They arrived and resettled, in large numbers, in New
York City. Within it, they concentrated heavily in a small section of Manhattan, the Lower East Side. In the heart of this district, the 10th Ward,
population density reached 523.6 people per acre by the turn of the century. Efforts to disperse this population met with very limited success.
Despite the initially harsh conditions, few Jewish immigrants abandoned
their community. Thousands took to street peddling, others opened small
shops, and many went to work in factories owned by German Jews.

The German Jewish community viewed the arrival of these impoverished masses with alarm, fearing that they would stigmatize the whole group in American eyes and jeopardize its own position. It promptly realized, however, that the best strategy lay not in rejecting the newcomers but in integrating them. Organizations such as the Hebrew American Aid Society, the United Hebrew Charities, the Independent Order of B'nai B'rith, the Baron de Hirsch Fund, and others ministered to the needs of the immigrants. They attended both to their material welfare and to the imperative need of teaching them the language and the ways of the new country. Although charity was often administered in an impersonal and even condescending manner, the Jewish organizations proceeded with such efficiency as to prompt outsiders to note that no other immigrant group had "proved so generous to their own kind."[10]

The newcomers, however, lost little time in emulating the earlier German immigrants. As they improved their economic position, German aid societies were replaced by Russian, Hungarian, and Galician ones. The Yiddish language, regarded by the Germans as a symbol of the patent inferiority of the new arrivals, became increasingly acceptable. In industry, the pattern of German-owned firms and Russian Jewish labor rapidly changed, as more Eastern Europeans became contractors and entrepreneurs. Jewish industry proliferated in the building and metal trades, in jewelry and printing, and in tobacco and cigar making. It was, however, the clothing industry that became "the great Jewish métier."[11] In 1920, of 23,479 factories in the borough of Manhattan, almost half, 11,172, were engaged in clothing production and employed more than 200,000 people. Except for the larger firms, employers were no longer German Jews, but overwhelmingly Eastern Europeans.[12]

The Jewish entrepreneurial drive led to significant economic mobility among first-generation immigrants. The ascent along the economic and social ladders was to be completed by the second and third generations. The original immigrants lacked the resources and time to take advantage of the public higher-education system in New York City. Their children, however, were able to do so and literally monopolized facilities at City College. By the third generation, Jewish students were attending top-rated schools, including those created by their own group. Thus, despite anti-Semitism, quota systems, and other restrictions, the remarkable progress of this immigrant group continued unabated. At the end of the 1930s, two-thirds of all Jewish workers were in white-collar positions. By the early 1940s, Jews comprised 65.7 percent of New York City's lawyers and judges, 55.7 percent of its physicians, and 64 percent of its dentists. By the 1960s, Jewish family income was the highest of any ethnic group, exceeding by 72 percent the national average.[13]

JAPANESE ENTERPRISE

Under very different circumstances, Japanese immigration to the West Coast followed a similar adaptation pattern. Significant Japanese immigration to the mainland did not start until 1890. From that year until 1908, about 150,000 male immigrants came. After the Gentlemen's Agreement of 1908, Japanese arrivals were predominantly the spouses of earlier immigrants, until the 1924 Immigration Act banned all further Asiatic immigration. During the entire period, there were fewer than 300,000 Japanese recorded as entering the United States.[14] This figure does not take into account the return flow and, hence, overestimates the actual size of net immigration. From 1908 to 1924, for example, the 160,000 Japanese immigrants resulted in a new inflow of only 90,000. The 1920 census counted 111,010 Japanese in the United States out of a total population of 106,000,000.[15]

Several authors have commented on the discrepancy between the tiny size of this group and the magnitude of the public reaction to it. Repeatedly, the California press and the labor movement engaged in virulent campaigns against the "Japanese invasion." In 1905, both houses of the California legislature passed a resolution asking Congress to limit further Japanese immigration. Included in a long bill of particulars was the following statement: "Japanese laborers, by reason of race habits, mode of living, disposition, and general characteristics, are undesirable. . . . They contribute nothing to the growth of the state. They add nothing to its wealth, and they are a blight on the prosperity of it, and a great impending danger to its welfare."[16]

One reason for such hostility was that, like Jews back East, the Japanese were highly concentrated and resisted efforts at dispersal. The vast majority lived in the three West Coast states, with the greatest number in California. Of the 111,010 Japanese counted by the 1920 census, 71,952 were in California. Even within this state, there was heavy concentration: one-third of Japanese residents of California in 1940 lived in Los Angeles County; six other counties accounted for another third.[17] But this was not the only reason for hostility, as the Japanese continued to be a tiny minority even in the areas of highest concentration. More basic problems had to do with their role in the economy: "So long as the Japanese remained willing to perform agricultural labor at low wages, they remained popular with California ranchers. But even before 1910, the Japanese farmhands began to demand higher wages. . . . Worse, many Japanese began to lease and buy agricultural land for farming on their own account. This enterprise had the two-fold result of creating Japanese competition in the produce field and decreasing the number of Japanese farmhands available."[18] Faced with such "unfair" competition, California ranchers turned to the ever-sympathetic state legislature. In 1913, the first Alien Land Law was passed, restricting the free acquisition of land by the Japanese. This legal instrument was perfected in 1920, when Japanese nationals were forbidden to lease agricultural land or to act as guardians of native-born minors in matters of property, which they themselves could not own.[19]

Restrictions in agriculture drove many Japanese into urban enterprise. Already in 1909, the Immigration Commission had found a total of about 3,000 small shops owned by Japanese in many Western cities. By 1919, 47 percent of hotels and 25 percent of grocery stores in Seattle were Japanese owned. Forty percent of Japanese men in Los Angeles were self-employed, operating dry-cleaning establishments, fisheries, and lunch counters. A large percentage of Japanese urban businesses were produce stands that marketed the production of Japanese farms.[20]

Two recurrent questions about the emergence of Japanese enterprise in agriculture and services were these: (1) how could they compete with larger and better-capitalized American farms? And (2) where did common laborers find the capital to start even small firms? Answers to both questions were found primarily in the strength of economic networks within the ethnic community. Rotating credit associations, variously known as *ko*, *tanomoshi*, or *mujin*, provided capital for urban businesses and farms where banks would offer none. Such associations depended heavily on mutual trust, and this was found within the immigrant community to an extent that effectively counterbalanced discrimination by the banks. Even relatively large undertakings, requiring sums close to $100,000, were financed on the basis of *tanomoshi*.[21]

Despite the many political restrictions and the continuous hostility, Japanese immigrants continued to improve their economic positions. Every effort to return the first generation *Issei* to the status of common laborers seemed to strengthen their resolve to move out of it. The major blows of wholesale confiscations and camp internments during World War II seriously disrupted this ethnic economy, but did not entirely eliminate it. Aging *Issei* and many of their children came out of the camps to create or reestablish small businesses. In addition, the end of the war brought about a rapid growth of labor demand, along with a reduction of hostility toward the Japanese.

The *Nisei* (the second generation) were thus able to explore alternative mobility paths. As second-generation Jews before them, the *Nisei* moved en masse toward higher education. Between 1940 and 1950, the number of professionals among the Japanese increased by 142 percent, while farmers and proprietors decreased by 14 percent and 29 percent, respectively. The third generation, *Sansei*, followed a similar course, with a remarkable 88 percent attending college. Still, a number of them continued the entrepreneurial tradition of their parents, though along new lines. In addition, there has been a significant movement toward ethnic reaffirmation and pride in the third generation.[22]

There are at present about 800,000 Japanese Americans. Since 1940, they have had more schooling than any other group in America, including native whites. The average in 1960 for both males and females was 12.5 years. Average occupational attainment trailed that of native whites in 1950, but exceeded it in 1960, being the highest for any ethnic group. By 1959, Japanese American males on the mainland earned 99 percent of the income of whites. By 1969, the average Japanese family income exceeded the national average by 32 percent, second only to the Jews among American ethnic groups.[23]

Social Capital

Neither the Jews of the Lower East Side, nor the Japanese of California could have performed these amazing economic feats without recourse to social ties to their fellows. Although values are commonly credited *post factum* as the source of internal solidarity and success in these communities, the primary forces creating social capital in such instances were situational: external hostility and discrimination meted on members of the same collectivity inevitably lead to the rise of strong bounded solidarity among them.[24]

By the same token, absence of any support or resources on the outside reinforces the power of the ethnic community to compel observance of its rules, leading to higher levels of enforceable trust. Rotating credit associations and a multitude of informal exchanges can thus be transacted in these environments without fear of malfeasance. Those tempted to do so are constrained by knowledge that precious little opportunity exists outside their own group. Justice Louis D. Brandeis, a prominent member of the Jewish community in the early twentieth century, justified tight normative enforcement in the following terms: "A single though inconspicuous instance of dishonorable conduct on the part of a Jew in any trade or profession has far reaching evil effects extending to the many innocent members of the race—since the act of each becomes thus the concern of all, we are perforce our brothers' keepers."[25]

Post factum chronicles of the economic success of such groups make much of their unique value endowment—the unique "love of learning" among Jews or the Japanese "Confucian ethic"—for example.[26] In reality, immigrants from the most varied religio/cultural backgrounds have been able to develop enclave or enclavelike economic hubs in America. In addition to the historical experience of Jews and Japanese, they include contemporary Protestant Koreans, Catholic and Buddhist Vietnamese, Catholic Cubans, and secular and Orthodox Russians.[27] If a unique value "ethic" were to be appended to the experiences of each of these groups, we would end up with a very messy theory indeed.[28]

The traits that all these communities have in common are situational and are linked to their condition as foreign and frequently derided minorities, leading to the rise of the social mechanisms noted previously. However, it is not the case that all discriminated and excluded foreign groups have created enclaves. As seen previously, they represent the exception in the economic adaptation process of immigrant groups: German and Russian Jews went that route, but neither Italians nor Poles arriving contemporaneously did so; Cubans and Koreans created ethnic enclaves in the late twentieth century, but neither Mexicans nor Filipinos followed that path.

These differences should alert us to the distinction between *sources* of social capital and the *resources* that can be accessed through their operation. This distinction, already noted in chapter 3, is crucial to avoid the circular reasoning of attributing collective success to the presence of social capital and collective failure to its absence. In fact, situational sources of social capital are commonly activated among *all* minorities confronting a difficult or hostile environment, but the resources accessed through its activation are very different. The key resource characterizing groups that have created enclaves has already been noted: the presence of a substantial number of immigrants with business expertise acquired in their country of origin. This type of human capital, combined with the situational social capital associated with immigration, leads the collectivity in the direction of self-employment and creation of business networks, rather than wage work. Absent this combination, immigrant social capital functions primarily as a survival mechanism—a means of gaining access to manual jobs and of finding some comfort and protection among one's fellows from a forbidding outside world.[29]

Authors like Carol Stack, Patricia Fernández-Kelly, and Mitchell Duneier have already documented the density of mutual assistance networks present in inner-city ghetto areas inhabited by domestic minorities.[30] However, the social isolation of these areas makes the information flowing from these networks largely redundant and the resources that can be accessed through them limited to modest mutual assistance. In like fashion, immigrant communities populated primarily by poorly educated manual workers can generate bounded solidarity and enforceable trust, but lack the internal human capital necessary to transform these social mechanisms into vehicles for upward mobility.

Class Heterogeneity

A second related feature in the onset of ethnic enclaves is the existence of class diversity within the immigrant population. Just as a uniform working-class background prevents the rise of these economic formations, a community made up exclusively of entrepreneurs would not create them either because it would lack both a consumer and a labor base. Access to a large captive market for ethnic goods and to a pliant coethnic labor force have been sine qua nons for the emergence of most ethnic enclaves.[31] In the absence of class diversity, immigrant enterprise is most likely to devolve into the middleman minority form, to be examined later.

Class heterogeneity in immigrant communities is commonly a function of the passage of time. Earlier cohorts usually come from higher-class backgrounds and have longer time to consolidate their position in the host society. Subsequent waves tend to possess less human capital, and their recent arrival makes them readily available for employment in enclave firms, where cultural ways are familiar and English is not necessary.[32] Among Cubans in Miami, for example, the earlier exile waves were composed of members of the upper bourgeoisie displaced by the revolution. Subsequent cohorts came from progressively lower-class backgrounds, creating a social gradient highly favorable to the emergence of an enclave.[33]

The Cuban example is not an isolated one. In a well-known article in this literature, Thomas Bailey and Roger Waldinger showed how enclaves served as "informal training mechanisms" teaching entrepreneurial skills to younger or more recently arrived members of the same ethnic group.[34] Social capital for enclave entrepreneurs flows from bounded solidarity and enforceable trust, enjoining these job seekers to work long hours diligently and without complaint. In turn, business owners are expected to pass along skills to coethnic workers and to support them once they had acquired the necessary means to set up businesses on their own. The fact that social capital "cuts both ways" in these situations is well illustrated by Min Zhou's study of the Chinatown enclave of New York.[35] Zhou shows how Chinese enclave firms function as veritable business engines where internal class differences provide ready labor for existing firms but also lead to skill transfers in favor of coethnic workers.

Returning to our two historical examples, we can readily see that the two causal factors noted—a combination of social capital with business human capital and a measure of internal class heterogeneity—were present in both. The presence of a strong "tradition of enterprise" among turn-of-the-century Jewish immigrants is well known. In the Pale of Settlement, Russian Jews, forced in part by laws restricting their ownership of land, had actively engaged in trade and commerce. An 1898 survey of the area found that one-third of all the factories were Jewish-owned.

Upon arrival in New York, Jewish immigrants with commercial, craft, and entrepreneurial skills easily surpassed comparable numbers among other immigrant groups. By 1914, they ranked first among printers, bakers, and cigar packers. They made up 80 percent of the immigrant hat makers, 68 percent of the tailors, and 60 percent of the watchmakers. They were up to half of the jewelers, photographers, dressmakers, and butchers. In total, Jews ranked first in twenty-six out of forty-seven trades recorded by the 1911 Immigration Commission.[36] The original class heterogeneity of the Jewish enclave was due to the marked differences between well-established German Jewish merchants and the newly arrived Russian immigrants As the latter moved on in the business world, they in turn hired recently arrived coethnics, leading to the "training system" described by Bailey and Waldinger.

The smaller size of the Japanese immigrant population and its more uniform character did not permit the level of complexity and class differentiation found in the Jewish Lower East Side. Japanese immigrants came mostly from rural areas. They were not, however, part of an impoverished subsistence peasantry, but members of a commercial farming class. They frequently sojourned to America to buy additional land or retire loans incurred in commercial production. Among Japanese requesting visas to travel to the United States between 1886 and 1908, 20 percent were classified as "merchants" and an additional 20 percent as "students."[37] Thereafter, the passage of time functioned in similar ways as among other entrepreneurial groups, with better-established merchants hiring and instructing more recent arrivals and would-be business owners of the *Nisei* generation.

How the Cuban Enclave Was Built

Three Stories

In 1966, Santiago Alvarez had had enough of the clandestine war conducted by the Central Intelligence Agency (CIA) against Castro's Cuba and decided to settle down. He was twenty-five and, for the last few years, had worked as a boat captain for the CIA infiltrating men and arms into Cuba. Aside from an intimate knowledge of the Cuban coast, he had few skills. "I didn't have much of an education. . . . I had to fight since a very young age," he said. In Miami, Santiago worked as a waiter, truck driver, and concrete salesman. Finally, in 1971, he opened his own construction firm, beginning with just himself, his pickup, and his connections. Such "back-of-the-truck" enterprises proliferated during the early 1970s, but did not yet challenge the dominance of established Anglo-owned companies. Alvarez's operation, however, never ceased growing. By 1985 he was one of South Florida's most active real estate developers, having taken over from older companies the building of shopping centers and department complexes in Hialeah.[38]

After spending eleven days in jail for antigovernment activities, Remedios Diaz-Oliver and her husband, Fausto, left Cuba in 1961. A graduate of two Havana business schools, she went to work as a bookkeeper for Richford Industries, a container distributor. Fausto found work at Bertram Yacht, located nearby; that meant the couple could manage with a single old car. Within a year, Remedios had been moved to Richford's international division. Fausto took his two weeks' vacation and the couple traveled to Central America with a bag of Richford's samples. They returned with $300,000 in orders from pharmaceutical companies in Honduras and Costa Rica. By 1965, Diaz-Oliver had been appointed Richford's vice president of domestic sales, in addition to her duties as president of the Latin American division.

These were the years in which former militant exiles were looking for permanent employment. From her Havana days, Remedios knew many people with the skills to make a business succeed. In 1966, she persuaded Richford to advance $30,000 in credit to one such person, with the promise that if he defaulted she would cover the debt with her own salary. The man paid, the account grew, and so did her commission. Following this experience and at her prodding, Richford agreed to advance credit to numerous exile clients. As these firms developed, the company's own business grew rapidly.

In 1976, however, Richford was sold to a division of Alco Standard Corporation of Omaha, Nebraska. The new employer required Remedios to sign a contract guaranteeing that she would not compete with Alco Standard if she left the company. Instead of signing, Diaz-Oliver decided to quit and form her own company. The construction trailer in which American International Container opened did not look like much, except that its owner had far more solid connections in the local market than the buttoned-down midwestern company. By 1978, American International had taken over the inventory of Alco Standard after driving it out of Miami. Diaz-Oliver became exclusive Florida distributor for some of the biggest names in packaging, including Owens-Illinois and Standard Container. Her company had warehouses in Miami, Orlando, and Tampa and annual sales of over $60 million.

Remedios has been president of Dade County's American Cancer Society, the Hispanic division of the Red Cross, and the social committee of the Big Five—the private club created in Miami in nostalgic remembrance of the Havana Yacht Club and its four extinct peers in Cuba.[39]

All that Diego R. Suarez has done in his life is design and manufacture agricultural equipment, especially for the sugarcane industry. A graduate of the Vocational School of Havana and of the Civic-Military Institute of Ceiba del Agua, Suarez founded and operated a company called Vanguard National Equipment prior to the revolution. After Fidel Castro came to power, Suarez started moving his capital out of Cuba, and he himself left in 1961. With the monies smuggled out and a loan from a small Puerto Rican bank, he established in Miami the Inter-American Transport Equipment Company, a manufacturer and supplier of harvest, transport, and field machinery for the sugar industry. The company began by exporting light equipment to Puerto Rico, then expanded to all Latin American countries except Brazil. At present, over 90 percent of the equipment manufactured is exported to more than forty countries worldwide. In Suarez's estimate, the large majority of field equipment used today in Florida's sugar industry comes from his factories.

The company's headquarters and main factory are located in the vicinity of Hialeah, where it employs between three hundred and four hundred workers. Trade names include Vanguard and Thomson (tractors, transport equipment, and other machinery) and Claas (harvesters). By

1986, most of this equipment was designed and manufactured at these facilities, except the harvesters, which were made in West Germany. Inter-American's engineers are Cuban, Mexican, American, and British.

In 1980, Suarez initiated the Inter-American Sugar Cane Seminars, which bring engineers, technologists, and sugar mill owners from all over the world to Miami to discuss scientific and technical issues ranging from sugarcane diseases to computer automation of sugar mills. Suarez also presides over companies affiliated with Inter-American Transport and is one of the founders and former directors of the Cuban American National Foundation.[40]

Character Loans

Diego Suarez was fortunate to have brought money and contacts from Cuba. In general, the largest and best-capitalized firms of the emerging Miami enclave were created by exiles experienced in business and having access to these resources. Many would-be entrepreneurs seeking a niche in Miami's economy during the early 1960s were not so fortunate, however. Unlike Asian immigrant communities that make extensive use of the rotating credit association as an instrument for pooling savings, Cubans did not have this cultural practice. In its absence, it seemed that business starts would have to rely on paltry family loans or small savings from wage labor.[41]

There was another way, however. What Remedios Diaz-Oliver was doing at Richford—extending credit on the basis of personal reputation—became institutionalized as Cuban managers gradually took over the loan portfolios of local banks. To be sure, these were not the dominant Anglo-owned banks for whom the exiles were just another downtrodden minority, but small banks created with South American capital. South American owners had deemed it wise to put the management of their firms in the hands of experienced but then unemployed Cuban bankers. Once their own positions became secure, these officers initiated a program of lending $10,000 to $30,000 to other Cubans for business start-ups.

Access to this credit was not based on the applicant's balance sheet or collateral, but on his or her business reputation in Cuba. This unique practice became known as "character" lending and allowed numerous exiles who spoke little English and had no standing in the American banking system to get a foothold in the local economy. A leading Cuban American banker who took part in this operation described it as follows:

At the start, most Cuban enterprises were gas stations; then came grocery shops and restaurants. No American bank would lend to them. By the mid-sixties, we started a policy at our bank of making small loans to Cubans who wanted to start their own businesses but did not have any capital. These loans of ten or fifteen thousand dollars were made because the person was known to us by his reputation and integrity. All of them paid back; there were zero losses. With some exceptions, they have continued being clients of the bank. People who used to borrow fifteen thousand dollars on a one-time basis now take out fifty thousand in a week. In 1973, the policy was discontinued. The reason was that the new exiles coming at that time were unknown to us.[42]

An early client, now a large factory owner, describes his impressions of differing banking styles:

The American banker looks only at the statement, the balance sheet of the company. If he doesn't like it, he doesn't give you the loan. The Cuban banker has a different technique: He looks for signs of your character. If he knows you, knows that you meet your obligations, he lends you without looking at the balance sheet. He knows you are not going to fail him. American banks have the habit of changing credit managers very often. They hire fresh college graduates who come here to Miami, know no one, and have to begin analyzing statements. There the Cuban banks have the advantage. Their loan officers know their clientele, they often even knew their families in Cuba—twenty, thirty years. It's a small technical detail, but important.[43]

Meanwhile, in the construction industry, skilled Cubans who sought jobs as carpenters, plumbers, and bricklayers were being blackballed by local unions dominated by native whites. Undeterred, the Cubans created their own home repair businesses by buying a truck and going door-to-door seeking work. Eventually, some of them gained access to character loans, Small Business Administration loans, or pooled family savings to establish more substantial firms. By 1979, about 50 percent of major construction companies in Dade County were Cuban-owned, and they accounted for over 90 percent of residential and commercial construction in the southwest zone of the county.

Developers like Santiago Alvarez gradually displaced older unionized companies. By 1985, six of the ten largest home builders in Dade were Cuban-owned, including West Miller Heights (P. Adrian), Atrium Homes (A. Sotolongo), H. G. Enterprises (H. Garcia), and Interam Builders (E. Pereira). These companies were uniformly nonunion. As they gradually expanded, unionized new construction in Miami plummeted from over 90 percent in 1960 to less than 10 percent in 1980. A Carpenter Union's organizer gloomily summarized the situation: "We paid dearly for not letting the Cubans in. They came to see us as the enemy, and workers in their companies would not touch us."[44] Grouped in the Latin Builders Association, the Cuban companies came to exert growing influence not only in the construction industry, but in local politics as well. Predictably, one of the goals of the association is to insure that the influence of the construction trades in Dade remains at a minimum.

There were other means of capitalizing new firms, both orthodox and unconventional. Established Cuban Jewish companies in Havana simply moved to Miami and continued their long-standing relationship with suppliers and creditors. This is the case of the Suave Shoe Company, a footwear manufacturer and one of the largest firms of the Miami enclave. Suave and similar manufacturers were able to secure credit from "factors," bankers who specialize in advancing capital on the basis of work orders, bypassing the usual 90 to 120 days' repayment period. "Factor" banking is not available to any business newcomer, however. Access to this credit system is available only to businesses with established networks and a solid commercial reputation. Thanks to this advantage, Suave became so successful that it went public and qualified to be listed on the New York Stock Exchange.[45]

But it was capital advanced by Cuban officials at the small South American banks that played the decisive role during the 1960s, fueling the development of a thick midlevel layer of enterprises between the transplanted large firms and the small family businesses. By 1977, the Census of Minority-Owned Enterprises counted 30,366 Cuban-owned firms in the United States, most of them in Miami. The area was home to half of the forty largest Hispanic firms in the nation and to the largest bank. There was one firm for every twenty-seven Cuban-born persons.[46]

Unexpected Consequences of Political Militancy

Clearly, social networks and social capital were essential in effecting the rapid transformation of political militants into ethnic entrepreneurs. Yet it is useful to delve deeper into the social context in which these events took place. Language and a common culture provided Cubans with a basis for solidarity but, by themselves, they were not enough to create a level of mutual support stronger than that typical among other immigrant communities. It was instead the common circumstance of exile and the collective experience of successive political defeats that cemented a strong sense of "we-ness" among these refugees. Expelled and despised by the government of their country, abandoned at the Bay of Pigs by a supposedly firm ally, traded off during the 1962 Missile Crisis, ridiculed by Latin American intellectuals who confined them to the dustbin of history, Cuban exiles had little to fall back on but themselves.[47]

Sharing a common political fate, and an unenviable one at that, had the unexpected consequence of promoting economic progress by cementing ties built originally on a common culture. The "discrimination" that Cubans suffered was not the usual type involving labor market opportunities or social acceptance. Instead, it concerned the failure of their overall political project and their inability to persuade others of its merit. Latin as well as North American intellectuals derided Cuban exiles as just a bunch of political losers stranded between two nations. This isolation defined the community and strengthened its internal solidarity in a way that even language or a well-defined national culture could not.

The physical boundaries of the Miami enclave are not clearly demarcated because Cuban businesses may be found throughout the metropolitan area. The social boundaries are, however, extremely clear; they define the operation and the limits of bounded solidarity and enforceable trust. Underlying the ease with which Cuban bank officials made character loans was the certainty that their clients would pay. Anyone defaulting or otherwise violating the implicit trust built into such deals could kiss good-bye his or her chances for business success; the entire Cuban community would know, and there was precious little opportunity outside of it. Hence, bankers were not simply being loyal to their friends but were also displaying good business acumen. The "zero losses" reported by our Cuban bank sources were predictable.

In his study of commercial enterprises in Bali, Clifford Geertz observed how successful entrepreneurs were assaulted by job- and loan-seeking kinsmen. The petitioners' claims were buttressed by strong norms enjoining mutual assistance within the extended family and among all community members. The result was to turn promising businesses into relief organizations languishing at the margins of solvency.[48] Family and ethnic obligations surely existed among Miami Cubans, but they did not go as far as to compromise the viability of business ventures. On the contrary, such ties worked in the entrepreneurs' favor because they functioned as sources of low-cost family labor and start-up capital. Most enclave firms could thereby prosper without fear that they would be turned into welfare hotels.[49]

The mechanisms of bounded solidarity and enforceable trust produced entrepreneurial success that was celebrated by the entire community and was presented to the world as a model to follow. In political defeat, success in business gradually emerged as a source of collective pride and as proof of the correctness of the refugees' ideological stance: while Cuba foundered economically and regimes friendly to Castro also failed, the Miami enclave flourished on the energies of exile entrepreneurs and their politically grounded solidarity.

THE INFORMAL ECONOMY

The examples of Inter-American Transport and the Suave Shoe Company—formal capital and business transfers from the country of origin to the immigrant enclave—are important, but exceptional. Far more common in the development of enclaves are the patterns exemplified by the "back of the truck" beginnings of Santiago Alvarez's construction firm or the character loans without collateral pioneered by Remedios Diaz-Oliver. Small and medium enclave enterprises begin invariably informal, either in their sources of credit, their access to labor, or their business practices. It could hardly be otherwise. Immigrant business initiatives face a foreign and often hostile world in which observance of formal rules, including fiscal requirements and labor covenants, would sink most such efforts.

For that reason, improvisation and nonobservance of formal rules is the norm, at least in the earlier stages of business creation. In the absence of money capital and social status in the host society, immigrant entrepreneurs mobilize their skills and social capital, seeking ways to bypass regulations in order to gain a competitive advantage. As Vittorio Capecchi noted in the case of the informal economy of central Italy, relationships of "complicity" among economic actors predominated in the early stages of development in this industrial district.[50] For the same reason, immigrant enclaves have been more common in the United States than in countries of northwestern Europe. Looser regulation of economic activity in America has provided the necessary space for the mix of immigrant human capital and social capital to produce a multitude of informal and semiformal enterprises whose viability would lead eventually to higher levels of formalization.

While the enclave of Miami is typical of these social arrangements, it is certainly not the only example. Studies of New York's Chinatown, Los Angeles's Koreatown, and the Dominican enclave of northern Manhattan also point to the proliferation of informal credit and informal modes of production and trade underlying the consolidation and growth of ethnic firms.[51] In terms of the functional typology of informal economies presented in chapter 7, immigrant enclaves fit squarely in the category of informal economies of growth. A common mistake in the past literature on immigrant and ethnic businesses was to define these initiatives as mere vehicles for economic survival.[52] While that may be true in the case of immigrant minorities composed mainly or exclusively of laborers, the defining feature of enclaves is precisely the capital accumulation and business development they make possible.

As in the case of Emilia-Romagna and other industrial districts that started as assemblages of small informal businesses, early enclave enterprises give way over time to larger formal firms. This leads, in turn, to the emergence of a class of wealthy first-generation immigrants and creates a platform for the subsequent entry into the professions of the second generation. The histories of the Jewish Lower East Side and the Japanese Little Tokyos of Los Angeles and San Francisco attest to this pattern. The evolution of the Miami enclave, of New York's Chinatown, and Los Angeles's Koreatown provide additional and compelling evidence.[53]

MIDDLEMAN MINORITIES

A tight-knit enclave is not, however, the only manifestation of viable ethnic entrepreneurship. In other areas where immigrant concentration is less dense, entrepreneurs tend to take over businesses catering to lower-income groups. In this role as "middlemen," these immigrants position themselves between dominant ethnic groups at the top of the class structure and impoverished minorities at the bottom. While this role entails substantial risks, as we will see next, it also offers the potential for significant profit since middleman businesses tend to operate without competition.[54]

Edna Bonacich, who coined the term, noted that middleman groups have existed in many historical contexts and have often been recruited by elites to cushion the conflict between haves and have-nots in specific circumstances. Jewish merchants in medieval cities commonly played this role. Indian merchants in East Africa successfully inserted themselves between the British colonial elites and the mass of native black population. Overseas Chinese are legendary in their capacity to create successful middleman enterprises throughout Southeast Asia.[55]

In these and other specific instances, middleman groups have been the target of intense hostility by the subordinate population to which they cater. This is a consequence of two interrelated factors: first, their daily presence and high visibility in impoverished areas where their businesses are located and, second, the high profits that they are known to derive from their quasi-monopolistic position. Thus, when discontent and frustration finally flare up, they are commonly targeted not on the economic elites ultimately responsible for the plight of the downtrodden, but on middlemen. This is the reason why, according to Bonacich, Jews in medieval and modern European cities, Indians in East Africa, and overseas Chinese throughout Asia suffered so many attacks and persecutions.

In America, immigrant groups endowed with sufficient human capital to follow the entrepreneurial path have commonly adopted a middleman role in the absence of a critical mass of coethnics to provide a captive market and a pliable labor force. Outside of their Lower Manhattan enclave, Jewish merchants played this role in pawnshops, grocery stores, and liquor stores scattered throughout largely black central cities.[56] As these immigrants aged, their businesses were taken over by more recently arrived entrepreneurial groups from Asia—Chinese and Koreans—outside of their respective enclave areas. Cuban merchants outside of Miami and, especially, in Puerto Rico, have fulfilled a similar role.[57]

Social capital plays a still stronger role among middlemen than among enclave entrepreneurs. This is so because, to the normal business needs for credit, information, and market opportunities, middleman enterprises add the requirement for mutual protection against widespread hostility by the population they serve. This sentiment strengthens, in turn, the sense of "we-ness" among entrepreneurs and, hence, their bounded solidarity. In the American inner city today, the spectacle of Korean and Chinese shop owners living in crowded apartments atop their businesses and working long hours to accumulate capital is common.[58] For these families, isolated in an ocean of foreign and commonly unfriendly faces, the only opportunity for sociability is in meetings with their fellows, often at Sunday church services. These rituals help reaffirm their sense of a common fate and are sites where the social capital created by this solidarity can be put to use.

The condition and role of middleman immigrant merchants were cast in sharp profile during the events surrounding the Los Angeles riots of 1992. The triggering episode was the verdict of an all-white jury to acquit a group of white policemen caught on tape beating a black motorist, Rodney King. As news of the verdict came out, black Central Los Angeles exploded. The impact of its fury was not felt, however, by the indicted policemen or the suburban white jury, but by Korean merchants in the immediate vicinity. Korean shops were looted and burned by the dozens, despite the fact that they had nothing to do with the beating or the acquittal. In response, Korean merchants created armed self-defense groups and organized politically.[59] Largely defenseless until then, they came to realize that the great vulnerability of their situation was not due to their beliefs or actions, but to the structural characteristics of the economic role that they had come to play.

The risks and dangers of middleman enterprise make it a one-generation phenomenon among American immigrant groups. First-generation shop owners toil in the inner cities with their sights on accumulating enough capital for their offspring to escape it. This is a common trend, illustrated by the mass move of second-generation Jews in an earlier period and Koreans and Chinese today into the universities and, subsequently into the professions. In this respect, they are similar to the one-generation pattern found among enclave entrepreneurs except that, among middlemen, it is strengthened by the very precariousness of their enterprises.

The Interface of Class and Ethnicity

In chapters 5 and 6, we saw that social classes are formed by aggregates of people with comparable life chances as determined by their possession of power-conferring resources.[60] While, in modern societies, the primary class-defining resource is wealth, social capital and cultural capital also come into play. As first noted by Pierre Bourdieu, a key characteristic of these resources is their "fungibility," meaning that under the right circumstances they can be transformed into each other.[61]

Immigrant business formations—enclaves and middleman minorities—represent instances of one such strategy, namely the use of coethnic social capital to alter the class position of an entire category of people. Under normal circumstances, immigrants are relegated to the class of common workers expected to live from paltry wages and to rise only slowly over several generations. Enclave and middleman entrepreneurs aim to bypass this situation by mobilizing the abundant sources of social capital in immigrant communities, due to a common fate in a strange land, and combining them with personal skills in order to create viable enterprises. Depending on the success of these firms, owners may find themselves in the class of petty entrepreneurs or be catapulted into that of rentiers or even regular capitalists (see the typology of class structure in chapter 5). In all cases, the goal is that, if the first generation does not make it beyond petty enterprise, the second will either by becoming elite professionals or full-fledged capitalists.

The unique character of these economic formations is best seen from the lens of the "normal" relationship between ethnicity and class. Normally, ethnic traits associated with foreignness and cultural difference from dominant elites compound social and economic disadvantage and serve to perpetuate a subordinate class position among immigrant groups. Enclaves and middleman minorities *reverse* that equation, grounding investments and economic transactions on bounded solidarity and trust. Instead of impersonal relationships governed by formal market rules, we find relationships of "complicity" guaranteed by the informal enforcement mechanisms of the community.

To be sure, not all members of even the most business-oriented groups become entrepreneurs themselves. Normally, only a minority does. But their success and that of their offspring gives to these communities a distinct social profile. Wealthy entrepreneurs become community leaders and role models; they commonly endow coethnic religious and civic institutions, and their success stories become part of the community lore and a source of collective pride. The histories of German and Russian Jews in America, followed by the Japanese, and contemporaneously, by Chinese, Cubans, and Koreans, attest to the power of these social arrangements and their capacity to provide a vehicle for both individual and collective mobility in the American class structure. The symbolic/cultural dimension stemming from repeated entrepreneurial success has had much to do with these groups' unique histories.

A second set of relationships between immigrant business formations and the class structure has to do with their potential legitimation of the existing order. As we have seen, middlemen can play a key role, softening the edges of the confrontation between elites and the subordinate population and often redirecting the frustration of the populace toward themselves. In a more indirect manner, enclaves play a similar role. Their visible presence in urban space blurs the sharp physical separation between wealthy suburbs and the impoverished inner city. Symbolically, enclaves offer tangible proof that the capitalist system is not closed to ethnic minorities and that opportunities exist for the willing and able. Elites can incorporate these achievements into their discourse, countering complaints about inequality and social oppression. This discourse is generally structured along the lines: "If minority *x* could move upward and achieve positions of wealth and influence, why could not minorities *y* and *z* do likewise?"

At a more concrete level, enclave entrepreneurs hire their own, thus reducing the level of ethnic minority unemployment, while creating a segment of the urban working-class refractory to organizational attempts by trade unions and populist organizations. The uniformly nonunion character of Cuban industrial and construction firms in Miami is a pattern that extends to most other enclaves: union organizers have had at best a precarious foothold in garment shops in New York's Chinatown or among Korean-owned industries in Los Angeles. Overall, the political effect of immigrant business formations is conservative. They tend to adapt rather than challenge the existing structures of power and contribute, directly or indirectly, to their legitimation. While the creation and success of immigrant firms are due to the characteristics of their community and the initiative of their owners, native elites are quick to apprehend the economic and political advantages these formations create.

In turn, successful immigrant entrepreneurs and their offspring tend to adopt and disseminate the same message. Ironically, the individualistic capitalist ethos, succinctly captured by the proverb "Where there's a will, there's a way," finds support in economic success built on the basis of

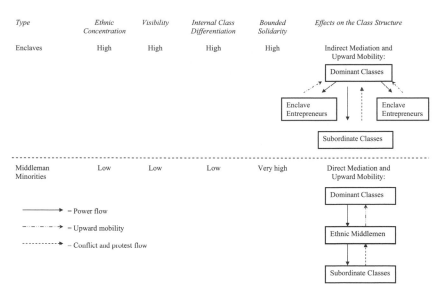

Figure 8.1 Characteristics of Immigrant Economic Formations

strong bounded solidarity. Social capital mutates into economic capital and, in turn, into political capital, legitimizing an order initially hostile to the immigrants' efforts and their bid to mobility. Figure 8.1 summarizes the relevant relationships.

Conclusion

The analysis of this second strategic research site continues the process of bringing into focus the meta-assumptions of economic sociology along with its explanatory mechanisms as applied to specific areas of economic life. It is apparent how the assumptions of social embeddedness, power, and unexpected consequences are reflected in the phenomenon of enclaves. Among the three explanatory mechanisms reviewed previously, only "institutions" has not been brought into the analysis. This is a consequence of the initially informal character of enclave and middleman firms that, in a sense, represent the opposite of "institutionalization." There are no formal legal blueprints for the creation of these immigrant enterprises that are mostly emergent and unanticipated, at least as seen from the lens of the mainstream economy.

As noted, enclaves and middlemen are relatively short-lived phenomena since they serve primarily for the consolidation of the economic position of their owners and as a platform for the advancement of the second generation via the educational system and the professions. This also conspires against the durability of these entrepreneurial initiatives and their institutionalization. Except for the very largest and most successful, enclave firms seldom devolve into permanent organizations that transcend the lives of their owners; middleman enterprises almost never do. Nevertheless, the success of these formations in propelling the second generation into positions of economic advantage can be remarkable. The appendix illustrates this fact with an emblematic case study.

Appendix

The original formulation of the concept of immigrant enclave dates back to the early 1980s and was primarily based on the experience of Cuban political exiles in Miami. It is appropriate to return to that city to examine what happened afterward since, if the notion that enclaves represent vehicles for upward mobility holds, the effect should be most visible among the group that gave rise to the concept in the first place.[62]

Data from the Public Use Microdata Sample (IPUMS) from the 2000 Census is appropriate for this purpose. Table 8.1 presents family incomes for the adult population in the Miami/Ft. Lauderdale Metropolitan Area (MSA), broken down by ethnic categories. Figures show that non-Hispanic whites have the highest incomes in this metropolitan area, significantly exceeding those of most other groups. The only exception is Cubans who arrived in the 1960s and 1970s, the creators of the enclave—whose incomes are not statistically different from non-Hispanic whites. Both groups exceed $80,000 on average. A close third is the U.S.-born Cuban second generation, mostly the children of pre-1980 arrivals, at over $78,700.

Table 8.2 disaggregates these figures further into the categories of self-employed and wage earners among adult males (there are not enough self-employed females to permit interethnic comparisons). Self-employed Cubans in Miami are, by definition, enclave entrepreneurs since, as seen previously, the original business networks of the enclave grew out of the city of Miami to encompass the entire metropolitan area. By contrast, Cuban waged and salaried workers may or may not be employees of the enclave economy.

The same ethnic hierarchy observed earlier holds, with non-Hispanic whites at the top, pre-1980 Cubans close behind, followed by their children and everyone else below. As repeatedly noted in prior studies, entrepreneurs (the self-employed) enjoy a substantial economic advantage over their waged coethnics. Non-Hispanic white business owners and first-generation Cuban entrepreneurs are the only groups to exceed family incomes of $100,000 per year, with the difference between the two groups just shy of $1,000. They are followed, at some distance, by second-generation Cubans, and then all others. Differences among waged and salaried workers follow exactly the same pattern: there is no statistical difference between the average incomes of non-Hispanic whites and pre-1980 Cuban workers, while all other groups fall significantly behind. This result indicates that Cuban workers who arrived at the time that the economic enclave was developing have done rather well economically, whether they were employed by coethnic firms or not.

Table 8.3 presents self-employment rates for adult males in the Miami metropolitan area in 2000. Two trends are apparent in these results: First, pre-1980 Cubans are the most entrepreneurial category, with a rate

TABLE 8.1
Family Incomes of Racial and Ethnic Groups in the Miami/Ft. Lauderdale Metropolitan Area (Adults 18–65)[1]

| Racial/Ethnic Group | Total MSA | Non-Hispanic White | Non-Hispanic Black | Cuban | | | Other Hispanic | Other |
				Pre-1980 Migrant	U.S. Born			
Family Income	68,720	84,842	51,361***	82,589	78,739***		56,371***	59,674***
	(67,753)	(82,165)	(41,434)	(74,208)	(62,310)		(54,670)	(59,775)
N	66,955	25,383	12,003	4,914	2,069		14,546	3,019

[1] Statistical significance of mean differences from non-Hispanic white incomes is indicated by asterisks.
***p < 0.001; **p. < 0.01; *p < 0.05, two tailed.
Note: Universe includes adults aged 18–64, who were not unemployed and whose annual income was greater than or equal to $500. Raw Ns included; person-weights used. Standard deviations in parentheses.
Source: IPUMS 2000.

TABLE 8.2
Family Incomes of Self-Employed and Salaried Males by Racial and Ethnic Group in the Miami/Ft. Lauderdale Metropolitan Area

Racial/Ethnic Group	Total MSA	Non-Hispanic White	Non-Hispanic Black[1]	Cuban			Other Hispanic	Other
				Pre-1980 Migrant	U.S. Born			
Working Adults	70,500	88,226	53,078***	87,404	77,688***	55,409***	58,974***
	(70,057)	(85,302)	(42,213)	(78,036)	(63,267)	(52,973)	(60,620)
Self-Employed	90,618	106,667	60,443***	105,921	94,683*	71,671***	79,990**
	(100,842)	(110,504)	(64,862)	(103,997)	(92,853)	(85,701)	(111,365)
Waged/Salaried	67,102	84,162	52,589***	82,363	75,569**	53,294***	55,868***
	(62,767)	(78,094)	(40,224)	(66,334)	(58,267)	(46,670)	(48,138)

[1] Non-Hispanic white is the reference category. Significant differences from this category are noted by asterisks.

*** p < 0.001; ** p < 0.01; * p < 0.05, two tailed.

Note: Universe includes adult males aged 18–64, who were not unemployed, and whose annual income was greater than or equal to $500. Person-weights used; standard deviations in parentheses.

Source: IPUMS 2000.

TABLE 8.3
Self-Employment Rates among Males by Racial and Ethnic Group in the Miami/Ft. Lauderdale Metropolitan Area (Adults 18–65)

Racial/Ethnic Group	Total MSA	Non-Hispanic White	Non-Hispanic Black[1]	Cuban			Other Hispanic	Other
				Pre-1980 Migrant	U.S. Born			
Self-Employment	0.14	0.18	0.06***	0.21***	0.11***		0.12***	0.13***
N	35,285	13,780	5,430	2,398	1,051		7,872	1,677

[1] Non-Hispanic white is the reference category. Significant differences from this category are noted by asterisks.
***p < 0.001; **p < 0.01; *p < 0.05, two tailed.
Note: Universe includes adult males aged 18–64, who were not unemployed, and whose annual income was greater than or equal to $500. Raw Ns included; person-weights used.
Source: IPUMS 2000.

significantly higher than even non-Hispanic whites. This result accords with the historical role of this group. Second, second-generation Cubans are among the *least* entrepreneurial category. This result is worth noting because it supports the historical role of immigrant enclaves established in the past literature. As with other entrepreneurial minorities before them, most Miami enclave firms have not lasted indefinitely, but rather have served as platforms for entry of the second generation into professional careers. The relatively high incomes of second-generation Cubans coupled with their low rates of entrepreneurship points toward that outcome.

The Cuban history in the United States is also unique in having been marked by a major hiatus that fractured the community. The defining event for this rupture was the Mariel exodus of 1980. The decision of the Cuban government to open the port of Mariel to all exiles wishing to take their relatives out of the island triggered a massive and chaotic exodus that brought 125,000 refugees in less than six months. The Cuban government took advantage of the episode to empty its jails and mental hospitals, putting the inmates aboard the boats. The spectacle of a chaotic flotilla of ragged people arriving in the Florida Keys triggered a strong negative reaction among the American public. The Carter administration refused to grant the new arrivals refugee status, categorizing them as "entrants, status pending." The public reaction to the Mariel episode shifted the perception of Cubans from a "model minority" and "the builders of the new Miami" to one of the most unpopular minorities in the nation.[63]

Perceiving the *marielitos*[64] and post-Mariel entrants as responsible for the rapid decline of the Cubans' public image in the United States and having few social links with them, pre-1980 exiles came to regard the newcomers as a category different from themselves. The separation was physical, as well as social: the old middle-class Cuban population settled in the comfortable suburbs of Coral Gables and Kendall; Mariel and post-Mariel refugees crowded in the poor city of Hialeah and the deteriorating "Little Havana" quarter of Miami. This rupture meant that Mariel and post-Mariel refugees reaped few benefits from the Cuban enclave and its internal ties of solidarity and mutual business support. No "character loans" were available to them; no business tips were granted to them either. While many Mariel and post-Mariel arrivals went to work for Cuban firms and some eventually became entrepreneurs, their social bonds to established enclave firms were nearly absent. These differences in the internal composition of the Cuban community spelled out the end of social capital and class heterogeneity as mechanisms for economic mobility of new arrivals.

This history is poignantly reflected in the economic performance of different segments of the Miami Cuban population over time. Table 8.4 presents regressions of family incomes in real dollars for the adult working population of Miami/Ft. Lauderdale on standard measures of human capital, self-employment, and ethnic origins.[65] The first model presents the effects of ethnic categories for all adults; the second restricts the sample to adult males.

Three findings emerge from this analysis: First, education and work experience have the expected positive net effects on incomes. College and postcollege graduates have an advantage measured in the tens of thousands of dollars relative to high school dropouts (the reference category). Females experience the familiar income handicap relative to statistically equivalent males. Second, after controlling for these predictors, self-employment continues to have a strong positive effect. Compared to workers of the same education, work experience, gender, and ethnicity, the self-employed have a net annual income advantage of approximately $15,000 in 2000. Third, there are stark differences among the three segments of the Cuban population. Pre-1980 Cubans have higher incomes than native whites, controlling for all other predictors; this difference becomes statistically significant among males. Their offspring, the second generation, do not differ significantly from the native white population, providing yet another indicator of their successful economic assimilation. Mariel and post-Mariel Cubans experience a significant economic disadvantage, higher than other Hispanic groups and comparable only to that suffered by African Americans. These differences are not due to recency of arrival or to variations in human capital endowment since the length of U.S.-specific work experience and the level of educational achievement are statistically controlled. With these controls in place, differences can be attributed directly to the rupture in modes of incorporation experienced by the most recent Cuban arrivals and the consequent absence of the social mechanisms accounting for the economic mobility of earlier exiles.

With this notable exception, results fit well the original theoretical expectations. A twenty-year retrospective provides an authoritative standpoint to assess the economic situation and performance of any immigrant group. From this perspective, the economic trajectory of earlier Cuban exiles in Miami has been enviable, placing them at par, if not higher, than the mainstream white population. Their children have gone on to join this

TABLE 8.4
Ordinary Least Squares Regressions of Family Income on Ethnicity
and Selected Variables

	Adults (18–64)	Males (18–64)
Ethnicity:[1]		
Pre-1980 Cuban	2023.88	3849.55*
	(1220.47)	(1777.46)
1980 or after Cuban	−14956.88***	−16442.62***
	(1027.94)	(1381.96)
U.S.-Born Cuban	−222.71	−372.66
	(1574.38)	(2272.18)
Black	−19062.42***	−17100.27***
	(676.70)	(974.96)
Hispanic	−14163.78***	−15565.28***
	(813.21)	(1115.40)
Other	−14091.57***	−15856.60***
	(1345.03)	(1834.92)
Female	−2408.99***	
	(528.30)	
Work Experience (U.S.)[2]	940.46***	934.68***
	(58.77)	(100.78)
Work Experience (U.S.) Squared	−15.81***	−13.00***
	(1.89)	(2.65)
Education:[3]		
High School	5787.45***	5109.78***
	(697.25)	(893.68)
Some College	15452.91***	14750.29***
	(717.47)	(938.03)
College	36585.79***	37062.47***
	(977.00)	(1295.85)
Post-Graduate	60334.30***	66736.50***
	(1469.41)	(2010.92)
Self-Employed [4]	14869.66***	15281.24***
	(1189.95)	(1451.51)
Intercept	50467.92***	49398.98***
	(1017.30)	(1371.06)
N	66,955	35,285
R^2	0.13	0.15

[1] Non-Hispanic White is the reference category.
[2] Years of U.S. residence after reaching adulthood (18 years).
[3] Less than high school is the reference category.
[4] Wage/salaried worker is the reference category.
Note: Universe includes adults aged 18–64, who were not unemployed, and whose annual income was greater than or equal to $500. Raw Ns included; person weight used.
***$p < 0.001$; **$p < 0.01$; *$p < 0.05$; two tailed
Source: IPUMS 2000 (5% microsample). Standard errors in parentheses.

population, becoming indistinct from it in terms of economic solvency. This overall pattern supports the original characterization of enclaves as vehicles for economic mobility, as it is clear that Cubans could not have moved ahead so rapidly without a history of rapid business formation grounded in bounded solidarity and enforceable trust. This route placed the earlier Cuban cohorts and their children firmly on top of an economically dynamic city. No other ethnic group, except native whites themselves, has matched this achievement.

CHAPTER NINE

Transnational Communities

A THIRD STRATEGIC research site is, in a sense, the obverse of the second. While ethnic enclaves and middleman minorities call attention to distinct economic activities of foreign-origin groups within receiving societies, transnationalism calls attention to the multiple social and economic networks they create across space and with places of origin.[1] *Globalization* has become the term of choice to refer to the process through which powerful economic actors, such as transnational corporations, progressively integrate nations and localities into a single homogenous system.[2] "Transnationalism" may be regarded as a form of "globalization from below" in which individuals and communities mobilize their grassroots networks to adapt and respond to the globalizing activities of corporation and governments.[3]

In the field of immigration studies, transnationalism is commonly seen as a novel perspective, capable of providing an alternative theoretical lens to the previously reigning assimilation framework.[4] For economic sociology, the value of the concept is to call attention to a set of phenomena that: (a) transcend national borders; (b) bypass formal, regulated international activities covered by the literature on globalization; (c) exemplify, in unique ways, the significance of its meta-assumptions and the operation of its explanatory mechanisms, as discussed in previous chapters. To highlight these three aspects, I will use the term *transnational communities* to refer to these concrete social formations, created by grassroots networks and superimposed, as it were, between two or more nation-states.[5]

Transnational communities represent a unique form of social embeddedness that mobilizes family and cultural ties to overcome the barriers of space and formal governmental regulation, thereby insuring a smooth flow of people, goods, and information across space. As we shall see, these flows often run counter to those promoted by states and corporate actors. The rise of these communities also represents an unexpected consequence of international migration. For both orthodox economic theory and the conventional sociological assimilation perspective, international migration represents primarily a one-way flow of people escaping hunger and want who arrive on the shores of the developed world to carve a new life, leaving the misery of their former existence behind.[6]

Contrary to these views, transnational communities give concrete expression to the fact that immigrants in the developed world do not abandon their kin and communities, nor their cultural loyalties and historical attachments. The consolidation of their economic and social positions abroad runs hand in hand with a growing process of institutionalization of cross-national ties through which migrants are able to lead dual lives, exploit differentials of advantage between places of origin and destination, and ultimately create novel social and economic structures.[7]

Among key ideal types and research sites examined in prior chapters, three bear directly on the rise and consolidation of transnational communities:

(a) Social capital
(b) Social institutions
(c) The informal economy

This chapter examines these interrelationships after further clarifying the concept of transnationalism by distinguishing it from related, but different, phenomena.

THE DEBATE ON TRANSNATIONALISM: THE PROBLEM OF MULTIPLE MEANINGS

The term *transnational* was not coined recently. As early as 1916, we find it in the title of a classic article by Randolph S. Bourne. In that piece, "Transnational America," Bourne argued that the country was doing a disservice to itself and its immigrants by pressuring them to conform to a homogenous world, losing in the process their distinct cultural heritage. In his words, "Just so surely as we tend to disintegrate these nuclei of nationalistic culture do we tend to create hordes of men and women without a spiritual country, cultural outlaws without taste, without standards but those of the mob. . . . Those who came to find liberty achieve only license. They become the flotsam of American life."[8] Subsequently, the concept has been used in multiple ways, referring in particular to the activities of global corporations. Partially in response to this earlier meaning, Luis Guarnizo and Michael Smith coined the terms *transnationalism from above* and *from below* to refer respectively to the cross-border initiatives of governments and corporations, on the one hand, and those of immigrants and grassroots entrepreneurs on the other.[9] However, a more refined typology is needed if confusion is to be avoided among multiple meanings. Actions conducted across national borders fall under four broad categories: those conducted by national states, those conducted by formal institutions that are based in a single country, those conducted by formal institutions that exist and operate in multiple countries, and those conducted by noninstitutional actors from civil society.

Examples of the first are the embassies, consulates, and diplomatic activities of national governments. Examples of the second are the exchange activities conducted with other countries by certain universities; the export drives of agricultural producers from a particular country; and the multicountry tours organized by performing groups (orchestras, dance troupes, etc.) based on a specific city or nation. Examples of the third kind of cross-border actors are global corporations with production and office facilities in multiple countries, the Catholic Church and other global religions, and the various specialized agencies of the United Nations. Examples of the fourth are grassroots activists coordinating environmental defense strategies from different countries and the grassroots trade conducted across borders by immigrant entrepreneurs.

To distinguish among these very different types of actors, we may reserve the term *international* to refer to the activities and programs of the first and second types—that is, those conducted by states and other nationally based institutions in other countries. The distinct characteristic of these activities is that they are carried out across borders in pursuit of the goals of large organizations that possess a clear national affiliation. The term *multinational* may be assigned to the third type of activity—that is, those conducted by institutions whose purposes and interests transcend the borders of a single nation-state. While these institutions may be headquartered in a specific national or urban space, say New York or the Vatican, the very character of their goals renders them simultaneously committed and active in the social, political, and economic life of a number of countries. Lastly, *transnational* activities would be those initiated and sustained by noncorporate actors, be they organized groups or networks of individuals across national borders. Many of these activities take place outside the pale of state regulation and control. Even when supervised by state agencies, the key aspect of transnational activities is that they represent goal-oriented initiatives that require coordination across national borders by individual members of civil society. These activities

TABLE 9.1
Cross-Border Activities by Different Types of Actors

		Areas	
Activities	Political	Economic	Sociocultural
International	Establishment of embassies and or-ganization of diplomatic missions abroad by national governments	Export drives by farming, ranch, and fishing organizations from a particular country	Travel and exchange programs organized by universities based on a specific country
Multinational	United Nations and other interna-tional agencies charged with moni-toring and improving specialized areas of global life	Production and marketing activi-ties of global corporations with profits dependent on multiple national markets	Schools and missions sponsored by the Catholic Church and other global religions in multiple countries
Transnational	a) Nongovernmental associations established to monitor human rights globally	a) Boycotts organized by grassroots activists in First World countries to compel multinationals to improve their Third World labor practices	a) Grassroots charities promoting the protection and care of children in poorer nations
	b) Hometown civic associations established by immigrants to im-prove their sending communities	b) Enterprises established by im-migrants to export/import goods to and from their home countries	b) Election of beauty queens and selection of performing groups in immigrant communities to take part in annual hometown festivals

are undertaken on their own behalf, rather than on behalf of the state or other large organizational bodies.

Thus defined, immigrant transnationalism represents just one manifestation of this type of action. Peter Evans has highlighted the potential effectiveness of grassroots transnational coalitions in exposing the abuses of multinational corporations in third world countries.[10] By publicly shaming multinational giants for their labor practices in poorer nations, these grassroots alliances of third world workers and first world activists have succeeded in producing significant changes in work conditions that otherwise would not have occurred. While there is nothing sacrosanct in the labels proposed, it is important to separate these sets of activities both to avoid terminological confusion and to facilitate analysis of their interactions. For example, the ways in which the *international* policies of national states affect the forms and scope of immigrant *transnational* initiatives has become a major analytic issue in this field of study. Similarly, the contest between corporate multinationals and transnational grassroots activists highlighted by Evans represents another significant terrain for future inquiry. Table 9.1 summarizes this typology with examples from three substantive areas.

The Debate on Transnationalism: The Problem of Adumbration

Shortly after the original statements in the early 1990s about the novelty and importance of transnational communities,[11] a loud chorus of critics rejected the value of the concept by pointing to the presence of similar practices among immigrant groups in the past. At the turn of the twentieth century, Polish, Italian, and Russian immigrants also forged multi-stranded relations linking together their societies of origin and settlement. They invested in land and businesses back home, crossed the Atlantic to visit families, and sponsored political causes favoring independence or a change of regime.[12] The independence of Poland and Czechoslovakia was actively supported by their large immigrant communities in America; and the struggle against Czarism found ardent partisans among Russian émigrés.[13] On the other side of the world, the overseas Chinese had for decades been creating complex trading communities spanning nations across the Pacific Rim.[14]

The point that there is really nothing new in the cross-border activities of contemporary immigrants was even embraced by some of the original proponents of the concept who failed to realize that, if these practices had always existed, then there was no novelty or justification for coining a new term. The debate surrounding transnationalism represents an exemplary instance of what Robert Merton referred to as the fallacy of adumbration. Merton dedicated the first chapter of his classic *Social Theory and Social Structure* to this problem, introducing it with a citation from Alfred North Whitehead: "But to come very near to a true theory and to grasp its precise application are two very different things. . . . Everything of importance has been said before by someone who did not discover it."[15]

The thrust of the argument is that, in science, it is a common occurrence for a significant finding to be preceded by a number of observations that pointed to the phenomenon in question, but failed to note its significance. Once a scientist or group of scientists have brought the nature and importance of the phenomenon to full public attention, it is a common occurrence to point to the trail of earlier "findings" that had identified it as well. The fallacy of adumbration consists in negating the novelty of a discovery by pointing to these earlier instances. In Merton's words, the adumbrator believes that, if something is new, it is not really true, and if something is true, it is not actually new. Precedents can always be found: "What is more common is that an idea is formulated definitely enough and emphatically enough that it cannot be overlooked by contemporaries, and it then becomes easy to find anticipations of it."[16]

Multiple historical instances of grassroots cross-border activities exist and have been extensively documented. Yet, until the concept of transnationalism was coined, the common character and significance of these phenomena remained obscure. For example, the parallels between Russian and Polish émigré political activism and the trading activities of the Chinese diaspora could not have been established because there was no theoretical lens that linked them and pointed to their similarities. In its absence, the respective literatures remained disparate and isolated from one another, as well as from present events.[17]

Once the concept of transnationalism made its appearance, it was a relatively straightforward task to point to these precedents and uncover commonalities among them. By itself, there is nothing wrong with this exercise and it can indeed provide useful results by exploring parallel threads linking contemporary events with similar ones in the past. The fallacy of adumbration consists in negating the value of the new concept by pointing to this evidence. Today, we rediscover and reappraise the transnational activities of Polish peasants, Chinese traders, and Russian émigrés not because such instances had been ignored in the past, but because their common relevance as instances of social fields across national borders has now been placed firmly before the eyes of the scientific community. Absent the transnational lens, this would not have been possible.

THE ROLE OF SOCIAL CAPITAL

"Migration and remittances represent the true economic adjustment program of the poor in our country."[18] With this trenchant remark, a young Salvadoran sociologist highlighted the significance of the transnational communities built by his compatriots over time. A first empirical fact established by research in this field is that migrant workers, lacking capital and legal standing, are unable to build transnational enterprises and similar initiatives on a contractual, formal basis. They thus substitute money capital with social capital in order to make these long-term activities viable. Social capital is cemented in preexisting kin and community ties, reenergized and reoriented for this purpose. The operation of social capital in this instance possesses three distinct characteristics:

1. The trust that it generates must be effective across long distances, making it difficult to sanction malfeasance.
2. While cemented in purely local ties, effects of this long-distance trust can have "structural" consequences for sending nations and immigrant settlements alike.
3. "Negative" social capital is present in the transnational field as a set of second-level unexpected consequences.

1. Precisely because they "float" over space and national borders, transnational communities are seldom able to bring sanctions to bear against those who shirk their obligations or violate the terms of the original agreements. Sending towns cannot penalize migrants who fail to send remittances or join civic hometown associations abroad, except by withdrawing social approval. Migrants are essentially at liberty to cut off ties and seek full integration into the host society, which is precisely what assimilation theory predicts. Similarly, migrant associations can seldom seek redress against their home country counterparts if the latter abscond with philanthropic contributions or rechannel them to their own ends.

The root of this situation lies in that social capital sustaining transnational ventures flow from *consummatory* rather than instrumental sources. Reciprocity expectations are difficult to enforce across space, and the overarching social structures that create enforceable trust are at best thin when the "assimilation alternative" is readily available to migrants. In this context, transnational civic initiatives and contributions flow, for the most part, out of unselfish motives grounded on values and, especially on bounded solidarity. A sense of duty to families and communities left behind is the primary motivator for transnational civic and philanthropic ventures. Even transnational economic enterprise is mostly grounded on trust flowing out of kin and coethnic solidarity.[19]

As we will see, the complexity and scope of transnational activities *increases* with the length of time, legal security, and economic power of immigrants in the host societies. This is precisely the outcome to be expected if these activities derive from consummatory rather than instrumental sources; absent bounded solidarity, older and better-established migrants would not invest their money and their time in communities long left behind, but would reorient them toward their new surroundings.[20] That they proceed otherwise attests to the power of family-grounded and community loyalties.

Clearly, remittances sent loyally year after year and sustained philanthropic contributions by hometown associations earn approval and status for migrants among those left behind. Migrants become "big men" when they return home and leaders of transnational organizations are greeted and feted by local authorities.[21] However, in most instances, these are derivative effects. Transnational organizations are not generally launched as an explicit quest for status and approval, but by genuine concern for the plight of kin and home communities. The operative motivation in the construction of such collective initiatives appears to be an extension of that underlying family remittances: "now that we're here and are doing better economically, we need to do something for our poor families and our forgotten hometowns."[22]

2. In principle, social structures built on such a basis could be expected to be fragile because unselfish motivations may be easily undermined by opportunism or malfeasance. As we will see next, this often happens. Nevertheless, in the aggregate, immigrant transnational activities and organizations tend to grow over time to the point that they acquire "structural" importance for the countries left behind and for the immigrant communities themselves.

First, remittances sent by expatriate communities currently add to billions of dollars and, in most sending countries, easily surpass foreign aid and rival major exports as sources of foreign exchange. Guarnizo notes the irony that the remittances of a migrant worker concerned with the welfare of his family at home are "banked" by financial institutions as a reliable source of foreign exchange and used as collateral by countries for soliciting international loans.[23] The financial magicians that rule the capitalist world have learned to rely not only on present remittances, but also on the expectation of future flows for rating the credit-worthiness of sending nations and their ability to repay loans. In this manner, millions of independent decisions by migrants seeking to improve their life chances can become transformed into a key "export" by their home countries and a major means of maintaining their financial health over time.[24]

Second, transnational ties sustained by bounded solidarity also become a key means for launching and developing immigrant enterprises. Surveys conducted recently among immigrants in the United States have found that upwards of 60 percent of entrepreneurs engage in a form of arbitrage linking economic opportunities at home with resources abroad in ways that could not be implemented in either site alone.[25] Case studies of "Chinatowns" and "Koreatowns" in the United States point in the same direction, showing the vital role of cross-national ties in sustaining these enterprises.[26] Hence, an important and generally unremarked character of ethnic enclaves is that they are, to a significant extent, "transnational"; they depend on these ties and simultaneously strengthen them, to the point of defining the socioeconomic profile of their respective communities.

Third, while many transnational organizations are small and short-lived, the consolidation of a few successful ones provides a model and incentive for other would-be leaders. Table 9.2 reproduces a 2006 inventory of all organizations created by Colombian, Dominican, and Mexican migrants in the United States. As shown in the table, there are hundreds of such organizations pursuing the most diverse activities and goals. Their structural significance lies in the capacity of the best established of these groups to enter into a dialogue with governments, endowing immigrant communities with "voice" in the affairs of their homelands.[27] Simultaneously, such organizations can play a vital role in guiding the social and political incorporation of their members in the host nations. Individual migrants seldom enter the political process on their own; they do so instead through the mediation of coethnic organizations in their immediate social environment.[28]

3. Trust sustained by value introjection and bounded solidarity is particularly subject to malfeasance.[29] Thus, it is not surprising that a number of such incidents have been reported in the transnationalism literature, leading to the breakup of cooperative relations. In the absence of formal contracts or strong overarching social structures guaranteeing reciprocal expectations, participants in the transnational field are commonly at the mercy of the goodwill and the good character of their long-distance transactors.[30]

More unexpected are other second-level consequences of transnational social capital that stem precisely from its anticipated *positive* effects. A reliable flow of remittances over time keeps families at home alive, but also generates dependence and discourages local productive investment. The conspicuous consumption stimulated by migrant gifts and imported cultural tastes easily leads to a sense of "relative deprivation" among nonmigrants and motivates them to move abroad as well.[31] Among young people, in particular, motivations to stay in school and pursue advancement locally may evaporate as they come to see their chances for mobility exclusively in leaving their country.[32]

Social networks linking migrants with nonmigrants facilitate this process, as they make each new journey abroad more predictable and less risky.[33]

TABLE 9.2
Inventoried Immigrant Organizations by Type

	Nationality			
Type	Colombian %	Dominican %	Mexican %	Total %
Civic/cultural organizations	47.30	30.00	6.82	16.23
Other cultural organizations	10.16	15.29	0.54	3.66
Economic organizations	4.44	2.35	0.70	1.52
Hometown associations	1.90	3.53	63.80	47.04
Federations of hometown associations	0.00	0.00	4.26	3.10
State-of-origin associations	0.32	1.18	8.68	6.48
International philanthropic organizations (Lions, Rotaries, Kiwanis)	6.98	3.53	0.00	1.58
Home country philanthropies	3.17	0.00	0.00	0.56
Political committees	7.93	10.00	0.46	2.70
Professional associations	8.89	14.12	0.70	3.44
Religious groups	1.59	1.18	0.23	0.56
Social service agencies	2.86	17.06	3.26	4.51
Sports groups	0.63	1.76	10.00	7.55
Student organizations	3.81	0.00	0.54	1.07
Total	100.00	100.00	100.00	100.00
N	315	170	1,290	1,775

Source: Comparative Immigrant Organizations Project (CIOP), Phase 2, 2006. Center for Migration and Development, Princeton University. Reported in Portes, Escobar, and Arana, "Bridging the Gap."

Although the immediate consequences of this form of social capital are positive for individuals, their second-level effects may be highly negative for communities as they continuously lose population. If the movement continues over time and is not counterbalanced by a sustained return flow, the result may be the hollowing out of sending communities. In the end, they become ghost towns or "tinsel towns," adorned only for the annual festivities, but otherwise populated only by the old and the infirm. Already up to one-half of Mexican municipalities are reported to have lost population during the last intercensal period.[34]

As elsewhere, effects of social capital in the transnational field "cut both ways." Highly positive for migrant kin and home communities that benefit from contributions and entrepreneurial investments, the process may become "too successful" over time. It can devolve into a dynamics of dependence, fostering inertia and depleting the very structures required for future investments and growth. This is the reason why many scholars from sending nations have rallied against migration as inimical to national development, despite its positive individual effects. The "Declaration of Cuernavaca," recently signed and circulated by a number of third world intellectuals, offers a case in point:

> The development model adopted in the immense majority of labor-exporting countries has not generated opportunities for growth nor economic or social development. On the contrary, it has meant the emergence of regressive dynamics; unemployment and job precarization; loss of qualified workers; productive disarticulation and stagnation; inflation and greater economic dependency. As a consequence, we experience a convergence between depopulation and the abandonment of productive activities in areas of high emigration.
>
> Declaration of Cuernavaca[35]

INFORMALITY AND INSTITUTIONALIZATION

Transnational activities, either of a civic/philanthropic or entrepreneurial kind, generally start informally. This is reflective of their grassroots character and their tendency, initially at least, to bypass official regulations and controls. To the extent that they remain survival strategies across national borders, they will remain informal. This explains, for example, the proliferation of unregulated couriers—known in Central America as *viajeros*—who commute back and forth between immigrant communities and towns of origin, delivering money and goods to expectant kin.[36] These long-distance informal transactions are usually highly reliable and certainly cheaper than Western Union wires or other formal channels.

Paralleling the evolution of enclave firms, as seen in chapter 8, transnational enterprises and organizations may grow and consolidate over time, expanding their scope of action and range of interlocutors. This necessarily entails a process of formalization, including the development of explicit institutional blueprints. A hometown committee formed by a few migrants and operating on a shoestring budget will remain informal, but a state-level confederation of such committees will not. This is especially the case if migrant leaders seek to become interlocutors of political authorities in their home countries and in host cities and states.[37] Similarly, successful transnational entrepreneurs cannot bypass legal rules governing international trade forever. At some point, the very growth of their firms will compel them to move above board and become visible to the law.[38]

The consolidation and institutionalization of transnational enterprises and civic/political organizations has an important corollary; namely, the substitution of bounded solidarity for enforceable trust and, subsequently, legal/contractual arrangements as guarantors of long-distance transactions. This process removes much of the vulnerability to malfeasance tied to trust grounded exclusively on good character and good will. A small *club de oriundos* or a fledgling migrant firm may be defrauded by their home country counterparts without any opportunity for redress; however, the Alianza Dominicana, the Centro Cívico Colombiano, or the Federation of Clubs of Zacatecas with lawyers on their staff and budgets in the hundreds of thousands or even millions are not so vulnerable. Venal local officials and other violators of agreements can be held to task and sanctioned by these organizations through a variety of means, economic and legal.[39]

The structural significance that transnational organizations can acquire depends precisely on this process of institutionalization, for the legitimacy and power thus acquired enables its leaders to engage in a dialogue with important political and economic actors. That mechanism has made it possible for migrant communities to extract the right to vote abroad from initially reluctant home governments and to encourage the latter to fund initiatives such as the *tres-por-uno* program in Mexico, through which each dollar raised by migrant organizations for public works at home is matched by one dollar from the Mexican federal government, one from the respective state, and another from the benefited municipality.[40] Similarly, migrant economic associations have been able to extract trade concessions from governments and to establish alliances with home country firms. As will be seen next, the residential construction industry in several migrant-sending countries has become increasingly dependent on demand from expatriates. Mediating between migrant demand and domestic construction firms can become a profitable and growing business for transnational real estate agencies.[41]

Transnational communities hence reflect and depend on the interplay between two of the causal mechanisms central to economic sociology: their emergence is inextricably tied to the cross-border operation of social capital grounded in altruistic sources; yet their consolidation over time requires the abandonment of purely informal practices and nonenforceable trust through a gradual processes of institutionalization. Contractual arrangements and organizations guided by formal blueprints endow these initiatives with legitimacy and allow them both to enforce agreements and engage the attention of powerful political and economic actors.

There is no evidence thus far that institutionalized transnational organizations or firms have attempted to neutralize the negative consequences of cross-border social capital, reviewed in the prior section. While, in principle, they could do so, the research literature registers no instance of migrant civic groups organizing return flows to repopulate home communities or transnational firms seeking to reenergize these towns' economies. The scope of institutionalization reached by transnational groups until now does not allow them to engage or attempt such experiments in macrosocial policy; instead, their reach has been limited to the projects and activities noted previously: promoting public works in the communities that still exist and empowering expatriates to gain the right to dialogue with political and civic authorities at home and in their areas of settlement abroad.

Transnational Entrepreneurship

Empirical Examples

This final section focuses more closely on economic transnationalism and its determinants. It is convenient at the start to illustrate the character of the phenomenon by drawing from the empirical literature. Instances of transnational entrepreneurship have been documented among a number of immigrant groups both in the United States and Western Europe. Four such cases are summarized next.

In their study of the large Salvadoran immigrant populations of Los Angeles and Washington, DC, Patricia Landolt and her associates discovered a "vibrant entrepreneurial community embedded in a web of social relations."[42] The study identified four types of transnational enterprises: *Circuit firms* are involved in the transfer of goods and remittances across countries and range from an array of informal international couriers, *viajeros*, to large formal firms, such as El Gigante Express, headquartered in Los Angeles. *Cultural enterprises* rely on their daily contacts with El Salvador and depend on the desire of immigrants to acquire and consume cultural goods from their country. Salvadoran newspapers are readily available in Los Angeles and Washington, DC, as are compact disks and videos with the latest musical hits. *Ethnic enterprises* are small retail firms catering to the immigrant community, which depend on a steady supply of imported goods, such as foodstuffs and clothing from El Salvador. Finally, *return migrant microenterprises* are firms established by returnees to El Salvador that rely on their contacts in the United States. They include restaurants, video stores, auto sales and repairs, Laundromats, and office supplies. Summarizing their findings on this last type of enterprise, the authors conclude that: "Typically, the idea for a microenterprise originates with the migrant's experience in the United States, and the investment capital comes from the migrant's personal savings. Given the precarious and often low rentability of their business ventures, expansion and maintenance costs often force the entrepreneur to seek wage work in the United States on a regular basis."[43]

A similar pattern was detected by José Itzigsohn and his associates in their study of the Dominican immigrant communities in the Washington Heights area of New York City.[44] These researchers also uncovered a number of informal transnational couriers operating between the United States and the Dominican Republic; the proliferation of stores selling imported Dominican foodstuffs, music, and newsprint in New York and Providence; and the rapid growth of remittance agencies, known locally as *financieras*. Return migrant firms in the capital city of Santo Domingo also include an array of businesses based on examples found in the United States. They include video stores, Laundromats, car detailing, home delivery of fast food, and computer software stores.

The residential construction industry, in particular, has become transnationalized through its increasing dependence on immigrant demand. Construction and real estate firms regularly advertise in the immigrant press in New York City. Entire residential neighborhoods in Santo Domingo have been built with the expatriate community in mind. Reflecting the growing importance of remittances and investments, the Dominican government has facilitated the election of a representative of the New York immigrant community to the national Congress and appointed an immigrant as its consul in New York City. In official parlance, Dominican immigrants are no longer "absent" (*ausentes*), but only "temporarily abroad."[45]

A third example with a unique cultural twist is provided by David Kyle's study of the Otavalan indigenous community in the highlands of Ecuador.[46] Traditionally, the town of Otavalo has specialized in the production and marketing of clothing, developing and adapting new production skills since the colonial period under Spain. During the last three decades or so, Otavalans have taken to traveling abroad to market their colorful wares in major cities of Europe and North America. In contrast to other indigenous producers who sell their crafts to intermediaries, Otavalans appropriate the full value of their production by bringing it themselves to first world consumers. During the same period, semipermanent Otavalan settlements began to emerge abroad. Their distinct feature is that members do not make their living from wage labor, but from the sale of goods brought from Ecuador. The back-and-forth movement required by their trade has turned Otavalans into a common sight, not only at the Quito airport but also in street fairs in New York, Paris, Amsterdam, and other first world cities.[47]

This dense transnational commerce has also had a profound impact on the town. Reversing the traditional racial hierarchy of the Andes, in Otavalo it is the indigenous entrepreneurs rather than local whites or mestizos who inhabit the better houses and have the best cars. In the streets of Otavalo, it is not uncommon to find white women attired in the regal traditional indigenous dress—the wives of transnational entrepreneurs who have brought them back from their journeys in Germany, England, or the Netherlands.[48]

A final example concerns the informal trans-Atlantic trade linking the islands of Cape Verde to their former colonial metropolis, Portugal, as well as to other Portuguese-speaking nations. This trade is conducted by women travelers. According to a research team from the University of Lisbon, these women have earned a distinct name in the local dialect, *rebidantes*, roughly translated as those who are able to overcome obstacles and create new life opportunities. The obstacles to be overcome are the costs of travel and the difficulties of buying goods in foreign countries; the opportunities relate to economic mobility and the acquisition of a "respectable" position for their families and communities.[49]

This informal transatlantic commerce is made possible by the presence of settled Cape Verdean communities abroad and the long-distance networks among kin and friends that they make possible. Initially, bounded solidarity within these networks enabled women of modest means to access wholesalers and other suppliers in distant countries; trust enforced by kin in various national locations turned these women into reliable international couriers carrying quantities of money and goods across the Atlantic. Air transportation and long distance communication have facilitated the growth of this transnational trade, which now employs thousands of women in the Cape Verde islands.[50]

These empirical examples not only illustrate the operation of social capital across long distances but also show that, even when initially based only on kin and coethnic solidarity, economic transnationalism has the potential to grow and consolidate into better institutionalized arrangements. They also show that, despite the potential negative consequences of social networks in weakening places of origin, enough economic dynamism continues to exist in many of them to sustain the operation of these enterprises. The obvious next question is what factors motivate individual migrants to become engaged in them.

Determinants of Economic Transnationalism

Transnational entrepreneurs are self-employed immigrants whose business activities require frequent travel abroad and who depend for the success of their firms on their contacts and associates in another country, primarily their country of origin. This section examines empirically the determinants of this form of economic adaptation, drawing on several hypotheses from past sociological theory and a data set uniquely suitable for this purpose.

A traditional assimilation approach would suggest that these activities are transitional and bound to disappear over time as immigrants become better integrated in the host society.[51] Thus we would expect that transnationalism would decline with years of U.S. residence and be most common among the most recent migrant cohorts. Immigrants with a precarious economic foothold, in particular those who experienced serious downward mobility upon arrival, should also be more likely to avail themselves of this option.

The more recent literature on immigrant entrepreneurship has taken a different tack, identifying gender, marital status, and human capital as important predictors. Past research consistently indicates that married males are overrepresented among entrepreneurs, gender, by itself, being the most powerful factor.[52] Human capital, in the form of years of education and high occupational skills, has also been found to play a significant role in immigrant business success. We reason that transnational entrepreneurship would be even more likely to depend on these human capital traits, as it involves greater risks and complexity.

Lastly, the economic sociology concepts discussed previously, in particular social capital and social embeddedness, should also bear directly on these individual decisions. Other things being equal, we should expect that individuals with more extensive and diversified networks would be in a better position to initiate and sustain transnational firms. The social contexts in which particular immigrant flows are embedded can also be expected to affect their economic options, regardless of other individual traits. Thus, groups who came escaping political upheaval and generalized violence in their home country may not have a transnational option at all, while those who are part of strong communities with multiple ties to a nation at peace can find numerous cross-border economic opportunities. The data set used next to examine determinants of economic transnationalism allows us to test these alternative propositions.

These data come from the Comparative Immigrant Entrepreneurship Project (CIEP), which interviewed representative samples of Colombian, Dominican, and Salvadoran family heads in their principal areas of concentration in the United States. When weighted, the 1,202 interviews completed in 2000–2001 are representative of over 187,000 adult immigrants from these nationalities.[53] The survey focused specifically on the question of immigrant economic adaptation and, in particular, forms of entrepreneurship. Table 9.3 presents preliminary evidence from this survey with respondents classified into wageworkers, purely domestic entrepreneurs, and transnational entrepreneurs. As the data show, the latter group is better educated, has better occupational qualifications, receives higher incomes, *and* is more likely to have acquired U.S. citizenship than the other two categories. These results run contrary to the assimilation perspective and provide additional support to the human capital approach to entrepreneurship, with the caveat that transnational merchants are even more qualified than those dedicated to purely domestic ventures.

The data allows us to go further and examine determinants of different forms of economic adaptation on the basis of the preceding hypotheses. Table 9.4 presents results of a multinomial logistic analysis using wageworkers as the reference and including indicators of all relevant causal dimensions. The table reveals that immigrant businesses of any kind are primarily the business of married males since both sex and marital status bear strongly on the pursuit of this economic path. This result is no

TABLE 9.3
Characteristics of Latin American Immigrants in the United States by Type
of Employment

	Wage Worker	Domestic Entrepreneur[1]	Transnational Entrepreneur[2]	Total
Years of Education	9.8	12.2	13.6	11.0
Professional/Executive Background, %	16	31	35	23
Monthly Income, U.S. $	1251	2836	3143	1918
U.S. Citizen, %	26	49	53	36
Years of Residence in U.S.	14.0	18.0	16.4	15.1
Satisfied with Life in U.S., %	29	49	49	37
N	744	181	277	1202

[1] Owners of firms with no transnational linkages.

[2] Owners of firms with regular transnational linkages: markets, sources of supplies and/or credit.

Source: Comparative Immigrant Entrepreneurship Project (CIEP), 1998. Center for Migration and Development, Princeton University. Reported in Portes, Haller, and Guarnizo, "Transnational Entrepreneurs."

different from that reported consistently in the literature on immigrant entrepreneurship, except that the gender effect is stronger on the probability of transnational than domestic enterprise.

Measures of socioeconomic background—education and professional/ executive experience—have the positive effects anticipated by the same literature. Both increase the probability of self-employment, but the effects are stronger on transnational than on domestic enterprise. Based on model coefficients, a married male with a college education and a professional background has a 37 percent greater probability to become a transnational entrepreneur; the figure increases to 45 percent if wage-workers are the reference category. Since all of these predictors refer to characteristics brought by immigrants from their home countries, the direction of causality is unambiguous.

The notion that transnational activities are a transitional pursuit, to be abandoned as assimilation takes hold, is not supported by the data. Longer periods of residence in the United States *increase* the probability of engaging in both domestic and transnational enterprise.[54] The coefficient associated with the most recent immigrant cohort, arriving during the 1990s, is both insignificant and negative. Nor are experiences of early downward mobility associated with transnationalism. The mobility indicator consists of the ratio of the last occupational status in the country of origin to the first in the United States. Higher scores thus signify greater downward mobility and should be associated with increased transnationalism. The effect is actually negative, indicating that each point drop in status *reduces* the probability of engaging in transnational business by 2 percent.

Rejection of this set of hypotheses shows that, contrary to what may be expected from an assimilation framework, it is not recency of arrival or the experience of occupational failure that prompts immigrants to become transnational entrepreneurs. Findings lead instead to the conclusion that this route is mainly open to immigrants who have established a secure foothold in the United States. While those experiencing serious downward mobility may be motivated to follow the same route, they lack the experiences, resources, and stability to follow it.

The effect of social networks lends support to the social capital argument. Business owners have more numerous social ties than wageworkers, and transnational entrepreneurs have more than domestic ones. As shown in table 9.4, the social network coefficient is very strong, exceeding five times its standard error. Each additional contact increases the probability of transnational enterprise by 1.5 percent.

Finally, with Dominicans as the reference category, results demonstrate sharp differences in forms of economic adaptation among the three nationalities in the sample. Other things equal, Salvadorans are 7 to 9 percent more likely to engage in transnational business activities, while Colombians are less likely to do so by about half that figure. Both coefficients are reliable, indicating the resilience of national differences after controlling for other factors. These results fit the known contexts of exit and incorporation under which each of these migrant flows have taken place: Salvadoran transnationalism has been supported by strong bonds of solidarity with their home communities forged during the country's civil war; these bonds were subsequently put to economic use once the country returned to democracy and internal peace. In contrast, Colombian transnationalism is weakened by continuing political convulsions and widespread violence in the home country.[55]

Hence, we find that both social capital, as indexed by strength of social networks, and social embeddedness, as represented by the distinct historical contexts in which specific migrant flows take place, have a

TABLE 9.4
Determinants of Transnational Enterprise among Colombian, Dominican, and Salvadoran Immigrants

Predictors:	Transnational Entrepreneurship (Binomial Logistic Regression)			Transnational Entrepreneurship (Multinomial Logistic Regression)			Domestic Entrepreneurship (Multinomial Logistic Regression)		
	Coefficient	S.E.	Δ^1	Coeff.	S.E.	Δ^1	Coeff.	S.E.	Δ^1
Demographic:									
Age	.017	.012		.013	.014		-.008	.013	
Sex (Male)	1.035***	.231	.08	1.245***	.239	.11	.876**	.260	.04
Marital Status (Married)	.440*	.215	.03	.615**	.223	.04	.749**	.243	.03
Number of Children	-.049	.070		-.046	.074		-.014	.072	
Human Capital:									
Education (Years)	.114***	.026	.01	.130***	.026	.01	.071*	.028	.008
Professional/Executive Background	1.191***	.331	.10	1.473***	.340	.14	.861*	.416	.04
Assimilation:									
Years of U.S. Residence	.036*	.017	.003	.048**	.018	.004	.041*	.019	.003
Post-1989 Arrival	-.437	.338		-.585	.353		-.743*	.373	-.02
Downward Mobility²	-.402**	.167	-.03	-.451**	.170	-.02	-.110	.202	
Experiences of Discrimination	.308	.207		.344	.217		.199	.222	

TABLE 9.4 (continued)

Predictors:	Transnational Entrepreneurship (Binomial Logistic Regression)			Transnational Entrepreneurship (Multinomial Logistic Regression)			Domestic Entrepreneurship (Multinomial Logistic Regression)		
	Coefficient	S.E.	Δ[1]	Coeff.	S.E.	Δ[1]	Coeff.	S.E.	Δ[1]
Social Networks:									
Size	.111***	.022	.01	.139***	.023	.015	.105***	.023	.008
Scope[3]	.226	.121		.153	.133		-.561*	.249	-.01
Nationality[4]:									
Colombian	-1.519***	.387	-.05	-1.685***	.384	-.04	-.846**	.331	-.02
Salvadoran	1.097***	.279	.09	.939**	.284	.07	-.619*	.306	-.015
Constant	-6.235	.686		-6.511	.692		-3.673	.817	
Chi Square (Degrees of Freedom)	141.67(14)***			257.17(28)***			257.17(28)***		
Pseudo R[2]	.256			.225					
N[5]	1,096.			1,096					

[1] Increase/decrease in the net probability of each outcome per unit change in significant predictors, evaluated at the mean of the weighted sample distribution.
[2] Ratio of occupational status in the country of origin to status of the first U.S. occupation.
[3] Ratio of number of contacts outside city of residence to local contacts.
[4] Dominican immigrants are the reference category.
[5] CIEP weighted sample.
* P < .05; ** P < .01; *** P < .001.
Source: Portes, Haller, and Guarnizo, "Transnational Entrepreneurs," based on data from CIEP.

bearing on individual forms of economic adaptation. These quantitative results support those of prior ethnographic studies concerning the role of the same factors in the rise and forms adopted by transnational communities as a whole. To summarize, transnational entrepreneurship is neither a marginal mode of economic adaptation nor one associated with poverty or recency of arrival. On the contrary, better-educated and more experienced immigrants are overrepresented in these activities. Yet, the opportunities to engage in them are also heavily conditioned by the sociopolitical conditions of the country of origin and the general historical circumstances in which each movement occurs. Depending on them, immigrants may move decisively in the transnational direction or avoid this alternative altogether for more traditional pursuits.

CONCLUSION

What would lead older, better-educated, and more established immigrants to engage in transnational enterprise and/or pursue civic and philanthropic projects in their home countries rather than to focus on their new lives, as expected by traditional assimilation theory? Concerning economic transnationalism, there is obviously the incentive of occupational independence and higher earnings in self-employment. As seen in the preceding chapter, migrant entrepreneurs consistently receive higher earnings than their waged coethnics; and, as seen in the previous section, transnational enterprise is more profitable, on average, than purely domestic pursuits. The human capital brought by educated and skilled immigrants is commonly "discounted" in the host labor market because of linguistic difficulties or racial discrimination.[56] Transnational entrepreneurship gives these immigrants an opportunity to put their human capital to use by combining it with the social capital available in their communities. Hence, the importance of extensive social networks, as documented in the preceding analysis.

Concerning the second course—the pursuit of transnational civic and philanthropic activism—I return to the importance of values and bounded solidarity discussed at the start of the chapter. The pursuit of such projects by economically secure immigrants is akin to the charitable activities engaged in by native middle-class households. While native philanthropy is guided by a broad gamut of concerns, immigrant transnationalism is naturally focused on the needs of their hometowns and the condition of their nation of origin. Not surprisingly, transnational organizations have much better luck recruiting among older and better-established migrants since they are the ones with the time and resources to engage in these pursuits.

Table 9.5 illustrates this pattern with data from a study of ninety large transnational organizations created by Latin American migrants in the United States. While there are significant differences among the three nationalities included in this survey, the common organizational profile is strongly geared toward naturalized citizens, long-term legal residents, and immigrants with higher levels of human capital.

In all cases, the consolidation and growth of transnational activities depend on the shift from consummatory to instrumental sources of social capital and, subsequently, to a legal/contractual basis. Otherwise, the initial enthusiasm and the good intentions stemming from bounded solidarity can easily dissipate when confronted with hard realities on the ground. Similarly, transnational businesses can only rely so far and so long on kin and coethnic solidarity. Sooner or later, enforceable trust must make its appearance followed, in the case of the more successful firms, by lawyers and contracts. This is the point of inflection in which grassroots economic activities of fledgling transnational entrepreneurs start to acquire the contours of the *multinational* enterprises driving the globalization process from above.

In conclusion, like the informal economy, ethnic enclaves and middle-man enterprises, immigrant transnationalism represents a generally neglected niche of economic activity that commonly escapes the attention of both authorities and academics concerned with large formal structures and macroprocesses. I argue that there is value in the study of these apparently marginal activities for two reasons: First, because they illustrate, with singular clarity, the social mechanisms underlying economic action. They offer a strategic site to put the meta-assumption of social embeddedness into motion and to show how the midrange explanatory concepts of economic sociology operate. Second, such apparently marginal sites are not devoid of importance and can actually affect formal economic structures and macroprocesses in unexpected ways. Like a large informal economy can wreak havoc with the calculations of government planners and the estimates of employment rates and gross economic activity, the consolidation of transnational communities can have a series of unanticipated consequences for the economies of home and host regions. Analysts who focus on the surface level of economic life, drawing their data from formal surveys and macroeconomic indicators are commonly taken by surprise by such phenomena as the emergence of remittances as a major source of foreign exchange, the colonization of entire sectors of

TABLE 9.5
Characteristics of Members of Transnational Organizations

	Colombian	Dominican	Mexican	Total
Age:				
30 years or less, %	12.1	11.1	24.8	15.2
40 years or more, %	53.2	53.8	33.6	48.3
Education:				
Less than high school, %	7.4	29.7	28.7	20.9
College degree or more, %	52.3	50.5	27.0	45.7
Occupation:				
Manual laborer, %	18.0	26.4	40.1	26.6
Professional/Business owner, %	49.8	61.5	36.0	50.3
Knowledge of English:				
Very little, %	11.9	18.7	5.0	12.4
Well or very well, %	64.2	49.7	60.9	58.5
Legal Status:				
Does not have entry visa, %	6.3	3.5	27.9	10.7
U.S. citizen, %	56.3	48.5	38.4	49.1
Length of U.S. Residence:				
Less than 5 years, %	10.1	5.8	10.4	8.7
Ten years or more, %	68.9	66.8	69.5	69.3
Average Trips to Home Country for Organizational Matters:				
Never or rarely, %	6.7	3.6	30.0	11.5
At least three trips a year, %	40.0	35.7	20.0	33.3
N	30	30	30	90

Source: Comparative Immigrant Organizations Project, Phase I, 2004. Center for Migration and Development, Princeton University. Reported in Portes, Escobar, and Walton Radford, "Immigrant Transnational Organizations."

home economies by migrant investments and firms, and the emergence of vibrant "parallel" economies in areas of immigrant concentration in the host countries. Economic sociology, on the contrary, can bring light to these processes and show how they interact with broader macroeconomic structures.

CHAPTER TEN

Markets, Models, and Regulation

IN CONCLUDING, I wish to return to the meta-assumptions that ground the field and to a so-far-unremarked aspect of them. It turns out that, in addition to being "lenses" to see the economic world from, they also may be transformed, under certain conditions, into midrange concepts amenable to measurement and inclusion into testable propositions. Classic authors associated with each can also be invoked to buttress this transformation of perspective into explanatory concept. I draw on a recently completed study of economic institutions and national development in Latin America to illustrate these points.[1]

EMBEDDINGS

Easily the assumption most susceptible to this transformation is economic sociology's most basic. As seen in chapter 2, Mark Granovetter's reworking of Polanyi had the effect of reclaiming for sociology the study of capitalist markets as social institutions. In a bold stroke, Granovetter did away with the previous Parsonian-sanctioned division between markets as a special sphere guided by rational maximization and the rest of society, guided by value introjection. In the process, however, "embeddedness" was transformed into an overarching perspective, vacuously applicable to any number of situations. Granovetter himself acknowledged this point. In his exchange with Brian Uzzi, who had been seeking to transform the notion into a variable, he remarked that the attempt to measure the "degree" of embeddedness may be a less productive approach than to conceive of embeddedness "as kind of an umbrella under which a lot of different and more precise kinds of research could be done on the ways in which social networks affect the conduct of the economy, economic behavior, economic actions, economic institutions."[2]

This is the view adopted so far in this book but, in moving embeddedness to the status of a meta-assumption, the field lost the more specific meaning that Polanyi had intended for it—namely the extent to which the capitalist market is subject to control by society, rather than vice versa. According to Polanyi, disembedded markets are intrinsically destructive and lead inevitably to catastrophic outcomes. For him, the real problem of modern capitalism is that "instead of the economic system being embedded in social relationships, these relationships are now embedded in the economic system."[3] In opposition to the fervent belief on self-regulated markets sponsored by economics in general and, as we will see shortly, finance theorists in particular, Polanyi took a very dim view of the paths toward which this reigning ideology was leading the world.

Embeddedness for Granovetter is a matter of social networks and sociability and how they permeate both markets and economic hierarchies; embeddedness for Polanyi is mostly a matter of how the state and other social institutions regulate and influence markets. This last definition is both amenable to measurement and usable as an explanatory variable for a number of economic outcomes. As such, it is less of an "umbrella" concept than an ideal type, on a par with those examined previously. Polanyi's embeddedness has less to do with networks than with power—the extent to which capitalists are able to impose their will on society rather than vice versa.[4]

The evolution of Latin American national tax authorities (as examined in the comparative study cited previously) provides an interesting example of how these power relationships play themselves in reality. Traditionally, the tax take of Latin American states has been low, representing a much smaller proportion of the Gross National Product than in richer nations. For the most part, firms and wealthy individuals in these countries were able to escape the tax man's reach, operating with fiscal impunity either de jure because of weak tax laws or de facto through bribery of state agents.[5] Rudolf Goldscheid's dictum that "the budget is the skeleton of the state stripped of all misleading ideology"[6] is as true in Latin America as elsewhere and, hence, states had to look elsewhere for alternative means to finance themselves.

Traditionally, this was accomplished through three means: (1) duties on imports and exports, (2) foreign indebtedness, and (3) inflation. Taxing the country's main export, usually a primary commodity, and its imports, mostly manufactures, turned the customshouse into the main real revenue source for the state. Foreign aid and foreign loans were also traditional staples in these states' weak financial systems, while inflation allowed them to settle their debts with a debased currency, effectively unloading the costs on the mass of the population. Meanwhile, local and foreign firms and speculators were pretty much free to do as they pleased.[7]

The advent of neoliberal reform throughout the continent following the Mexican default of 1982 had a series of consequences that effectively did away with these traditional practices. International assistance to overcome the cascading defaults and subsequent economic depression of the early 1980s in Latin America was made conditional on the opening of its markets to foreign competition in order to "get the prices right."[8] New external loans depended on state progress in balancing its books and eliminating deficit spending, even at the cost of social unrest. In effect, bringing down external trade barriers and drastically reducing domestic inflation deprived governments of their principal sources of finance. Under these conditions, states had no recourse but to turn to internal revenues through new value-added taxes and corporate and personal income tax. Extracting these resources from a most unwilling population and from a recalcitrant capitalist class required, in turn, the massive application of state power. To cite but one example: "In 1987, the International Monetary Fund noted that 'given that the Dominican Republic cannot cut its expenses on a mass scale, a tributary reform to replace the loss of taxes to external trade is the only way to rebuild and maintain social services and state investment.'"[9]

In country after country, the previously dormant tax authority was replaced by semiautonomous and powerful entities whose directors were commonly appointed by the president of the republic and whose functionaries were insulated from the rest of the state apparatus. In the Dominican Republic, the fiscal reform began in 1997 with the unification of separate tributary agencies into the National Directorate of Internal Revenues (DGII in the Spanish acronym) which was subsequently given operational and budgetary autonomy and whose director was and is appointed by the president. A charismatic figure was named to the post and has held it, with brief interludes, until now. In the words of this functionary: "The institution has a commitment to be a prestigious organization whose goal is to increase revenues on a sustained basis and reduce evasion by heightening the perception of risk . . . tributary authorities have as their *raison d'être* to tax and, hence, to increase fiscal revenues must be their strategic goal."[10]

In response, as shown in table 10.1, the share of government revenue accounted for by internal taxes increased to 50 percent of the total in just one decade while tax evasion declined by 10 percent. Income tax declarations filed by firms increased from 11,403 in 1996 to 29,175 in 2004. Since 80 percent of the total tax take is accounted for by two dozen large firms, the DGII created a Directorate of Large Contributors whose

TABLE 10.1
Composition of Central Government Revenues, Dominican Republic

Year	Customs %	Internal Taxes %	Treasury Obligations %
1998	35.1	42.5	21.6
1999	34.1	41.3	12.9
2000	34.8	44.0	10.8
2001	23.1	46.9	13.8
2002	23.9	44.7	17.6
2003	20.2	44.3	30.6
2004	31.4	45.2	19.8
2005	32.0	49.9	17.1
2006	21.7	47.4	29.7
2007	20.0	50.0	29.0

Source: Guzmán, "Recaudación y desarrollo," p. 23 (based on official Treasury data).

function, according to the director general is: "To insure fulfillment of these firms' tax obligations, establishing teams of fiscal technicians who operate as account officers and provide them with all the necessary information."[11] Technological innovations that allow the Directorate to cross-tabulate fiscal data from different sources insure that today the directives of DGII auditors pack the necessary punch.

At the other end of the continent, in Chile, the story is very much the same. The return of democracy after the Pinochet dictatorship was followed by a political pact between the government and the corporate elites to increase both the income tax and the value-added tax to a level sufficient to restore the "social equilibrium" of the country. Government programs designed to reduce social inequality could only be financed internally because of drastic cuts in custom tariffs aimed at increasing foreign trade. Business elites agreed to this compromise because of their weakened political position, given their past association with the dictatorship, and because of a government guarantee that tax rates would go no higher.[12]

The reorganized Internal Revenue Service (SII in the Spanish acronym) took full advantage of this pact. As in other countries of the region, the director of the SII is appointed and accountable to the president of the republic and, as in the Dominican Republic, the position was filled by a knowledgeable and powerful figure, in this case a civil engineer, who has held it for the last twelve years.[13] In Chile, only the top 18 percent of income earners are liable for income tax and just 6 percent account for 92 percent of the total income tax receipt, figures reflecting the weight of large corporations and wealthy individuals. In response, the SII also created a Directorate of Large Contributors that functions, as in the Dominican Republic, to provide information and assistance to corporate taxpayers, but also to insure timely payment.[14]

As a result, income tax receipts more than doubled between 1987 and 2005, and the internal tax take increased from 15 percent to 19 percent of the Gross Internal Product during the last decade. A recent study that examined opinions of state agencies among members of the Chilean business elite found that, despite the higher tax load placed on them by the post-Pinochet administrations, the large majority believe that the SII is one of the best state agencies and the one that has registered most progress in recent years.[15] Reasons for this conclusion are mostly based on the remarkable technical progress experienced by the agency: "This process has had as its fundamental axis a modernization of the technical infrastructure that has allowed the Service to improve its mechanisms of fiscal control and oversight . . . today, a large number of taxpayers receive their annual tax declaration, prepared and sent via Internet by the SII; all they have to do is examine it, sign it, and send it back. This presupposes a level of information by the agency that is ever more encompassing and reliable."[16]

To a greater or lesser degree, the same evolution is apparent in the other tax authorities included in this comparative study, such as those of Argentina, Colombia, and Mexico.[17] In all cases, fiscal imperatives have prompted the state to "re-embed" their economic elites in society, taking away from them the fiscal immunity they enjoyed for so long. Whether the capitalist class arrived at a fiscal pact with the state, as in Chile, or was forced into compliance, as in Argentina, the result has been the same. Although cases of fraud, tax evasion, and tax elusion are still common, the overall trend is unmistakable.[18]

Ironically, the global campaign, led by the International Monetary Fund, to "free markets" and "get the prices right" ended up constraining formerly free market actors and reincorporating them into society via newly energized fiscal institutions. As a consequence of market reform aimed at "getting the state out of the economy," the state has been compelled to exercise vastly greater control over markets in order to finance itself and fulfill at least some of its distributional functions.[19] The end result of this process has been a new form of regulated capitalism that bears closer resemblance to the advanced economies of Western Europe than to the freewheeling practices of Latin American elites in the past. For our purposes, the methodological lesson to be derived from this experience is that Polanyi's "de-embedding" and "re-embedding" of markets and market actors can be readily examined, measured, and incorporated into explanatory propositions in ways that Granovetter's version is not. As a midrange concept, embeddedness is relevant to myriad situations, as it embodies the perennial tension between states and markets in capitalist societies.

SELF-FULFILLING PROPHECIES AND PERFORMATIVITY

Unintended consequences is the second meta-assumption of economic sociology. As seen in chapter 2, the concept is also so general as to be unfalsifiable. The typology of possible alternatives to rational purposive action presented in that chapter is a way of systematizing the general idea and, in the process, seeking to bring it closer to the level of explanatory concepts. A variant that includes elements of several of these types was also analyzed by Robert Merton under the term, "the self-fulfilling prophecy."[20] This occurs when the end-state of an action comes close to that initially envisioned, which was actually false. As Merton carefully defines it, "The self-fulfilling prophecy is in the beginning a *false* definition of the situation evoking a new behavior which makes the original false conception come *true*."[21]

As an illustration, Merton offers the "sociological parable" of the Last National Bank of Millingville, which was a perfectly stable institution until false rumors about its economic health made depositors stage a run on it; the run brought about the bank's demise.[22] Initially false definitions may be conveyed intentionally or may simply arise out of the culture of the times; the important point is that action by relevant actors based on these premises makes them come true. While Merton's examples generally highlighted the negative consequences of this phenomenon, this need not be the case, at least in the short run. For instance, financial markets may become rule-bound and predictable not because they were so in the first place, but because academic models of market behavior became accepted, by market players and regulators alike, as isomorphic with reality itself.

The extent to which a "prophecy" becomes self-fulfilling is, in principle, measurable and capable of inclusion into testable propositions. The specific genre of self-fulfilling prophecy to which I wish to call attention here—the extent to which academic models of the economy prefigure the actual economy—was presciently identified by Émile Durkheim in his critique of the economics discipline of his time. Even before the mathematization of the field and its dominance by formal models, Durkheim noted that "economists substitute their own ideas for empirical reality; they then draw conclusions from these—and present results as applicable to the society that they chose *not* to study in the first place."[23]

Since Durkheim's time at least, economics has become accustomed to this form of self-fulfillment in which its intellectual models of markets come to determine, or at least influence, how markets actually behave. The process reached its zenith with the advent of finance theory in the post–World War II period: "a distinct academic specialty of 'financial economics,' which had begun to emerge in the 1950s, gathered pace in the 1960s and 1970s. At its core were elegant mathematical models of markets."[24]

Milton Friedman's declaration that economic theory was "an engine to analyze the world, not a photographic reproduction of it,"[25] took a life of its own as models developed by academic economists began to be accepted as "the way things are" by market practitioners. By 1998, the French sociologist Michel Callon could assert that "economics . . . shapes and formats the economy rather than observing how it functions."[26] The British sociologist Donald MacKenzie elaborated the idea in a series of detailed case studies of how academic models have transformed the way markets work. For instance, the elegant Black-Scholes-Merton model of options pricing has, according to MacKenzie, not only altered the ways options ("call" and "put") work, but considerably facilitated their growth:

> [T]he Black-Scholes-Merton model's assumption of zero transaction costs is now close to true for the hedging of derivatives by major investment banks, in part because the use of that model and its descendants by those banks allows them to manage their portfolios in a way that minimizes transaction costs . . . customers can in consequence purchase derivatives *as if* those individuals could trade continuously without costs (italics in original).[27]

MacKenzie labeled this form of self-fulfillment "performativity." He took issue with Daniel Miller's call to "radically separate out the market as a ritual and ideological system constructed by economists and the actual practice of economies," precisely because economic theory is so closely interwoven with the actual practice of markets. For this to happen, that is, for the academic discipline to be able to "perform" the economy, it had to start by disregarding contrary empirical facts. This is actually a precondition for all self-fulfilling prophecies: in order to mold reality according to their own definition of the situation, they must begin by negating or ignoring present reality and its constraints.

In economics, this feat was accomplished primarily by Milton Friedman, who argued that it did not matter whether a model's assumptions were implausible or not, provided that they led to verifiable predictions. In his words: "Truly important and significant hypotheses will be found to have 'assumptions' that are wildly inaccurate descriptive representations of reality. . . . A hypothesis is important if it 'explains' much by little . . . and makes valid predictions on the basis of them alone. *To be important, therefore, a theory must be descriptively false in its assumptions*" (quotation marks in original; italics mine).[28]

The patently false assumption of continuously costless trade led to the important Black-Scholes-Merton model, which, among other consequences, turned that assumption into actual practice in investment banking. Friedman's statement is still more forceful because it makes the wrongness of a theory's original assumptions one of the preconditions for its success. While he might have had in mind the need for simplification in order to construct viable models, actual events can go further since a successful theory can bring about *post factum* the accuracy of its own assumptions.

MacKenzie gets a bit carried away in the last sentences of his otherwise excellent study by asserting that "the notion of performativity prompts the most important question of all: What sort of a world do we want to see performed?"[29] While the statement may be permissible as a final rhetorical flourish, it is problematic because it implies the full malleability of economic reality. It is not. The unreality of initial assumptions so contemptuously dismissed by Friedman can return with a vengeance when economic prophecies cease to become self-fulfilling and, consequently, markets crash. The regular collapse of markets and market institutions, despite following the expectations of the best theories, attests to the resilient power of facts on the ground. When economic phenomena are not studied, but "performed," long-term consequences can be dire.

As I pen these lines in October 2008, the financial world is crashing down in a cascading series of bankruptcies of epochal proportions. Who could have anticipated that giant investment banks, like Lehman Brothers, would simply evaporate in a matter of days? There has been nothing more "performed" than the complex set of derivatives and other instruments on which financial capitalism, investment banks at the forefront, has been based in recent years. Proliferating hedge funds employing mathematical models created their own reality, multiplying many times the value of the original loans. But when the underlying collateral for those loans plunged in value and the debtors defaulted en masse, reality came back with a vengeance. This was a situation that could not be simply manipulated at will.[30]

Prophecies can also become self-defeating. In his original analysis, Merton used the concept of the self-defeating prophecy to refer to those situations in which repeated announcements of a final outcome lead to a series of deliberate steps that prevent the foretold result from materializing.[31] The classic example is Marx and Engels's repeated announcement of the end of capitalism and the advent of the dictatorship of the proletariat. So transparent were the forces identified by the Marxist analysis of capitalism and so threatening its implications for the dominant classes that resolute measures were taken to change the course of events and thus prevent the proletariat from fulfilling its "historical" role.[32] Anticipating the role of Keynesianism half a century later, Marx's dire predictions helped save capitalism from itself.[33]

In the case of performativity, a self-defeating prophecy materializes when the remolding of markets by theory confronts hard constraints in the real economy, triggering a cumulative reaction. The Friedmanesque "engine" has hit a wall more than once. The 2008 collapse of the highly leveraged financial markets, once assumed to be safe and even "conservative,"[34] is only the latest and most visible example. Others include the catastrophic failure of the neoliberal model for economic development in Argentina, Indonesia, Mexico, and other third world countries and its substitution, under the press of circumstances, by statist policies and the renationalization of recently privatized assets.[35]

For our purposes, the important lesson is that self-fulfilling and self-defeating prophecies bring down the general assumption of unintended consequences to the level of explanatory mechanisms. As Callon, MacKenzie, and his followers have demonstrated, it is possible to examine the extent to which a particular theory or model can transform the economic phenomena that it allegedly describes. "Performativity" is not an umbrella concept, but a measurable and testable dimension of economic life. In like fashion, we can examine a number of other definitions of the situation from which a set of purposive actions or policies depart and establish their capacity to transform reality or, alternatively, give rise to vigorous resistance. Propositions concerning these processes can be formulated accordingly.

To return to Charles Tilly's favorite example of "Hidden Elbow" in chapter 2, it is possible that the original imagery of France as a unified, compliant, and centralized entity under the absolute authority of the king—held with unfaltering conviction by Louis XIV and Colbert— ended up by transforming a contentious France into precisely that entity.[36] To cite a contemporary example of the opposite outcome, in the early 1990s, Argentine economy minister Domingo Cavallo announced that, henceforth, the Argentine peso would be worth a dollar and that this "convertibility" scheme, added to other market-opening measures, would usher the entrance of the nation into the ranks of the developed world. Ten years later, the Argentine economy came crashing down in the worst downturn of its history, bringing the country to its knees. As in the United States in 2008, economic realities on the ground trumped performance.[37] Self-fulfilling prophecies based on economic theories have a way of turning into self-defeating ones.

POWER AND MARKETS

The third meta-assumptions of economic sociology—power—can also be brought down to the level of testable propositions. This can be done both at the level of interpersonal relations and of structural processes. To begin with, power is a factor intermingled with the ways in which the other concepts guiding the field can also be converted into explanatory mechanisms. As seen previously, the extent to which markets are able to tear free of state society controls or, alternatively, are re-embedded into them, depends fundamentally on the alignment of relevant actors and the power with which they back their respective interests. Similarly, the extent to which a particular economic prophecy becomes self-fulfilling or not hinges on the relative power of actors willing to embrace its premises and act accordingly.

Few academic models become self-fulfilling. In particular, those that predict the demise of capitalism brought about by its own contradictions and the rebellion of the exploited classes have seldom materialized. Such predictions become self-defeating precisely because dominant classes can marshal the necessary power to derail the foretold outcome. Economic elites are not invulnerable, but their displacement comes about in different ways, often as an unintended consequence of their own actions. Under certain historical circumstances, the rational pursuit of self-interest by dominant actors can conjure the rise of still more powerful forces that marginalize the former elites.

We have already seen the paradox of how the adoption of free market policies in Latin America ended up fiscally constraining the very classes that supported such reforms in the first place. A still more compelling illustration is provided by the evolution of stock markets in the region. I use material from the same comparative study cited previously to describe the dynamics of power in this instance and the self-defeating consequences of its use by its former holders. Latin American stock exchanges have traditionally been the fief of a small privileged group that used them as much for sociability and networking as for rent seeking. Profits in these exchanges depended on access to privileged information, and those wishing to take part had to pay high rents to the few well-connected brokerage houses. In the words of Colombian sociologist César Rodríguez Garavito, these exchanges were "gentlemen's clubs" that functioned less to finance domestic industry than to serve as vehicles for interest representation of the economic elite.[38] Their membership commonly provided a useful guide to the names of the local aristocracy.

Nowhere was this clearer than during the period of Socialist government under President Salvador Allende of Chile. The Santiago stock exchange became during these years the focal point of opposition to the leftist regime and the exchange's president the most articulate spokesman on the anti-Socialist camp. Stock values during this period declined to near zero, until a few weeks before the military coup that overthrew Allende. At that point, stock values started to rise again, as members of the restricted "Gentlemen's Club" gained knowledge of the imminent coup.[39] They duly celebrated its success and welcomed with open arms the arrival of General Pinochet to power and the imposition of free market reform by its advisers.

During the years of the Pinochet dictatorship, the brokerage houses of the Santiago Exchange remained, however, well insulated from the play of market forces. They were, after all, one of the firmest pillars of the regime. With the advent of democracy, their fortunes changed. The open-market policies initiated by the "Chicago Boys"[40] under Pinochet and continued by the subsequent democratic governments brought to Chile a growing number of foreign investment banks. As these firms became involved in trading and issuing shares in the Santiago Exchange, they confronted the power of entrenched local brokers:

The most significant "island of power" is formed by the traditional brokers who immediately opposed the entry of the banks. . . . A tension emerged between the reproduction of the traditional *ethos* proper of a "gentlemen's club" and a modern perception that viewed the Exchange as a competitive business place. To the extent that world financial markets operate under this modern *ethos*, the interest of some in preserving the Exchange as a traditional space, based on informal mechanisms of control, could only slow down the integration of the national market into global financial circles (italics and quotation marks in original).[41]

Foreign banks became seriously interested in the exchange after the Chilean government privatized social security, compelling the newly established private pension administrators to invest in the stock market and government securities. From one day to the next, as it were, the volume of transactions in the Santiago Exchange took a quantum leap: "[T]he law that authorized the investment of pension funds in the stock market turned the AFPs (the pension administrators) into financial actors of the first rank. . . . In total, institutional investors increased their stock holdings in the Santiago Exchange from U.S. 1.04 billion in 1980 to 14 billion in 1991."[42]

In response to the recalcitrance of the entrenched elite, foreign investors and emerging national banks allied with them created the new Electronic Exchange (Bolsa Electronica) in direct competition with the traditional institution. The evident advantages in speed and transparency of electronic trades over "voice" trading threatened the Santiago Exchange with immediate obsolescence.[43] The finance ministry, no longer beholden to traditional elite power, allowed the creation of the Electronic Exchange as a way of quickening the nation's integration into global financial circles.

The prospect of losing most of their business to the Electronic Exchange forced the hand of the established brokers. Live transactions in the Santiago Exchange's "pits" gave way to electronic trades. New penalties against inside trading and new rules on access to information seriously restricted the privileged transactions of the past. Four of the eleven seats on the board were granted to the new institutional investors who also came to control the bulk of transactions. Brokerage houses declined from seventy-two in 1960 to just thirty-four in 2005, as many of the traditional operators abandoned the business: "In fact, the new institutional investors that have assumed the leadership of the Exchange are the great commercial and investment banks. Hence, this decline in the number of market operators has not reflected contraction, but actual expansion and rationalization of trade."[44]

TABLE 10.2
Sixteen Largest Brokerage Houses in the Santiago Exchange, 2004

Broker	Type	Gross Income (Billion Pesos)[1]	Profit Rate, 2003–4 %
Banchile	Domestic Commercial Bank	41,104	9.52
Larrain Vial	Traditional Broker	14,404	4.77
Bice	Domestic Commercial Bank	27,038	4.50
Consorcio	Investment Group	9,976	4.06
BCI	Domestic Commercial Bank	19,100	3.86
Valores Security	Foreign Investment Bank	31,268	3.48
IM Trust	Foreign Investment Bank	7,039	2.66
Santander Investment	Foreign Commercial Bank	11,596	2.33
CorpBanca	Domestic Commercial Bank	15,896	2.24
Banco Estado	Domestic Commercial Bank	9,059	1.90
BBVA	Foreign Commercial Bank	6,817	1.65
Citigroup	Foreign Commercial Bank	6,841	1.61
Celfin	Domestic Investment Bank	9,077	1.49
Deutsche	Foreign Investment Bank	11,852	1.02
Alfa	Investment Group	7,820	0.88
Ureta and Bianchi	Traditional Broker	1,071	0.77

[1] The exchange rate in 2004 was U.S. $1.00 = Chilean $609.
Source: Wormald and Brieba, "La Bolsa de Comercio de Santiago de Chile," table 3.

Several traditional brokerage houses survived the confrontation, but their trade volume and relative importance were greatly diminished. Table 10.2 lists the sixteen largest operators in the Santiago Exchange in 2004. Only two traditional brokers make the list and one of them is dead last. Only one member of the old economic elite, Larrain Vial, ranks at the top of the list; the rest are investment and commercial banks, both foreign and domestic.

Chilean brokers must have seriously reconsidered what they prayed for. The free market they welcomed with open arms removed the protective barriers under which they thrived in the past and placed them in direct competition with far larger and more technologically savvy multi-national actors. It was the power of these competitors, not the policies of the defunct socialist regime, that finally eclipsed the Chilean financial elite, relegating it to a secondary role in its own country.

While the evolution of the Santiago Exchange illustrates this power confrontation with unique clarity, it is not an isolated example. In country after country, stock exchanges experienced a similar evolution, eliminating traditional practices and displacing entrenched elites lest the institutions themselves be shut out from global financial markets. Latin American exchanges copied Wall Street and copied each other, watching out for the latest technological innovations and moving inexorably toward electronic trading and universalistic access to information. As they modernized, they also denationalized since effective power devolved into the hands of multinational investors and banks. As Rodríguez Garavito concludes for the case of the Bogotá Exchange:

> As a consequence of a process of diffusion and international competition, the Colombian Stock Exchange [BVC in the Spanish acronym] has been transformed from a purely domestic institution into a node of the global financial networks. . . . The entry of the new global actors has been the most transformative force for the BVC and the Colombian financial scene. Dissatisfied with the preferential treatment granted by the Exchange to its stockholders, the new actors forced changes in corporate governance and operational functioning, accompanying the Exchange's de-mutualization.[45]

REPRISE

In conclusion, I return to the broad themes sounded in chapter 2. Economic sociology is not likely to move forward as a field if it continues to insist on ritualistic invocation of its founding assumption accompanied by a growing but disparate set of case studies. The latter support the tenability of the assumption, but do not extend its range, reducing its heuristic power through repetition. It is important to establish a clear hierarchy between abstract perspectives and concepts that "work," that is, that carry explanatory and predictive power in multiple settings. Following Max Weber and Robert K. Merton, I have chosen to call these concepts midrange ideal types. Perspectives and ideal types should also be differentiated from research sites. The latter possess no explanatory power of their own; they are simply places where broader ideas can be applied, possibly yielding new propositions.

In my view, a suitable theoretical program to advance the agenda of economic sociology can be built around the following steps:

- Putting to use the explanatory concepts of the field in specific areas of the economy and developing, in the process, new propositions and theories.
- Using these empirical explorations to modify, retain, and extend the scope of existing ideal types.
- Developing new such concepts, thereby increasing the explanatory power and reach of the field.
- Identifying new strategic areas where the perspective and conceptual tools of economic sociology can be fruitfully applied.

The combination of these activities may not only move the discipline ahead of its present state but also bring it into the public domain as an alternative to the questionable policies stemming from theoretical economics. It appears increasingly clear that the economic collapse of 2008 had some of its roots in an unshakable, almost religious belief in these theories. They include not only the financial models "performing" markets without benefit of plausible empirical grounding but also the more general assumption that markets are all-knowing, self-regulating entities whose efficiency is inevitably compromised by government meddling. Consequences of these beliefs have been exactly what Polanyian "disembeddedness" has led us to anticipate.

A sociological approach based on focused application of the concepts of social class, social institutions, and the self-defeating consequences of untamed markets would have gone a long way toward counteracting the headlong march into economic disaster. While *events*, such as the collapse of Lehman Brothers, could not be predicted with certainty, the overall *trend* was unmistakable. In a similar vein, the generalized crisis of confidence in the markets in 2009 was fundamentally a sociological phenomenon that for long eluded the best efforts of mainstream economists in charge of policy at the U.S. Treasury and Federal Reserve to overcome.

This historical contingency is not the only example. As applied to the field of health care, the economic theory of "moral hazard" has provided the ideological underpinnings for effective resistance to universal health care and for the harmful definition of care as a market commodity. The sorry state of the American health system in the early twenty-first century, more expensive and more inegalitarian than its counterparts in other Western democracies, can be traced, at least in part, to the ideological sway of such notions.[46] A sociological approach to health and health care, drawing on midrange concepts such as social class, institutions, and Polanyian embeddedness could provide a much-needed theoretical corrective in this field as well.

In sum, the agenda for economic sociology is both extensive and urgent. It is a field whose time has come and whose promise should be fulfilled. It will not do so by following the present path and, for that reason, a change of course is needed.

Notes

CHAPTER ONE
Economic Sociology: Past Achievements and Present Challenges

1. Smelser and Swedberg, *Handbook of Economic Sociology*, 1994, 2005.
2. Granovetter, "Economic Action and Social Structure."
3. Merton, "On Sociological Theories of the Middle Range"; Weber, "Objectivity in Social Science."
4. Swedberg and Smelser, *Handbook*, 1994, 2005.
5. Swedberg, *Principles*.
6. Ibid.; Swedberg and Smelser's "Introduction" to the *Handbook*, 2005.
7. Weber, "Objectivity," 80.
8. Ibid., 93.
9. Portes and Haller, "The Informal Economy."
10. Weber, "Objectivity."
11. Weber, *The Protestant Ethic*; Bendix, *From Max Weber*.
12. Rumbaut, "Assimilation and Its Discontents"; Pahl, "Employment, Work, and the Domestic Division of Labor"; Roberts, "The Other Working Class."
13. Merton, "On Sociological Theories of the Middle Range."
14. Collins, "Prediction in Macro-Sociology."
15. Kennedy, *The Rise and Fall of the Great Powers*.
16. Tilly, "To Explain Political Processes."
17. Portes, "On Grand Surprises and Modest Certainties."
18. See, for example, Arrighi, *The Long Twentieth Century*, chap. 4; and Wallerstein, "The Rise and Future Demise of the World Capitalist System."
19. O'Connor, *The Fiscal Crisis of the State*.
20. In a dialogue with institutional economists, economic sociologists have examined, for example, the origins of firms, the stability of corporate hierarchies, and the development of stable market practices. Significant theoretical development in economic sociology in the past owes at least as much to the analysis of steady states and continuities as to that of processes with change. See Granovetter, "Business Groups"; DiMaggio and Louch, "Socially Embedded Consumer Transactions"; Swedberg, "Markets as Social Structures"; and White, "Where Do Markets Come From?"

CHAPTER TWO
The Assumptions That Ground the Field

1. This chapter is based on two prior publications: Portes, "Economic Sociology

and the Sociology of Immigration"; and Portes, "The Hidden Abode: Sociology as the Analysis of the Unexpected."

2. Altman, *A Reconstruction Using Anthropological Methods of the Second Economy*, 4–6. See also Lomnitz, "Informal Exchange Networks in Formal Systems."

3. Portes and Sensenbrenner, "Embeddedness and Immigration," 1339.

4. Capecchi, "The Informal Economy and the Development of Flexible Specialization." See also Sabel, "Flexible Specialization and the Re-Emergence of Regional Economies."

5. Capecchi, "The Informal Economy and the Development of Flexible Specialization," 200–201.

6. Ibid.; Brusco, "The Emilian Model of Productive Decentralization."

7. Díaz, "Restructuring the New Working Classes in Chile"; Portes, "Neoliberalism and the Sociology of Development."

8. Díaz, "Chile: Hacía el Pos-Neoliberalismo?"

9. Morrill, "Conflict Management."

10. Ibid., 600.

11. Frank, "Rethinking Rational Choice." See also Sen, "Rational Fools."

12. Weber, *The Theory of Social and Economic Organization*, 88–115.

13. Ibid., 324–29. See also Hart, "The Idea of Economy."

14. Blau, *Exchange and Power in Social Life*; Gouldner, "The Norm of Reciprocity"; Portes and Sensenbrenner, "Embeddedness and Immigration."

15. Parsons and Smelser, *Economy and Society*.

16. Polanyi, *The Great Transformation*; Polanyi, "The Economy as Instituted Process."

17. Granovetter, "Economic Action and Social Structure."

18. Ibid.; Granovetter, "The Old and the New Economic Sociology."

19. Dalton, "Men Who Manage," 334.

20. Abolafia, *Making Markets*, 10.

21. Mills, *The Sociological Imagination*; Wolff, *The Sociology of Georg Simmel*.

22. Merton, "The Unanticipated Consequences"; Merton, "Social Structure and Anomie"; Merton, "Unanticipated Consequences and Kindred Sociological Ideas."

23. See, for example, Granovetter's study of the birth of the electrical industry in the United States; Zelizer's study of money and intimate relationships; Morrill's previously cited study of corporate behavior; and Massey et al.'s study of the failure of U.S. immigration policy: Granovetter, "Coase Revisited"; Zelizer, *The Purchase of Intimacy*; Morrill, "Conflict Management"; Massey et al., *Beyond Smoke and Mirrors*.

24. The original reference is from the first volume of *Capital*: "Accompanied by Mr. Moneybags and by the possessor of labor power, we therefore take leave for a time of this noisy sphere, where everything takes place on the surface and in

view of all men, and follow them both into the hidden abode of production, on whose threshold there stares us in the face 'No admittance except on business.' " Marx, *Capital*, vol. 1.

25. Harvey, *The Condition of Postmodernity*.

26. Bourdieu, *Distinction*.

27. Durkheim, *The Rules of the Sociological Method*; Durkheim, *Suicide*, 171–202; Mauss, *The Gift*; Lévi-Strauss, *The Elementary Structures of Kinship*.

28. Meyer, "The World Polity"; Meyer and Hannan, *National Development*.

29. Weber, *The Protestant Ethic and the Spirit of Capitalism*. See also Bendix, *Max Weber: An Intellectual Portrait*.

30. Michels, *Political Parties*; Lopreato, *Vilfredo Pareto*, 1–35.

31. Simmel, "The Stranger"; Simmel, "The Significance of Numbers in Social Life"; Coser, *The Functions of Social Conflict*.

32. Merton, "Social Structure and Anomie."

33. Coleman, "A Rational Choice Perspective."

34. Castells, *End of Millennium*, 3:31.

35. Tilly, "Invisible Elbow."

36. Ibid., 590.

37. Ibid.

38. There are alternative versions of what happened on that day. The present account draws from that broadcasted by the History Channel during a series titled "Secrets of World War II," which provides additional evidence in support of this account of events. The documentary was transmitted on March 24, 1999.

39. Pozas, "Sociología económica y migración internacional"; Block, "The Role of the State in the Economy"; Block, *Postindustrial Possibilities*.

40. This schema will be presented and discussed in chapter 4.

41. Weber, "Class Status, and Party."

42. Ibid. See also Weber, "Capitalism and Rural Society in Germany"; Gramsci, "State and Civil Society"; Mills, *The Power Elite*.

43. Durkheim, *The Rules of the Sociological Method*; Durkheim, *The Division of Labor in Society*.

44. Marx, *The Eighteenth Brumaire*; Marx, *Grundrisse*.

45. Weber, "Social Stratification and the Class Structure"; Weber, "Class, Status, and Party."

46. Williamson, *Markets and Hierarchies*.

47. Bourdieu, *Distinction*; Bourdieu, "Les trois états du capital culturel."

48. Gramsci, *Prison Notebooks*; Wright, *Classes*; Mills, *The Power Elite*.

CHAPTER THREE
Social Capital

1. This chapter is based on the following prior publications: Portes and

Sensenbrenner, "Embeddedness and Immigration"; Portes, "Social Capital: Its Origins and Application in Modern Sociology."

2. Portes, "Social Capital," 6.

3. Marx and Engels, *Manifesto*; Marx, *The Grundrisse*.

4. Bourdieu, "Le capital social"; Coleman, "Social Capital in the Creation of Human Capital."

5. Bourdieu, "The Forms of Capital."

6. Portes, "Social Capital."

7. Coleman, "The Rational Reconstruction of Society"; Coleman, "The Design of Organizations and the Right to Act."

8. Putnam, *Bowling Alone*; Putnam, "The Prosperous Community."

9. Putnam, *Bowling Alone*; Portes, "The Two Meanings of Social Capital."

10. Bourdieu, "The Forms of Capital"; Bourdieu, "Les trois états du capital culturel"; Portes, "The Two Meanings of Social Capital."

11. Coleman, "Social Capital in the Creation of Human Capital," S104.

12. Wrong, "The Oversocialized Conception of Man."

13. Wolff, *The Sociology of Georg Simmel*; Simmel, "The Sociology of Conflict"; Blau, *Exchange and Power in Social Life*; Homans, *Social Behavior*; Schiff, "Social Capital, Labor Mobility, and Welfare"; Coleman, "The Realization of Effective Norms."

14. Coleman, *Foundations of Social Theory*, 273–72; Portes and Sensenbrenner, "Embeddedness and Immigration."

15. Durkheim, *The Division of Labor in Society*; Durkheim, *The Rules of the Sociological Method*.

16. Zhou and Bankston, "Social Capital and the Adaptation of the Second Generation," 207.

17. Coleman, "Social Capital in the Creation of Human Capital," S110.

18. Hao, *Kin Support*.

19. Gold, "Gender and Social Capital."

20. Granovetter, *Getting a Job*.

21. Burt, *Structural Holes*.

22. Lin et al., "Social Resources and Strength of Ties."

23. Light, "Immigrant and Ethnic Enterprise"; Light and Bonacich, *Immigrant Entrepreneurs*.

24. Zhou, *New York's Chinatown*; Light and Bonacich, *Immigrant Entrepreneurs*; Portes and Stepick, *City on the Edge*; Perez, *Cuban Miami*.

25. Stack, *All Our Kin*; Fernández-Kelly and Konczal, "Murdering the Alphabet."

26. Wacquant and Wilson, "The Cost of Racial and Class Exclusion." See also Fernández-Kelly, "Social and Cultural Capital."

27. Sullivan, *Getting Paid*.

28. Ibid.; Granovetter, *Getting a Job*.

29. Fernández-Kelly, "Social and Cultural Capital."

30. Grootaert and Bastelaer, *Understanding and Measuring Social Capital*.

31. Evans, "Development as Institutional Change"; Portes and Mooney, "Social Capital and Community Development."

32. Waldinger, "The 'Other Side' of Embeddedness," 557.

33. Smith, *The Wealth of Nations*, 332.

34. Geertz, *Peddlers and Princes*.

35. Granovetter, "The Economic Sociology of Firms"; Weber, *The Theory of Social and Economic Organization*, part 1; Weber, *The Protestant Ethic*.

36. Boissevain, *Friends of Friends*; Portes, "Economic Sociology."

37. Simmel, "The Metropolis and Mental Life."

38. Rumbaut, "Ties That Bind," 39.

39. Bourgois, "In Search of Respect," 32.

40. Stepick, "The Refugees Nobody Wants"; Stepick et al., "Shifting Identities and Intergenerational Conflict"; Suarez-Orozco, "Towards a Psychosocial Understanding"; Matute-Bianchi, "Ethnic Identities and Patterns of School Success."

41. Lozano was initially convicted by a Miami jury, but an appeals court threw out the conviction on the grounds that he could not get a fair trial in the city. Throughout the process, Lozano continued to make appeals for financial support through Spanish-language radio stations in Miami. Portes and Stepick, *City on the Edge*, 2–3, 9.

42. Nee and Nee, *Longtime Californ'*; Boswell, "A Split Labor Market Analysis"; Zhou, *New York's Chinatown*.

43. Portes and Zhou, "Entrepreneurship and Economic Progress in the 1990s."

44. Rischin, *The Promised City*; Howe, *World of Our Fathers*.

45. Zhou and Bankston, "Social Capital"; Portes and Stepick, *City on the Edge*; Stepick et al., *This Land Is Our Land*.

46. Portes and Guarnizo, "Tropical Capitalists."

47. According to the Federation of Dominican Industrialists and Merchants, New York City hosts some 20,000 Dominican-owned businesses, including about 70 percent of Spanish grocery stores, or *bodegas*; 90 percent of taxicabs in upper Manhattan; several supermarket chains; newspapers and radio stations. See Guarnizo, "Los 'Dominican Yorkers'"; Guarnizo, *One Country in Two*.

48. Granovetter, "Entrepreneurship, Development, and the Emergence of Firms," 26. See also Granovetter, "The Economic Sociology of Firms and Entrepreneurs."

CHAPTER FOUR
The Concept of Institutions

1. Revised and expanded version of a prior publication, Portes, "Institutions and Development: A Conceptual Reanalysis."

2. Evans, "The Challenges of the 'Institutional Turn'"; Nee and Ingram, "Embeddedness and Beyond."

3. Hoff and Stiglitz, "Modern Economic Theory and Development," 389; Evans, "The Challenges of the 'Institutional Turn.'"

4. Evans, *Dependent Development*; Portes, "Neoliberalism and the Sociology of Development"; Hirschman, *The Strategy of Economic Development*.

5. Roland, "Understanding Institutional Change," 110.

6. Hodgson, "Institutional Blindness in Modern Economics," 148.

7. North, *Institutions, Institutional Change*, 3.

8. Durkheim, *The Rules*; *Suicide*.

9. Ibid., 116.

10. Roland, "Understanding Institutional Change," 116.

11. Scott, *Institutions and Organizations*.

12. Hollingsworth, "On Institutional Embeddedness."

13. Dolsak and Ostrom, *The Commons in the New Millennium*; Elster et al., *Institutional Design in Post-Communist Societies*.

14. Ostrom, *Governing the Commons*; Ostrom et al., *The Drama of the Commons*.

15. Weber, *The Sociology of Religion*; Parsons, *The Social System*.

16. Newcomb, Turner, and Converse, *Social Psychology*; MacIver and Page, *Society*.

17. Cooley, *Human Nature and the Social Order*; Simmel, "The Stranger"; Goffman, *Encounters*.

18. Linton, *The Cultural Background*; Newcomb, *Social Psychology*, chap. 3.

19. Cottrell, "Roles and Marital Adjustment"; Linton, "The Cultural Background"; Merton, "The Role-Set"; Goffman, *The Presentation of Self*; Goode, "A Theory of Role Strain."

20. DiMaggio and Powell, "The Iron Cage Revisited."

21. Bourdieu, *Distinction*; Bourdieu, "Les trois états du capital culturel"; Swidler, "Culture in Action."

22. Scott, *Organizations and Institutions*; DiMaggio, "Cultural Aspect."

23. Weber, "Social Stratification and Class Structure"; Veblen, *The Theory of the Leisure Class*; Mills, *The Power Elite*.

24. Weber, "Social Stratification"; Bendix, *Max Weber*, chaps. 9–10.

25. Weber, "Social Stratification"; Wright, "Varieties of Marxist Conceptions"; Wright, *Classes*; Poulantzas, *Classes in Contemporary Capitalism*.

26. Williamson, *Markets and Hierarchies*; Williamson, *The Economic Institutions of Capitalism*.

27. Hout et al., "The Persistence of Classes"; Bourdieu, "The Forms of Capital"; Wright, *Classes*.

28. Hout et al., "The Persistence of Classes"; Grusky and Sorensen, "Can Class Analysis Be Salvaged?"

29. MacIver and Page, *Society*; Newcomb et al., *Social Psychology*, 333–41; Merton, "The Role Set."

30. MacIver and Page, *Society*; Merton, "Social Structure and Anomie"; North, *Institutions*; Scott, *Institutions and Organizations*.

31. Giddens, *The New Rules of the Sociological Method*.

32. Meyer and Rowan, "Institutionalized Organizations."

33. Selznick, *TVA and the Grassroots*, 16–17.

34. Scott, *Institutions and Organizations*, chap. 2; DiMaggio and Powell, "The Iron Cage Revisited."

35. Granovetter, "Economic Action and Social Structure"; Granovetter, "Coase Revisited."

36. Meyer and Rowan, "Institutionalized Organizations"; Selznick, *TVA and the Grassroots*.

37. Evans, "Development as Institutional Change."

38. Roland, "Understanding Institutional Change."

39. O'Donnell, "The State, Democratization"; Portes, "Neoliberalism and the Sociology of Development"; Evans, "The Challenges of the 'Institutional Turn.'"

40. DeJanvry and Garramon, "Laws of Motion of Capital"; Centeno, *Democracy within Reason*; Evans, *Embedded Autonomy*; Evans, "Predatory, Developmental and Other Apparatuses."

41. Hoff and Stiglitz, "Modern Economic Theory and Development," 420.

42. Weber, "Social Stratification and Class Structure"; Gramsci, "State and Civil Society"; Poulantzas, *Classes in Contemporary Capitalism*.

43. Sen, *Development as Freedom*.

44. Evans, "Development as Institutional Change"; Baiocchi, *Radicals in Power*.

45. Ostrom, *Governing the Commons*.

46. Evans, "Development as Institutional Change," 40.

47. MacLeod, *Downsizing the State*; Ariza and Ramirez, "Urbanización, mercados de trabajo."

48. MacLeod, *Downsizing the State*.

49. Ibid., 123, 133.

50. Ibid., 96.

51. Ibid., 71, 75–76.

52. Ibid., 81–82.

53. Ariza and Ramirez, "Urbanización, mercados de trabajo"; Shaiken, *Mexico in the Global Economy*; Delgado-Wise, "The Relation between Mexico-U.S. Economic Integration."

54. Shaiken, *Mexico in the Global Economy*; Delgado-Wise, "The Relation between Mexico-U.S. Economic Integration."

55. Campbell, *Institutional Change*.

56. Meyer et al., "World Society and the Nation-State"; Meyer and Hannan, *National Development and the World System*.

57. Meyer et al., "World Society and the Nation-State"; Sassen, *The Mobility of Labor and Capital*.

58. Castells, *The Internet Galaxy*; Castells, *The Information Age*.

59. Weber, "Religious Rejections of the World"; Weber, *The Sociology of Religion*; Weber, *The Protestant Ethic*.

60. Wuthnow, *Meaning and Moral Order*; Wuthnow, *After Heaven*; Roof, *Spiritual Marketplace*; Kepel, *Les banlieus de l'Islam*.

61. Campbell, *Institutional Change*, 35–38.

62. Williamson, *Markets and Hierarchies*; Granovetter, "Economic Action and Social Structure"; Swedberg, *Principles of Economic Sociology*.

63. Block, "The Roles of the State in the Economy"; Block, "Introduction" to Polanyi's *The Great Transformation*; Pozas, "Sociología económica y migración internacional."

64. Nee and Ingram, "Embeddedness and Beyond"; Nee, "The New Institutionalisms"; Campbell and Lindberg, "Property Rights."

65. Nee, "The New Institutionalisms," 55.

CHAPTER FIVE
The Concept of Social Class

1. This chapter is a revised and expanded version of a prior publication: Portes, "The Resilient Importance of Class: A Nominalist Interpretation."

2. For a discussion of Marshal Michel Ney and his relationship with Napoleon Bonaparte, see Schom, *Napoleon Bonaparte*, 439–40, 481–84, 639–42, 737.

3. For an account of the monarchist restoration in France and Europe after the Vienna Congress, see Nicolson, *The Congress of Vienna*; Kissinger, *A World Restored*.

4. Meyer and Rubinson, "The World Educational Revolution"; Meyer et al., "World Society and the Nation State"; Mayer, "A Comparison of Poverty and Living Conditions"; Jencks et al, *Inequality*; Reskin, "Sex Segregation in the Workplace."

5. Jenkins and Leicht, "Class Analysis and Social Movements."

6. Grusky and Sørensen, "Can Class Analysis Be Salvaged?" 1201.

7. Ibid.; Wright, "Rethinking Once Again the Concept of Class Structure."

8. Harvey, *The Limits to Capital*; O'Connor, *The Fiscal Crisis of the State*.

9. Lenin, *What Is to Be Done?*

10. Smith and Edmonston, *The Immigration Debate*.

11. Veblen, *The Theory of the Leisure Class*; Sennett and Cobb, *The Hidden Injuries of Class*; Western, et al., "Système pénal et marché du travail."

12. Sassen, *The Global City*.

13. Tilly, *The Contentious French*.

14. Bourdieu, *Distinction*; Bordieu, "Les troits états du capital culturel."

15. Dobb, *Studies in the Development of Capitalism*.

16. Mandel, *Late Capitalism*.

17. Marx, *Capital*, vol. 3; Marx, *The Eighteenth Brumaire*; Marx, *Class Struggle in France*.

18. Sennett and Cobb, *The Hidden Injuries*.

19. Marx, *The Grundisse*, 29, 61, 66.

20. Bourdieu, "Les trois états"; Bordieu, "Le capital social." See also Portes, "Social Capital."

21. Mills, *The Power Elite*; Domhoff, *Who Rules America Now?*

22. Mills, *The Power Elite*, 30–39; Schumpeter, "An Economic Interpretation of Our Time."

23. Schumpeter, "An Economic Interpretation of Our Time"; Mills, *The Power Elite*; Mandel, *Late Capitalism*; Lamarche, "Property Development."

24. Lenin, *What Is to Be Done?*; Mandel, *Late Capitalism*; Edwards, *Labor Market Segmentation*; Wright, "Varieties."

25. Bluestone and Harrison, *The De-Industrialization of America*; Sassen, *The Global City*; Evans, "The Challenges of the 'Institutional Turn.' "

26. A useful cutting point in the early 2000s in America is 3 million dollars, a figure that would have allowed its possessors to live in relative comfort without work. It can thus be operationally defined as a criterion for the class of rentiers. Data from the Internal Revenue Service indicates that adult Americans who own such wealth represent a tiny fraction of the population, estimated at no more than 2 percent. See also Updegrave, "Assessing Your Wealth."

27. Poulantzas, *Classes in Contemporary Capitalism*; Wright, *Classes*; Cutler et al., *Marx's Capital and Capitalism Today*, vol. 1.

28. Davis and Moore, "Some Principles of Stratification"; Wright and Perrone, "Marxist Class Categories."

29. This approach is congruent with Weber's use of "market power" as the defining criterion of class, but extends it by pointing to the sources of such power and the major cleavages to which they give rise. See Weber, *The Theory of Social and Economic Organization*, part 1; Bendix, *Max Weber*, 85–87.

30. See Castells, *The Internet Galaxy*; Evans, "The Challenges."

31. Carchedi, *On the Economic Identification*; Burawoy, *Contemporary Currents*; Poulantzas, *Classes*.

32. Edwards, *Labor Market*; Jaffee, "The Political Economy of Job Loss"; Lozano, *The Invisible Work Force*.

33. Rosenblum, *Immigrant Workers*; Bonacich, "Advanced Capitalism and Black-White Relations;" Grusky and Sørensen, "Can Class Analysis Be Salvaged?"

34. Class divisions can actually exist *within* occupations, especially those requiring advanced training. The star surgeon in an elite hospital is in an objectively different situation from the common internist because extraordinary abilities endow her with sufficient market power to bid for a higher class position. The same division occurs among lawyers, college professors, and actors, among others. Identifying occupation with class achieves a certain formal elegance by placing all individuals with the same formal job title into one category. However, this serves to obscure, not clarify, class cleavages because the formal title conceals differences in access to power-conferring resources.

35. Lozano, *The Invisible Work Force*; Hirst and Zeitlin, "Flexible Specialization"; Bluestone and Harrison, *The Deindustrialization*; Castells and Portes, "World Underneath."

36. Pahl and Wallace, "Household Work Strategies; Fernández-Kelly and Garcia, "Informalization at the Core"; Castells and Portes, "World Underneath."

37. Hannan and Freeman, "The Population Ecology of Organizations"; Sassen, "New York City's Informal Economy"; Granovetter, "The Economic Sociology of Firms and Entrepreneurs"; Light, "Immigrant and Ethnic Enterprise."

38. Wright, "Varieties"; Wright, *Classes*; Wright, "Rethinking Once Again"; Poulantzas, *Classes*.

39. Marx and Engels, *The Communist Manifesto*; Marx, *The Grundrisse*; Dobb, *Studies*; Nun, "Superpoblación relativa."

40. Harrison and Bluestone, *The Deindustrialization*; Sassen, *The Global City*; Castells and Laserna, "The New Dependency"; Fligstein, "States, Markets, and Economic Growth."

41. Hirst and Zeitlin, "Flexible Specialization"; Romo and Schwartz, "The Structural Embeddedness of Business Divisions"; Harvey, *The Limits to Capital*; Edwards, *Labor Market*; Harrison and Bluestone, *The Great U-Turn*.

42. Conclusions of a survey of Chicago-area employers conducted in the late 1980s and directed by William J. Wilson, then of the University of Chicago.

43. Kircheman and Neckerman, "We Love to Hire Them, But," 231.

44. Sustained growth of the American economy in recent years has led to labor scarcities in some sectors that open opportunities to members of this class. Nevertheless, they are commonly hired when no other sources of labor are available and under "flexible" arrangements quite different from the previously protected industrial working class. See Waters, "West Indian Immigrants, African Americans"; Stewart, "African Americans and Post-Industrial Labor Markets"; Blau, *Illusions of Prosperity*.

45. Declines in open unemployment as a result of sustained economic expansion in the late 1990s conveyed a partially distorted image of the labor market, obscuring the phenomenon of labor redundancy. Statistics were based on employed individuals and those actively seeking work, omitting discouraged workers and those who never sought formal employment. The burgeoning informal and petty criminal economies in low-income areas of American cities, as described in recent ethnographies, points to the continuing existence of marginalized classes and the illusory character of "full employment." See Bourgois, *In Search of Respect*; Fernández-Kelly, "Social and Cultural Capital"; Wilson, *When Work Disappears*; Edin and Lien, "Work, Welfare, and Single Mothers."

46. "The World as a Single Machine," special survey of *The Economist*, June 20, 1998, p. 3.

47. Sassen, *The Global City*; Reich, *The Work of Nations*; Piore and Sabel, *The Second Industrial Divide*.

48. Piore and Sabel, *The Second Industrial Divide*; Edwards, *The Labor Market*; Reich, *The Work of Nations*; Romo and Schwartz, "The Structural Embeddedness."

49. De Janvry and Garramon, "Laws of Motion of Capital"; Portes and Bach, *Latin Journey*, chaps. 1–2.

50. Evans and Leighton, "Some Empirical Aspects of Entrepreneurship"; Portes and Sassen, "Making It Underground"; Granovetter, "The Economic Sociology."

51. Fligstein, "States, Markets"; Bluestone and Harrison, *The Great U-Turn*.

52. Bluestone and Harrison, *The Great U-Turn*; Fernández-Kelly and Garcia, "Informalization at the Core"; Storper and Scott, "Work Organization and Local Labor Markets"; Hill, "Global Factory and Company Town"; Wilson, *Where Work Disappears*.

53. *Money* magazine, *Everybody Is Getting Rich*. This cover banner in *Money* did not go unchallenged. An indignant reader wrote back, "What planet are you living on? 'Everyone's Getting Rich?' I found this message offensive. True, some people are getting very rich. But many more in America remain very poor indeed—not to mention Africa, Mexico, and innumerable other places." Rogers, "Is Everyone Getting Really Rich?"

54. Updegrave, "Assessing Your Wealth."

55. The work of Bruce Western and Katherine Beckett introduced a novel dimension to the condition of this class by taking into account the size of the incarcerated population of working age. By 1993, the incarceration rate in the United States was 519 per 100,000 or approximately *five* times the highest rate in Western Europe corresponding to the United Kingdom. Among American blacks, the rate reached 1,947 per 100,000 for an absolute total of over 625,000 inmates. If the number of working-age prisoners is added to the unemployment rate, the figure increases from 5.6 percent to 7.5 percent in 1995. This number still excludes discouraged workers and those who never held paid employment. If the latter are added, the empirical estimate of the class of redundant workers would hover around 10 percent of the labor force in the mid-1990s. Western and Beckett, "How Unregulated Is the U.S. Labor Market?"

56. Castells and Laserna, "The New Dependency"; Portes and Roberts, "The Free Market City"; Harrison and Bluestone, *The Deindustrialization*; Gereffi and Korzeniewicz, *Commodity Chains and Global Capitalism*.

57. Fligstein, "States, Markets"; Evans, "The Challenges."

58. Gereffi, "International Trade and Industrial Upgrading"; Waldinger and Lichter, *How the Other Half Works*; Fernández-Kelly, *For We Are Sold*; Portes, "The Free Market City."

59. The rise of the Reform Party with the figure of Ross Perot as its presidential candidate in 1992 garnered strong support from this class alliance. One of Perot's most popular campaign messages was "the giant sucking sound from the South" as U.S. jobs and small firms were swallowed by Mexico in the wake of NAFTA. See also Hufbauer and Schott, *NAFTA: An Assessment*; Shaiken,

"Advanced Manufacturing and Mexico"; Massey et al., *Beyond Smoke and Mirrors*.

60. Massey, *Categorically Unequal*; Freeman, *America Works*.

61. Portes and Rumbaut, *Immigrant America*, 3rd ed., chaps. 2–3.

62. Ibid.; Rosenfeld and Tienda, "Mexican Immigration"; Massey et al., *Beyond Smoke*.

63. Portes and Rumbaut, *Immigrant America*, chap. 4. Espenshade and Rodriguez, "Completing the Ph.D."; Alarcón, "Recruitment Processes among Foreign-Born Engineers."

64. Office of Immigration Statistics, *2002 Annual Report*; *2006 Annual Report*.

65. Ibid.; Rosenfeld and Tienda, "Mexican Immigration"; Portes and Zhou, "Entrepreneurship and Economic Progress in the 1990s."

66. Kircheman and Neckerman, "We Love to Hire Them"; Cornelius, "The Structural Embeddedness"; Portes and Rumbaut, *Immigrant America*, chap. 10; Frey and Liaw, "The Impact of Recent Immigration."

67. Massey et al., *Beyond Smoke*; Portes and Rumbaut, *Immigrant America*; Congressional Budget Office, *Economic Growth and Immigration*.

68. Congressional Budget Office, *Economic Growth and Immigration*; Rosenfeld and Tienda, "Mexican Immigration"; Butcher, "An Investigation on the Effects of Immigration."

69. Passel, "The Economic Downturn and Immigration Trends."

70. Swedberg, *Principles of Economic Sociology*.

71. Fligstein, "States, Markets," 138.

72. Ibid.; Abolafia, *Making Markets*.

CHAPTER SIX
Social Class (Continued)

1. This chapter is a revised and abridged version of a prior publication: Portes and Hoffman, "Latin American Class Structures: Their Composition and Change during the Neoliberal Era."

2. See Sunkel, "The Unbearable Lightness of Neoliberalism"; Robinson, *Promoting Polyarchy*; Portes, "Neoliberalism and the Sociology of Development."

3. Portes and Hoffman, "Latin American Class Structures."

4. See Carchedi, *On the Economic Differentiation of Social Classes*; Wright, *Classes*; Grusky and Sørensen, "Can Class Analysis Be Salvaged?"

5. Hall, "The Reworking of Class Analysis."

6. Wright, *Classes*; Wright, "Rethinking Once Again"; Goldthorpe, "Class and Politics in the Advanced Industrial Societies"; Clark and Lipset, "Are Social Classes Dying?"

7. See Luxembourg, *The Accumulation of Capital*; Emmanuel, *Unequal Exchange*; Wolpe, *The Theory of Internal Colonialism*.

8. Wallerstein, "Semi-Peripheral Countries"; Hopkins and Wallerstein, "Patterns of Development."

9. Economic Commission for Latin America and the Caribbean, *Social Panorama of Latin America*, 63.

10. Ibid., 64–65.

11. Birbeck, "Garbage, Industry, and the 'Vulture'"; Cross, *Informal Politics*; Portes and Walton, *Labor, Class, and the International System*, chap. 3.

12. International Labour Organization/Lima, *Panorama Laboral*; Klein and Tokman, "La estratificación social bajo tensión."

13. Klein and Tokman, "La estratificación social bajo tension," 18.

14. Economic Commission for Latin America and the Caribbean, *Social Panorama*, 67–68.

15. See Nun, "Superpoblación relativa"; Benería, "Subcontracting and Employment Dynamics"; Birbeck, "Garbage Industry"; Peattie, "What Is to Be Done with 'the Informal Sector?'"

16. Castells and Portes, "World Underneath"; Portes and Walton, *Labor, Class*.

17. International Labour Organization/Lima, *Panorama Social*.

18. Klein and Tokman, "La estratificación cocial," 17.

19. Galbraith, "A Perfect Crime"; Korzeniewicz and Smith, "Poverty, Inequality, and Growth."

20. Klein and Tokman, "La estratificación social." 20; Economic Commission for Latin America and the Caribbean, *Social Panorama*, 19.

21. The poverty line is calculated on the basis of the cost of a basket of goods and services for the average individual. As working-class households have more than four members on average in all countries considered, an income of less than 4 p.l.s (poverty lines) for the principal breadwinner is insufficient to lift the household out of poverty. Families respond to this situation through alternative income-earning activities, such as sending other members into the labor force or engaging in street vending or other informal activities.

22. Economic Commission for Latin America and the Caribbean, *Social Panorama*, 76–77; Díaz, "Chile: Hacia el pos-neoliberalismo?"

23. Galbraith, "A Perfect Crime"; Firebaugh, "Empirics of World Income Inequality."

24. Economic Commission for Latin America and the Caribbean, *Social Panorama*, 63.

25. Sunkel, "The Unbearable Lightness"; Portes and Roberts, "The Free Market City."

26. Portes and Roberts, "The Free Market City."

27. Merton, "Social Structure and Anomie."

28. Economic Commission for Latin America and the Caribbean, "Agenda social: Seguridad ciudadana y violencia," 208.

29. Gaviria and Pagés, "Patterns of Crime Victimization."

30. Ibid.; Arriagada and Godoy, "Prevention or Repression?"; De Roux, "Ciudad y violencia en América Latina."

31. Gaviria and Pagés, "Patterns," 6, 10.

32. Cerrutti and Grimson, "Neoliberalismo y después"; Sabatini and Wormald, "Santiago de Chile"; Kaztman et al., "La ciudad fragmentada"; Portes and Roberts, "The Free Market City."

33. Arriagada and Godoy, "Prevention or Repression"; Valladares et al., "Rio de Janeiro"; De Roux, "Ciudad y violencia."

34. Fundación Paz Ciudadana, "Delincuencia y opinión publica."

35. Gaviria and Pagés, "Patterns"; Sabatini and Wormald, "Santiago de Chile"; Cerrutti and Grimson, "Buenos Aires."

36. Cerrutti, "Report on Argentina," 46.

37. Tilly, *Durable Inequality*; Massey, *Categorically Unequal*.

38. Portes and Roberts, "The Free Market City"; Kaztman et al., "La ciudad fragmentada."

39. Latin American Weekly Report, "Argentina: An Era of Continuity and Change," December 13, 2007.

40. Roberts, "Social Inequalities without Class Cleavages"; Latin American Weekly Report, "MAS Approves New Constitution in Bolivia"; "Correa Redefines Meaning of Full Powers," December 13, 2007.

CHAPTER SEVEN
The Informal Economy

1. This chapter is an abridged and modified version of Portes and Haller, "The Informal Economy."

2. Fernández-Kelly and Garcia, "Informalization at the Core"; Gereffi, "International Trade."

3. Chavez, "Settlers and Sojourners."

4. Lozano, *The Invisible Work Force*, 54, 59.

5. Hart, "The Idea of the Economy," 158.

6. Hart, "Informal Income Opportunities," 68.

7. Sethuraman, *The Urban Informal Sector*; Klein and Tokman, "Sector informal."

8. Tokman, "Unequal Development"; Garcia, *Reestructuración*; Klein and Tokman, "Sector informal"; PREALC, *Mas allá de la crisis*.

9. Hart, "The Idea of the Economy," 158.

10. De Soto, *The Other Path*; Portes and Schauffler, "Competing Perspectives."

11. Feige, "Defining," 990.

12. Castells and Portes, "World Underneath," 12.

13. Feige, "Defining," 991.

14. Ibid., 992.

15. Castells and Portes, "World Underneath"; Blanes Jimenez, "Cocaine, Informality"; Grossman, "Informal Personal Incomes."

16. Portes, Castells, and Benton, "The Policy Implications of Informality"; Roberts, "Employment Structure"; Cross, *Informal Politics*; Sassen, "New York City's Informal Economy."

17. Sabel, "Flexible Specialization"; Capecchi, "The Informal Economy."

18. Benton, "Industrial Subcontracting"; Sabel, "Learning by Monitoring"; Brusco, "The Emilian Model."

19. Hart, "The Idea of the Economy," 158.

20. Stepick, "Miami's Two Informal Sectors"; Millman, "New Mex City"; Cornelius, "The Structural Embeddedness."

21. Granovetter, "Economic Action and Social Structure"; Granovetter, "The Nature of Economic Relationships."

22. Capecchi, "The Informal Economy"; Brusco, "The Emilian Model"; Sabel, "Changing Modes of Economic Efficiency."

23. Sabel, "Changing Modes of Economic Efficiency."

24. Capecchi, "The Informal Economy," 200–201.

25. Lomnitz, "Informal Exchange Networks", Altman, *A Reconstruction*.

26. Altman, *A Reconstruction*.

27. Roque, "Economia informal en Cuba"; Henken, "Condemned to Informality."

28. Roque, "Economia informal," 10–11.

29. Evans, "Predatory, Developmental, and Other Apparatuses," 582.

30. Buchanan, Tollison, and Tullock, *Toward a Theory of the Rent-Seeking Society*.

31. Evans, "Predatory."

32. Polanyi, *The Great Transformation*.

33. Adams, "Harnessing Technological Development."

34. Lomnitz, "Informal Exchange," 54.

35. Makaria, *Social and Political Dynamics*; Perez-Sainz, *Informalidad urbana*; Centeno and Portes, "The Informal Economy in the Shadow of the State."

36. Evans, "Predatory"; De Soto, *The Other Path*.

37. Standing, "The British Experiment."

38. Pahl, "Employment, Work."

39. Roberts, "The Other Working Class."

40. Rev, "The Advantages of Being Atomized"; Stark, "Bending the Bars"; Treml, "Purchases of Food."

41. Sassen, "New York"; Zhou, *New York's Chinatown*; Zhou and Bankston, "Entrepreneurship."

42. Molefsky, "America's Underground Economy," 25.

43. Gutmann, "Statistical Illusions," 22.

44. MacDonald, "Fiddly Jobs, Undeclared Working."

45. Mingione, "The Case of Greece"; Leonard, *The Informal Economy in Belfast.*

46. Gutmann, "Are the Unemployed Unemployed?" Greenfield, *Invisible, Outlawed, and Untaxed.*

47. Greenfield, *Invisible, Outlawed, and Untaxed*, 80–81.

48. Fernández-Kelly and Garcia, "Informalization in the Core"; Sassen and Smith, "Post-Industrial Growth and Economic Reorganization."

49. General Accounting Office, "Sweatshops in the United States."

50. Portes and Sassen, "Making It Underground."

51. McCrohan, Smith, and Adams, "Consumer Purchases in Informal Markets."

52. Gutmann, "The Subterranean Economy"; Gutmann, "Statistical Illusions"; Feige, "How Big Is the Irregular Economy?" Tanzi, *The Underground Economy.*

53. Feige, "Defining and Estimating," 997.

54. Feige, "Revised Estimates of the Underground Economy."

55. Karoleff et al., "Canada's Underground Economy"; Smith, "Assessing the Size," table 3.

56. Castells and Portes, "World Underneath"; Portes and Sassen, "Making It."

57. Porter and Bayer, "A Monetary Perspective"; Burton, "The Underground Economy in Britain"; Enste and Schneider, "Increasing Shadow Economies"; Centro de Estudios Economicos del Sector Privado (CEESP), *La economia subterranea.*

58. Feige, "Defining and Estimating," 993.

59. Rev, "The Advantages"; Stark, "Bending the Bars"; Burawoy and Lukacs, "Mythologies of Work."

60. Doan, "Class Differentiation"; McKeever, "Reproducing Inequality"; Meagher, "Crisis, Informalization"; Cheng and Gereffi, "The Informal Economy in East Asian Development"; Díaz, "Restructuring and the New Working Classes"; Makaria, *Social and Political Dynamics.*

61. Centeno and Portes, "The Informal Economy."

62. Portes and Walton, *Labor, Class*, chap. 2; Birbeck, "Garbage, Industry"; Cross, *Informal Politics*; Kempe, "Growth and Impact of the Subterranean Economy."

63. MacDonald, "Fiddly Jobs."

64. Lozano, *The Invisible Work Force.*

65. Brusco, "The Emilian Model"; Capecchi, "The Informal Economy"; Castells and Portes, "World Underneath."

Chapter Eight
Ethnic Enclaves and Middleman Minorities

1. This chapter draws on the following: Portes and Bach, *Latin Journey*, chap. 2; and Portes and Stepick, *City on the Edge.*

2. Light, "Asian Enterprise in America." Light and Gold, *Ethnic Economies.*

3. Portes and Stepick, *City on the Edge*, chap. 6; Díaz-Briquets, "Cuban-Owned Businesses in the United States."

4. Frazier, *The Negro in the United States*.

5. Portes and Bach, *Latin Journey*, chap. 2.

6. Ibid.

7. Goldscheider, *Jewish Continuity and Change*; Daniels, "The Japanese-American Experience."

8. Rischin, *The Promised City*.

9. Dinnerstein, "The East European Jewish Migration."

10. Rischin, *The Promised City*, chap. 6.

11. Ibid., 61.

12. Ibid., 67; Dinnerstein, "The East European Jewish Migration."

13. Dinnerstein, "The East European Jewish Migration"; Goldscheider, *Jewish Continuity and Change*; Sowell, *Ethnic America*, chap. 4.

14. Daniels, "The Japanese-American Experience."

15. Petersen, *Japanese Americans*, 16.

16. Cited in Daniels, "The Japanese-American Experience," 257.

17. Ibid., 251.

18. Light, *Ethnic Enterprise in America*, 9.

19. Petersen, *Japanese Americans*, 52.

20. Light, *Ethnic Enterprise in America*, 29.

21. Ibid., chap. 2; Petersen, *Japanese Americans*, 54.

22. Petersen, *Japanese Americans*, 54; Daniels, "The Japanese-American Experience."

23. Daniels, "The Japanese-American Experience"; Sowell, *Ethnic America*, chap. 7; Bonacich and Modell, *The Economic Basis of Ethnic Solidarity*, chaps, 7 and 15.

24. Light, *Ethnic Enterprise in America*; Light, "Disadvantaged Minorities in Self-Employment"; Portes and Sensenbrenner, "Embeddedness and Immigration."

25. Cited in Dinnerstein, "The East European Jewish Migration," 226.

26. Sowell, *Ethnic America*; Howe, *World of Our Fathers*. For a review of these theories see Bonacich and Sowell, *The Economic Basis of Ethnic Solidarity*, chap. 2.

27. Portes and Bach, *Latin Journey*, 40.

28. Ibid.; Light, "Immigrant and Ethnic Enterprise in America."

29. Light, "Immigrant and Ethnic Enterprise in America"; Portes and Sensenbrenner, "Embeddedness and Immigration."

30. Stack, *All Our Kin*; Fernández-Kelly, "Social and Cultural Capital in the Urban Ghetto"; Duneier, *Slim's Table*.

31. Bonacich and Modell, *The Economic Basis of Ethnic Solidarity*; Light, "Disadvantaged Minorities in Self-Employment"; Light and Gold, *Ethnic Economies*; Portes, "The Social Origins of the Cuban Enclave Economy."

32. Portes, "The Social Origins of the Cuban Enclave Economy"; Rischin, *The Promised City*; Light and Bonacich, *Immigrant Entrepreneurs*.

33. Perez, "Cuban Miami"; Pedraza, "Cuba's Exiles"; Portes and Stepick, *City on the Edge*, chap. 6.

34. Bailey and Waldinger, "Primary, Secondary, and Enclave Labor Markets."

35. Zhou, *New York's Chinatown*.

36. Rischin, *The Promised City*, 59; Howe, *World*.

37. Petersen, *Japanese Americans*, 14; Daniels, "The Japanese-American Experience."

38. This and the following stories are drawn from field interviews conducted in Miami in the late 1980s and early 1990s and related articles and reports. The names are real since each of these entrepreneurs has made his or her life and career experiences public. The stories have been previously published in Portes and Stepick, *City on the Edge*, 129–32.

39. Ibid.

40. Ibid.

41. This section is drawn from ibid., 132–35.

42. Field interview in Miami, February 7, 1989, in ibid., 133.

43. Field interview in Miami, January 14, 1987, in ibid.

44. Field interview in Hialeah, August 15, 1984, in ibid., 134.

45. Ibid., 134–35.

46. Ibid. Updated evidence of the evolution and consequences of the Cuban enclave of Miami is presented in the appendix.

47. This section is drawn from Portes and Stepick, *City on the Edge*, 137–40.

48. Geertz, *Peddlers and Princes*.

49. Portes and Sensenbrenner, "Embeddedness and Immigration."

50. Capecchi, "The Informal Economy and the Development of Flexible Specialization."

51. Zhou, *New York's Chinatown*; Light and Bonacich, *Immigrant Entrepreneurs*; Bonacich and Modell, *The Economic Basis of Ethnic Solidarity*; Portes and Guarnizo, "Tropical Capitalists."

52. Borjas, "The Self-Employment Experience of Immigrants"; Borjas, *Friends or Strangers*; Bates, "Self-Employed Minorities"; Bates and Dunham, "The Changing Nature of Business Ownership."

53. Recent empirical results on the Miami enclave experience are summarized in the appendix.

54. This section is partially drawn from Portes and Manning, "The Immigrant Enclave."

55. Bonacich, "A Theory of Middleman Minorities"; Granovetter, "The Economic Sociology of Firms and Entrepreneurs."

56. Howe, *World*; Dinnerstein, "The East European Jewish Migration."

57. Cobas, "Participation in the Ethnic Economy"; Boswell and Curtis, *The Cuban-American Experience*.

58. Kim, *New Urban Immigrants*; Min, "Factors Contributing to Ethnic Business"; Light, "Disadvantaged Minorities in Self-Employment."

59. Bobo and Johnson, "Racial Attitudes in a Prismatic Metropolis."

60. Weber, *The Theory of Social and Economic Organization*, part 4; Marx, *Capital*, vol. 3, chaps. 51, 52.

61. Bourdieu, "Le capital social"; "Les trois états du capital cultural."

62. This material is a summary of Portes and Shafer, "Revisiting the Enclave Hypothesis."

63. For a full account of the Mariel exodus and its aftermath, see Portes and Stepick, *City on the Edge*. For effects of the Mariel exodus on the educational attainment of the Cuban second generation, see Portes and Rumbaut, *Legacies*, chap. 9.

64. This was the dismissive label applied to the arrivals during the exodus. See Camayd-Freixas, *Crisis in Miami*.

65. For a rationale and justification for using real rather than logged dollars in income regressions, see Portes and Zhou, "Self-Employment and the Earnings of Immigrants." See also Hodson, "Some Consideration concerning the Functional Form of Earnings."

CHAPTER NINE
Transnational Communities

1. This chapter is based on the following prior publications: Portes, Haller, and Guarnizo, "Transnational Entrepreneurs"; Portes, Escobar, and Walton Radford, "Immigrant Transnational Organizations and Development."

2. In modern sociology, the pioneer of this idea was Immanuel Wallerstein. See Wallerstein, *The Modern World-System*, vol. 1; Wallerstein, *Geopolitics and Geoculture*. Another influential contributor to this literature was Saskia Sassen. See Sassen, *The Mobility of Labor and Capital*; Sassen, *The Global City*.

3. Smith and Guarnizo, *Transnationalism from Below*; Portes, "Global Villagers"; Vertovec, "Migrant Transnationalism and Modes of Transformation."

4. Basch, Glick-Schiller, and Blanc-Szanton, *Nations Unbound*; Levitt and Glick-Schiller, "Conceptualizing Simultaneity."

5. Portes, Guarnizo, and Landolt, "Transnational Communities"; Portes, "Global Villagers."

6. Gordon, *Assimilation in American Life*; Alba and Nee, *Remaking the American Mainstream*; Waldinger and Fitzgerald, "Transnationalism in Question."

7. Guarnizo, Portes, and Haller, "Assimilation and Transnationalism"; Levitt, "Transnational Migration"; Portes, Escobar, and Arana, "Bridging the Gap."

8. Bourne, "Transnational America."

9. Guarnizo and Smith, "The Locations of Transnationalism."

10. Evans, "Fighting Marginalization."

11. Basch et al., *Nations Unbound*; Glick-Schiller and Basch, "Towards a Transnationalization of Migration."

12. Foner, "What's New about Transnationalism?" Waldinger and Fitzgerald, "Transnationalism in Question."

13. Glazer, "Ethnic Groups in America"; Kivisto, "Theorizing Transnational Migration."

14. Granovetter, "The Economic Sociology of Firms and Entrepreneurs"; Zhou, "Revising Ethnic Entrepreneurship"; Geertz, *Peddlers and Princes*.

15. In Merton, *Social Theory and Social Structure*, 13.

16. Ibid., 12.

17. Portes, "Theoretical Convergencies"; Smith, "Diasporic Memberships."

18. Ramos, "Rapporteur's Comments."

19. On this point, see the detailed studies of transnational communities by Smith, Levitt, Landolt, and Kyle among others. Smith, *Mexican New York*; Levitt, *The Transnational Villagers*; Landolt, *The Causes and Consequences of Transnational Migration*; Kyle, *Transnational Peasants*.

20. Guarnizo, Portes, and Haller, "Assimilation and Transnationalism"; Itzigsohn and Saucido, "Immigrant Incorporation."

21. Smith, *Mexican New York*; Landolt, "Salvadoran Economic Transnationalism"; Levitt, *The Transnational Villagers*.

22. Portes, "Theoretical Convergencies"; Menjivar, *Fragmented Ties*; Margolis, *Little Brazil*.

23. Guarnizo, "The Economics of Transnational Living."

24. Ibid.; Vertovec, "Migrant Transnationalism"; Portes, "The Debates and Significance."

25. Portes, Haller, and Guarnizo, "Transnational Entrepreneurs."

26. Zhou, *New York's Chinatown*; Kim, *New Urban Migrants*; Light and Bonacich, *Immigrant Entrepreneurs*.

27. Portes, Escobar, and Arana, "Bridging the Gap."

28. Rosenblum, *Immigrant Workers*; Dahl, *Who Governs?*; Glazer and Moynihan, *Beyond the Melting Pot*.

29. Granovetter, "Economic Action and Social Structure"; Granovetter, "The Nature of Economic Relationships."

30. Menjivar, *Fragmented Ties*; Guarnizo, Sanchez, and Roach, "Mistrust, Fragmented Solidarity."

31. Stark, "Migration Decision Making"; Massey and Garcia España, "The Social Process of International Migration"; Lungo and Kandel, *Transformando El Salvador*.

32. Lungo and Kandel, *Transformando El Salvador*; Delgado-Wise and Cypher, "The Strategic Role of Mexican Labor"; Guarnizo and Díaz, "Transnational Migration."

33. Massey, "Understanding Mexican Migration"; Pessar and Grasmuck, *Between Two Islands*; Repak, *Waiting on Washington*.

34. Delgado-Wise and Cypher, "The Strategic Role"; Delgado-Wise and Covarrubias, "The Mexico-United States Migratory System."

35. Delgado-Wise and Covarrubias, "The Mexico-United States Migratory System."

36. Landolt, Autler, and Baires, "From 'Hermano Lejano' to 'Hermano Mayor.'"

37. Goldring, "The Mexican State and Transmigrant Organizations"; Itzigsohn and Saucido, "Immigrant Incorporation"; Ostergaard-Nielsen, "Transnational Practices."

38. Portes, Haller, and Guarnizo, "Transnational Entrepreneurs"; Zhou, "Revisiting Ethnic Entrepreneurship."

39. Portes, Escobar, and Walton Radford, "Immigrant Transnational Organizations and Development"; Goldring, "The Mexican State and Immigrant Transnational Organizations"; González Gutiérrez, "Fostering Identities."

40. González Gutiérrez, "Fostering Identities."

41. Portes, Haller, and Guarnizo, "Transnational Entrepreneurs"; Grasmuck and Pessar, *Between Two Islands*; Guarnizo, "Los 'Dominican Yorkers' "; Landolt, *The Causes and Consequences of Transnational Migration*.

42. Landolt, *The Causes and Consequences of Transnational Migration*; Landolt, "Salvadoran Economic Transnationalism."

43. Landolt, Autler, and Baires, "From 'Hermano Lejano' to 'Hermano Mayor,' " 299.

44. Itzigsohn, Dore Cabral, Hernández, and Vázquez, "Mapping Dominican Transnationalism."

45. Ibid.; Portes and Guarnizo, "Tropical Capitalists."

46. Kyle, *The Transnational Peasant*.

47. Ibid.

48. Ibid.; Portes and Sensenbrenner, "Embeddedness and Immigration."

49. Marqués, Santos, and Araújo, "Ariadne's Thread."

50. Ibid.

51. Alba and Nee, *Remaking the American Mainstream*; Gordon, *Assimilation*.

52. Portes and Jensen, "The Enclave and the Entrants"; Zhou, "Revisiting Ethnic Entrepreneurship"; Light, *Ethnic Enterprise*.

53. Portes, Guarnizo, and Haller, "Transnational Entrepreneurs."

54. In other model specifications, we substituted U.S. citizenship acquisition for years of U.S. residence. The two variables cannot be added simultaneously because of collinearity. The direction of effects is the same as those observed here, with U.S. naturalization increasing the probability of transnationalism by 10 percent after controlling for other variables.

55. Guarnizo and Díaz, "Transnational Migration"; Landolt, *The Causes and Consequences*.

56. Light and Bonacich, *Immigrant Entrepreneurs*; Light, *Ethnic Enterprise in America*; Zhou, "Revisiting Ethnic Entrepreneurship"; Portes and Zhou, "Entrepreneurship and Economic Progress."

CHAPTER TEN
Markets, Models, and Regulation

1. Portes and Smith, "Institutions and Development in Latin America."
2. Cited in Swedberg, *Principles of Economic Sociology*, 37.
3. Polanyi, "Our Obsolete Market Mentality," 70.
4. Ibid.; Polanyi, "The Economy as Instituted Process."
5. Velasco, "Servicio de Administración Tributaria de México."
6. Goldschied, "A Sociological Approach to Problems of Public Finance."
7. Velasco, "Servicio de Administración"; Guzmán, "Recaudación y desarrollo"; Furtado, *Obstacles to Development in Latin America*.
8. Balassa et al., *Toward Renewed Economic Growth*; Williamson, *The Political Economy of Policy Reform*.
9. Guzmán, "Recaudación y desarrollo," 11.
10. Ibid., 17.
11. Ibid., 38.
12. Wormald and Cardenas, "Formación y desarrollo del servicio de impuestos internos," 13.
13. Ibid.
14. Ibid., 12–13.
15. Abraham Waissbluth, "La reforma del estado en Chile," cited in ibid.
16. Ibid., 3.
17. Velasco, "Servicio de Administración Tributaria en Mexico"; Roig, "La dirección general impositiva de la Argentina"; Rodríguez Garavito and Rodríguez Blanco, "Entre el clientelismo y la modernización."
18. Elusion refers to the practice of hiring experts to find loopholes in the tax laws so as to legally bypass, avoid, or lighten the fiscal burden. See Roig, "La dirección general impositiva"; Guzmán, "Recaudación y desarrollo."
19. Wormald and Cardenas, "Formación y desarrollo."
20. Merton, "The Self-Fulfilling Prophecy."
21. Ibid., 195.
22. Ibid.
23. Durkheim, *Rules of the Sociological Method*, 24, cited in Swedberg, *Principles*, 20.
24. MacKenzie, *An Engine, Not a Camera*, 5. I am indebted to Viviana Zelizer for bringing the literature on performativity to my attention.
25. Friedman, "The Methodology of Positive Economics," 35, cited in MacKenzie, *An Engine*, 11.
26. Callon, "The Embeddedness of Economic Markets," 2.
27. MacKenzie, *An Engine*, 258.
28. Friedman, "The Methodology," 14, cited in MacKenzie, *An Engine*, 9–10.
29. Ibid., 275.

30. Jacobson, "Risk in the Mortgage Industry"; Crooks, "A Prophet Reborn." Alan Greenspan's mea culpa before Congressman Waxman's Sub-Committee confessing that he had "found a flaw" in his free market is one of the most intellectually poignant moments of this crisis.

31. Merton, *Social Theory and Social Structure*, 477; Merton, "The Unanticipated Consequences."

32. Dahrendorf, *Class and Class Conflict*; Gouldner, *The Two Marxisms*; Portes, "The Resilient Significance of Class."

33. Heilbronner, *The Worldly Philosophers*, chap. 9.

34. Jacobson, "Risk in the Mortgage Industry"; Wadhwani, "How Efficient Market Theories."

35. Cerrutti and Grimson, "Neoliberalismo y después"; MacLeod, *Downsizing the State*; Portes, "Neoliberalism and the Sociology of Development."

36. "Invisible Elbow."

37. Cerrutti and Grimson, "Neoliberalismo y después."

38. Rodríguez Garavito, "De Club de Caballeros a Foro Electronico."

39. Wormald and Brieba, "La Bolsa de Comercio de Santiago de Chile."

40. These were Chilean economists trained under Milton Friedman at the University of Chicago. They formed part of a student group sponsored by the U.S. Agency for International Development and U.S. Embassy. Back in Chile, they duly proceeded to put into practice the ideas of their mentor, restructuring the Chilean economy. See also MacKenzie, *An Engine, Not a Camera*, 16.

41. Wormald and Brieba, "La Bolsa de Comercio," 44.

42. Ibid., 17.

43. Ibid.

44. Ibid., 23.

45. Rodríguez Garavito, "De Club de Caballeros," 20.

46. The point is developed at greater length in Portes, Light, and Fernández-Kelly, "Immigration and the Health System."

Bibliography

Abolafia, Mitchell. *Making Markets: Opportunities and Restraint on Wall Street.* Cambridge, MA: Harvard University Press, 1996.

Adams, Richard N. "Harnessing Technological Development." In *Rethinking Modernization: Anthropological Perspectives*, edited by J. Poggie and R. Lynch, 37–68. Westport, CT: Greenwood Press, 1975.

Alarcón, Rafael. "Recruitment Processes among Foreign-Born Engineers and Scientists in Silicon Valley." *American Behavioral Scientist* 42 (June/July 1999): 1381–97.

Alba, Richard, and Victor Nee. *Remaking the American Mainstream: Assimilation and Contemporary Immigration.* Cambridge, MA: Harvard University Press, 2003.

Aluman, Jonathan. "A Reconstruction Using Anthropological Methods of the Second Economy of Soviet Georgia." PhD diss., Enfield, England, Middlesex Polytechnic Institute, 1983.

Ariza, Marina, and Juan Manuel Ramirez. "Urbanización, mercados de trabajo y escenarios sociales en el México finisecular." In *Las ciudades latinoamericanas a comienzos del siglo*, edited by A. Portes, B. R. Roberts, and A. Grimson. Buenos Aires: Prometeo Editores, 2005.

Arriagada, Irma, and Lorena Godoy. "Prevention or Repression? The False Dilemma of Citizen Security." *CEPAL Review* 70 (April 2000): 111–36.

Arrighi, Giovanni. *The Long Twentieth Century: Money, Power, and the Origins of Our Times.* London: Verso Books, 1994.

Bailey, Thomas, and Roger Waldinger. "Primary, Secondary, and Enclave Labor Markets: A Training System Approach." *American Sociological Review* 56 (1991): 432–45.

Baiocchi, Gianpaolo. *Radicals in Power: The Workers Party and Experiments in Urban Democracy in Brazil.* London: Zed, 2003.

Balassa, Bela, Gerardo M. Bueno, Pedro-Pablo Kuczynski, and Mario H. Simonsen. *Toward Renewed Economic Growth in Latin America.* Washington, DC: Institute for International Economics, 1986.

Basch, Linda G., Nina Glick-Schiller, and Cristina Blanc-Szanton. *Nations Unbound: Transnational Projects, Post-Colonial Predicaments, and De-Territorialized Nation-States.* Langhorne, PA: Gordon and Breach, 1994.

Bates, Timothy. "Self-Employed Minorities: Traits and Trends." *Social Science Quarterly* 68 (1987): 539–51.

Bates, Timothy, and Constance Dunham. "The Changing Nature of Business Ownership at a Route to Upward Mobility of Minorities." Presented at the

Conference on Urban Labor Markets and Labor Mobility, Sponsored by the Urban Institute, March 7–8, Arlie House, VA, 1991.

Bendix, Reinhard. *Max Weber, an Intellectual Portrait*. Garden City, NY: Anchor Books, 1962.

Beneria, Lourdes. "Subcontracting and Employment Dynamics in Mexico City." In *The Informal Economy: Studies in Advanced and Less Developed Countries*, edited by A. Portes, M. Castells, and L. A. Benton, 173–88. Baltimore: Johns Hopkins University Press, 1989.

Benton, Lauren. "Industrial Subcontracting and the Informal Sector: The Politics of Restructuring in the Madrid Electronics Industry." In *The Informal Economy: Studies in Advanced and Less Developed Countries*, edited by A. Portes, M. Castells, and L. A. Benton, 228–44. Baltimore: Johns Hopkins University Press, 1989.

Birbeck, Chris. "Garbage, Industry, and the 'Vultures' of Cali, Colombia." In *Casual Work and Poverty in Third World Cities*, edited by R. Bromley and C. Gerry, 161–83. New York: John Wiley, 1979.

Blanes Jimenez, Jose. "Cocaine, Informality, and the Urban Economy in La Paz, Bolivia." In *The Informal Economy: Studies in Advanced and Less Developed Countries*, edited by A. Portes, M. Castells, and L. A. Benton, 135–49. Baltimore: Johns Hopkins University Press, 1989.

Blau, Joel. *Illusions of Prosperity: America's Working Families in an Age of Economic Insecurity*. New York: Oxford University Press, 1999.

Blau, Peter M. *Exchange and Power in Social Life*. New York: Wiley, 1964.

Block, Fred. "Introduction." In K. Polanyi, *The Great Transformation*. Boston: Beacon Press, 2000.

———. *Postindustrial Possibilities: A Critique of Economic Discourse*. Berkeley: University of California Press, 1990.

———. "The Roles of the State in Economy." In *The Handbook of Economic Sociology*, edited by N. J. Smelser and R. Swedberg, 691–710. New York: Russell Sage Foundation; Princeton, NJ: Princeton University Press, 1994.

Bluestone, Barry, and Bennett Harrison. *The Deindustrialization of America*. New York: John Wiley, 1982.

Bobo, Lawrence D., and Devon Johnson. "Racial Attitudes in a Prismatic Metropolis." In *Prismatic Metropolis: Inequality in Los Angeles*, edited by L. D. Bobo, M. L. Oliver, and J. H. Johnson, 1–163. New York: Russell Sage Foundation, 2000.

Boissevain, Jeremy. *Friends of Friends, Networks, Manipulators, and Coalitions*. New York: St. Martin's Press, 1974.

Bonacich, Edna. "Advanced Capitalism and Black-White Relations: A Split Labor Market Interpretation." *American Sociological Review* 41 (1976): 34–51.

———. "A Theory of Middleman Minorities." *American Sociological Review* 38 (1973): 583–94.

Bonacich, Edna, and John Modell. *The Economic Basis of Ethnic Solidarity: Small Business in the Japanese-American Community.* Berkeley: University of California Press, 1980.

Borjas, George J. *Friends or Strangers: The Impact of Immigrants on the U.S. Economy.* New York: Basic Books, 1990.

———. "The Self-Employment Experience of Immigrants." *Journal of Human Resources* 21 (1986): 485–506.

Boswell, Terry E. "A Split Labor Market Analysis of Discrimination against Chinese Immigrants, 1850–1882." *American Sociological Review* 51 (1986): 352–71.

Boswell, Thomas D., and James R. Curtis. *The Cuban-American Experience.* Totowa, NJ: Rowman & Allanheld, 1984.

Bourdieu, Pierre. "Le capital social: Notes provisoires." *Actes de la Recherche en Sciences Sociales* 31 (1980): 2–3.

———. *Distinction, A Social Critique of the Judgment of Taste.* Translated by R. Nice. 1970. Reprint, Cambridge, MA: Harvard University Press, 1984.

———. "The Forms of Capital." In *Handbook of Theory and Research for the Sociology of Education,* edited by J. G. Richardson, 241–58. New York: Greenwood Press, 1985.

———. "Les trois états du capital culturel." *Actes de la Recherche en Sciences Sociales* 30 (1979): 3–6.

Bourgois, Phillippe I. *In Search of Respect: Selling Crack in El Barrio.* Cambridge: Cambridge University Press, 1995.

Bourne, Randolph S. "Transnational America." *Atlantic Monthly* (July 1916): 86–97.

Brusco, Sebastiano. "The Emilian Model: Productive Decentralization and Social Integration." *Cambridge Journal of Economics* 6, no. 2 (1982): 167–84.

Buchanan, James M., Robert D. Tollison, and Gordon Tullock. *Toward a Theory of the Rent-Seeking Society.* College Station: Texas A&M University Press, 1980.

Burawoy, Michael. "Contemporary Currents in Marxist Theory." *American Sociologist* 13 (1978): 50–64.

Burawoy, Michael, and Janos Lukacs. "Mythologies of Work: A Comparison of Firms in State Socialism and Advanced Capitalism." *American Sociological Review* 50 (1985): 723–37.

Burt, Ronald S. *Structural Holes; The Social Structure of Competition.* Cambridge, MA: Harvard University Press, 1992.

Burton, John. "The Underground Economy in Britain." In *The Underground Economy: Global Evidence of Its Size and Impact,* edited by O. Lippert and M. Walker, 209–15. Vancouver, Canada: The Fraser Institute, 1997.

Butcher, Kristin F. "An Investigation of the Effect of Immigration on the Labor Market Outcomes of African-Americans." In *Help or Hindrance? The Economic Implications of Immigration for African-Americans,* edited by D. S. Hamermesh and F. D. Bean, 149–81. New York: Russell Sage Foundation, 1998.

Callon, Michel. *The Laws of the Market*. Oxford: Blackwell, 1998.

Camayd-Freixas, Yohel. *Crisis in Miami: Community Context and Institutional Response in the Adaptation of Mariel Cubans and Undocumented Haitian Entrants in South Florida*. Commissioned report. Boston Urban Research and Development, 1988.

Campbell, John L. *Institutional Change and Globalization*. Princeton, NJ: Princeton University Press, 2004.

Campbell, John L., and Leon N. Lindberg. "Property Rights and the Organization of Economic Activity by the State." *American Sociological Review* 55 (1990): 634–47.

Capecchi, Vittorio. "The Informal Economy and the Development of Flexible Specialization." In *The Informal Economy: Studies in Advanced and Less Developed Countries*, edited by A. Portes, M. Castells, and L. A. Benton, 189–215. Baltimore: Johns Hopkins University Press, 1989.

Carchedi, G. *On the Economic Identification of Social Classes*. London: Routledge and Kegan Paul, 1977.

Castells, Manuel. *End of Millennium: The Information Age*. Oxford: Blackwell Publishers, 1998.

———. *The Internet Galaxy*. New York: Oxford University Press, 2001.

Castells, Manuel, and Roberto Laserna. "The New Dependency: Technological Change and Socio-Economic Restructuring in Latin America." *Sociological Forum* 4 (1989): 535–60.

Castells, Manuel, and Alejandro Portes. "World Underneath: The Origins, Dynamics, and Effects of the Informal Economy." In *The Informal Economy: Studies in Advanced and Less Developed Countries*, edited by A. Portes, M. Castells, and L. A. Benton, 11–37. Baltimore: Johns Hopkins University Press, 1989.

Centeno, Miguel Ángel. *Democracy within Reason: Technocratic Revolution in Mexico*. University Park: Pennsylvania State University Press, 1994.

Centeno, Miguel Ángel, and Alejandro Portes. "The Informal Economy in the Shadow of the State." In *Out of the Shadows: Political Action and the Informal Economy in Latin America*, edited by P. Fernández-Kelly and J. Shefner, 23–48. University Park: Pennsylvania State University Press, 2006.

Centro de Estudios Económicos del Sector Privado (CEESP). *La economía subterránea en México*. Mexico City: Editorial Diana, 1987.

Cerrutti, Marcela. "Report on Argentina." Final report for the project "Latin American Urbanization in the Late Twentieth Century," delivered at the final project conference, Montevideo, Uruguay, August 2003.

Cerrutti, Marcela, and Alejandro Grimson. "Buenos Aires: Neoliberalismo y después." In *Ciudades latinoamericanas: Un análisis comparativo en el umbral del nuevo siglo*, edited by A. Portes, B. R. Roberts, and A. Grimson, 75–147. Buenos Aires: Prometeo Libros, 2005.

Chavez, Leo R. "Settlers and Sojourners: The Case of Mexicans in the United States." *Human Organization* 47 (1988): 95–108.

Cheng, Lu-lin, and Gary Gereffi. "The Informal Economy in East Asian Development." *International Journal of Urban and Regional Research* 18 (1994): 194–219.

Clark, Terry N., and Seymour M. Lipset. "Are Social Classes Dying?" *International Sociology* 6 (December 1991): 397–410.

Cobas, José. "Participation in the Ethnic Economy, Ethnic Solidarity, and Ambivalence toward the Host Society: The Case of Cuban Émigrés in Puerto Rico." Presented at the American Sociological Association, San Antonio, 1984.

Coleman, James. "The Design of Organizations and the Right to Act." *Sociological Forum* 8 (1993): 527–46.

———. *Foundations of Social Theory.* Cambridge, MA: The Belknap Press of Harvard University Press, 1990.

———. "A Rational Choice Perspective on Economic Sociology." In *Handbook of Economic Sociology,* edited by N. J. Smelser and R. Swedberg, 166–80. New York: Russell Sage Foundation; Princeton, NJ: Princeton University Press, 1994.

———. "The Rational Reconstruction of Society." *American Sociological Review* 58 (1993): 1–15.

———. "Social Capital in the Creation of Human Capital." *American Journal of Sociology* 94 (Supplement) (1988): S95–121.

Collins, Randall. "Prediction in Macrosociology: The Case of the Soviet Collapse." *American Journal of Sociology* 100 (May 1995): 1552–93.

Congressional Budget Office. *Economic Growth and Immigration: Bridging the Demographic Divide.* Report Summary (November 15), Washington, DC: U.S. Congress, 2005.

Cooley, Charles H. *Human Nature and the Social Order.* New York: Charles Scribners and Sons, 1902.

Cornelius, Wayne A. "The Structural Embeddedness of Demand for Mexican Immigrant Labor: New Evidence from California." In *Crossings, Mexican Immigration in Interdisciplinary Perspectives,* edited by Marcelo M. Suárez-Orozco, 115–55. Cambridge, MA: Center for Latin American Studies, Harvard University, 1998.

Coser, Lewis. *The Functions of Social Conflict.* New York: Free Press, 1956.

Cottrell, Leonard S. "Roles and Marital Adjustment." *Publications of the American Sociological Society* 28 (1933).

Crooks, Ed. "A Prophet Reborn." *Financial Times,* October 19, 2008.

Cross, John C. *Informal Politics: Street Vendors and the State in Mexico City.* Stanford, CA: Stanford University Press, 1998.

Cutler, Anthony, Barry Hindess, Paul Hirst, and Athar Hussain. *Marx's Capital and Capitalism Today.* Vol. 1. London: Routledge and Kegan Paul, 1977.

Dahl, Robert A. *Who Governs? Democracy and Power in the American City.* New Haven, CT: Yale University Press, 1961.

Dahrendorf, Ralf. *Class and Class Conflict in Industrial Society.* Stanford, CA: Stanford University Press, 1959.

Dalton, Melville. *Men Who Manage: Fusions of Feeling and Theory in Administration.* New York: Wiley, 1959.

Daniels, Roger. "The Japanese-American Experience, 1890–1940." In *Uncertain Americans: Readings in Ethnic History,* edited by Leonard Dinnerstein and Frederic C. Jaher, 250–76. New York: Oxford University Press, 1977.

Davis, Kingsley, and Wilbert M. Moore. "Some Principles of Stratification." *American Sociological Review* 10 (1945): 242–49.

De Janvry, Alain, and Carlos Garramón. "Laws of Motion of Capital in the Center-Periphery Structure." *Review of Radical Political Economics* 9 (Summer 1977): 29–38.

De Roux, Gustavo. "Ciudad y violencia en América Latina." Paper presented to the first Latin American and Caribbean Conference on Violence and the City, Cali, Colombia, December 1993.

De Soto, Hernando. *The Other Path.* New York: Harper and Row, 1989.

Delgado Wise, Raúl. "The Relation between Mexico-U.S. Economic Integration and International Migration under NAFTA." Paper presented at the CUMBRE 2005 Conference, Office of Latino and Latin American Studies, University of Nebraska–Omaha, April 22, 2005.

Delgado Wise, Raúl, and Humberto Márquez Covarrubias. *The Reshaping of Mexican Labor Exports under NAFTA: Paradoxes and Challenges.* Zacatecas, Mexico: University of Zacatecas, International Network of Migration and Development, 2006.

Delgado Wise, Raúl, and James M. Cypher. "The Strategic Role of Mexican Labor under NAFTA: Critical Perspectives on Current Economic Integration." *Annals of the American Academy of Political and Social Sciences* 610 (March 2007): 120–42.

Díaz, Alvaro. "Chile: Hacia el pos-neoliberalismo?" Paper presented at the Conference on Responses of Civil Society to Neo-Liberal Adjustment. Department of Sociology, University of Texas at Austin, April 1996.

———. "Restructuring and the New Working Classes in Chile: Trends in Waged Employment and Informality." Working Paper #DP47, United Nations Research Institute for Social Development, October 1993.

Díaz-Briquets, Sergio. "Cuban-Owned Business in the United States." *Cuban Studies* 14 (1985): 57–64.

DiMaggio, Paul. "Cultural Aspects of Economic Action and Organization." In *Beyond the Marketplace,* edited by R. Friedlander and A. F. Robertson, 113–36. New York: Aldine de Gruyter, 1990.

DiMaggio, Paul, and Hugh Louch. "Socially Embedded Consumer Transactions: For What Kind of Purchases Do People Most Often Use Networks?" *American Sociological Review* 63 (October 1998): 619–37.

DiMaggio, Paul, and Walter W. Powell. "The Iron Case Revisited: Institutional Isomorphism and Collective Rationality in Organizational Fields." *American Sociological Review* 48 (April 1983): 147–60.

Dinnerstein, Leonard. "The East European Jewish Migration." In *Uncertain Americans: Readings in Ethnic History*, edited by L. Dinnerstein and F. C. Jaher, 216–31. New York: Oxford University Press 1977.

Doan, Rebecca. "Class Differentiation and the Informal Sector in Amman, Jordan." *International Journal of Middle East Studies* 24 (February 1992): 27–38.

Dobb, Maurice *Studies in the Development of Capitalism*. 1947. Reprint, New York: International Publishers, 1963.

Dolsak, Nines, and Elinor Ostrom. *The Commons in the New Millennium: Challenges and Adaptation*. Cambridge, MA: MIT Press, 2003.

Domhoff, G. William. *Who Rules America Now?* Englewood Cliffs, NJ: Prentice-Hall, 1983.

Duneier, Mitchell. *Slim's Table: Race, Respectability, and Masculinity*. Chicago: University of Chicago Press, 1992.

Durkheim, Émile. *The Division of Labor in Society*. 1893. Reprint, New York: Free Press, 1984.

———. *The Rules of the Sociological Method*. 1903. Reprint, New York: Free Press, 1982.

———. *Suicide: A Study in Sociology*. Translated by J. A. Spaulding and G. Simpson. 1897. Reprint, New York: Free Press, 1965.

Economic Commission for Latin America and the Caribbean (ECLAC). "Agenda social: Seguridad ciudadana y violencia." In *Panorama social de América Latina*, 205–40. Santiago, Chile: ECLAC, 2001.

———. *Social Panorama of Latin America, 1999–2000*. Annual Report, Santiago, Chile: ECLAC, 2000.

Edin, Kathryn, and Laura Lien. "Work, Welfare, and Single Mothers' Survival Strategies." *American Sociological Review* 62 (1997): 253–66.

Edwards, Richard. *Labor Market Segmentation*. Lexington, MA: D. C. Health, 1975.

Elster, Jon, Claus Offe, and Ulrick K. Preuss. *Institutional Design in Post-Communist Societies: Rebuilding the Ship at Sea*. Cambridge: Cambridge University Press, 1998.

Emmanuel, Arghiri. *Unequal Exchange: A Study of the Imperialism of Trade*. London: New Left Books, 1972.

Enste, Dominik, and Friedrich Schneider. "Increasing Shadow Economies All Over the World—Fiction or Reality?" Discussion Paper #26, Institute for the Study of Labor, Bonn, Germany, 1998.

Espenshade, Thomas J., and Germán Rodriguez. "Completing the Ph.D.: Comparative Performance of U.S. and Foreign Students." *Social Science Quarterly* 78 (June 1997): 593–605.

Evans, David S., and Linda S. Leighton. "Some Empirical Aspects of Entrepreneurship." *American Economic Review* 79 (June 1989): 519–35.

Evans, Peter. "The Challenges of the 'Institutional Turn': Interdisciplinary Opportunities in Development Theory." In *The Economic Sociology of Capitalist*

Institutions, edited by V. Nee and R. Swedberg, 90–116. Princeton, NJ: Princeton University Press, 2004.

———. *Dependent Development: The Alliance of Multinational, State, and Local Capital in Brazil*. Princeton, NJ: Princeton University Press, 1979.

———. "Development as Institutional Change: The Pitfalls of Monocropping and the Potentials of Deliberation." *Studies in Comparative International Development* 38 (Winter 2004): 30–52.

———. *Embedded Autonomy: States and Industrial Transformation*. Princeton, NJ: Princeton University Press, 1995.

———. "Fighting Marginalization with Transnational Networks: Counter-Hegemonic Globalization." *Contemporary Sociology* 29 (2000): 230–41.

———. "Predatory, Developmental, and Other Apparatuses: A Comparative Political Economy Perspective on the Third World State." *Sociological Forum* 4 (1989): 561–87.

Feige, Edgar L. "Defining and Estimating Underground and Informal Economies: The New Institutional Economics Approach." *World Development* 18, no. 7 (1990): 989–1002.

———. "How Big Is the Irregular Economy?" *Challenge* 22 (1979): 5–13.

———. "Revised Estimates of the Underground Economy: Implications of U.S. Currency Held Abroad." In *The Underground Economy: Global Evidence of Its Size and Impact*, edited by O. Lippert and M. Walker, 151–208. Vancouver, Canada: The Fraser Institute, 1997.

Fernández-Kelly, M. Patricia. *For We Are Sold, I and My People: Women and Industry in Mexico's Frontier*. Albany: State University of New York Press, 1983.

———. "Social and Cultural Capital in the Urban Ghetto: Implications for the Economic Sociology of Immigration." In *The Economic Sociology of Immigration: Essays in Network, Ethnicity, and Entrepreneurship*, edited by Alejandro Portes, 213–47. New York: Russell Sage Foundation, 1995.

Fernández-Kelly, M. Patricia, and Anna M. Garcia. "Informalization at the Core: Hispanic Women, Homework, and the Advanced Capitalist State." In *The Informal Economy: Studies in Advanced and Less Developed Countries*, edited by Alejandro Portes, M. Castells, and L. A. Benton, 247–64. Baltimore: Johns Hopkins University Press, 1989.

Fernández-Kelly, M. Patricia, and Lisa Konczal. "'Murdering the Alphabet': Identity and Entrepreneurship among Second Generation Cubans, West Indians, and Central Americans." *Ethnic and Racial Studies* 28 (November 2005): 1153–81.

Firebaugh, Glenn. "Empirics of World Income Inequality." *American Journal of Sociology* 104 (May 1999): 1597–630.

Fligstein, Neil. "States, Markets, and Economic Growth." In *The Economic Sociology of Capitalism*, edited by V. Nee and R. Swedberg, 119–43. Princeton, NJ: Princeton University Press, 2006.

Foner, Nancy. "What's New about Transnationalism? New York Immigrants To-day and at the Turn of the Century." *Diaspora* 6 (1997): 355–75.

Frank, Robert H. "Rethinking Rational Choice." In *Beyond the Marketplace: Rethinking Economy and Society*, edited by R. Friedland and A. F. Robertson, 53–87. New York: Aldine de Gruyter, 1990.

Frazier, E. Franklin. *The Negro in the United States.* New York: Macmillan, 1949.

Freeman, Richard. *America Works: The Exceptional U.S. Labor Market.* New York: Russell Sage Foundation, 2007.

Frey, William H., and Kao-Lee Liaw. "The Impact of Recent Immigration on Population Distribution in the United States." In *The Immigration Debate*, edited by J. P. Smith and B. Edmonston, 338–448. Washington, DC: National Academy Press, 1998.

Fundación Paz Ciudadana. "Delincuencia y opinión publica." Report. Santiago, Chile: Centro de Documentación Pas Ciudadana, 1998.

Furtado, Celso. *Obstacles to Development in Latin America.* New York: Monthly Review Press, 1970.

Galbraith, James K. "A Perfect Crime: Global Inequality." *Daedalus* 131 (Winter 2002): 11–25.

Garcia, Norberto. *Restructuración, ahorro, y mercado de trabajo.* Santiago, Chile: PREALC, 1991.

Gaviria, Alejandro, and Carmen Pagés. "Patterns of Crime Victimization in Latin America." Working Paper #408, Inter-American Development Bank, Washington, DC, October 29, 1999.

Geertz, Clifford. *Peddlers and Princes.* Chicago: University of Chicago Press, 1963.

General Accounting Office. "Sweatshops in the United States: Opinions on Their Extent and Possible Enforcement Options." Briefing Report HRD-89-101 BR. Washington DC: U.S. Government Printing Office, 1989.

Gereffi, Gary. "International Trade and Industrial Upgrading in the Apparel Commodity Chain." *Journal of International Economics* 48 (1999): 37–70.

Giddens, Anthony. *Las nuevas reglas del método sociológico.* Buenos Aires: Amorrortu, 1987.

Glazer, Nathan. "Ethnic Groups in America." In *Freedom and Control in Modern Society*, edited by T. A. M. Berger, and C. Page, 158–73. New York: Van Nostrand, 1954.

Glazer, Nathan, and Daniel P. Moynihan. *Beyond the Melting Pot: The Negroes, Puerto Ricans, Jews, Italians, and Irish and New York City.* Cambridge, MA: MIT Press, 1970.

Glick-Schiller, Nina, and Linda Basch. "Towards a Transnationalization of Migration: Race, Class, Ethnicity, and Nationalism Reconsidered." *Annals of the New York Academy of Sciences* (1992): 645.

Goffman, Erving. *Encounters: Two Studies in the Sociology of Interaction.* Indianapolis: Bobbs-Merrill, 1961.

———. *The Presentation of Self in Everyday Life*. Garden City, NY: Doubleday, 1959.

Gold, Steven J. "Gender and Social Capital among Israeli Immigrants in Los Angeles." *Diaspora* 4 (1995): 267–301.

Goldring, Luin. "The Mexican State and Transmigrant Organizations: Negotiating the Boundaries of Membership and Participation." *Latin American Research Review* 37 (2002): 55–99.

Goldscheid, Rudolf. "A Sociological Approach to Problems of Public Finance." In *Classics in the Theory of Public Finance*, edited by R. A. Musgrave and A. T. Peacock. London: Macmillan, 1958.

Goldscheider, Calvin. *Jewish Continuity and Change: Emerging Patterns in America*. Bloomington: Indiana University Press, 1986.

Goldthorpe, John. "Class and Politics in Advanced Industrial Societies." In *The Breakdown of Class Politics*, edited by T. N. Clark and S. M. Lipset, 105–20. Washington, DC: Woodrow Wilson Center Press; Baltimore: Johns Hopkins University Press, 2001.

González Gutiérrez, Carlos. "Fostering Identities: Mexico's Relations with Its Diaspora." *Journal of American History* 86 (September 1999): 545–67.

Goode, William J. "A Theory of Role Strain." *American Sociological Review* 25 (August 1960): 483–96.

Gordon, Milton M. *Assimilation in American Life: The Role of Race, Religion, and National Origins*. New York: Oxford University Press, 1964.

Gouldner, Alvin. "The Norm of Reciprocity: A Preliminary Statement." *American Sociological Review* 25 (1960): 161–79.

———. *The Two Marxisms*. New York: Oxford University Press, 1982.

Gramsci, Antonio. *Prison Notebooks*. Translated and edited by Q. Hoave and G. N. Smith. 1927–33. Reprint, New York: International Publishers, 1971.

———. "State and Civil Society." In *Prison Notebooks*, translated and edited by Q. Hoave and G. N. Smith, 206–76. 1927–33. Reprint, New York: International Publishers, 1971.

Granovetter, Mark. "Business Groups." In *Handbook of Economic Sociology*, 1st ed., edited by N. J. Smelser and R. Swedberg, 453–75. New York: Russell Sage Foundation; Princeton, NJ: Princeton University Press, 1994.

———. "Coase Revisited: Business Groups in the Modern Economy." In *The Sociology of Economic Life*, edited by M. Granovetter and R. Swedberg, 327–56. Boulder, CO: Westview Press, 2001.

———. "Economic Action and Social Structure: The Problem of Embeddedness." *American Journal of Sociology* 91 (1985): 481–510.

———. "The Economic Sociology of Firms and Entrepreneurs." In *The Economic Sociology of Immigration: Essays in Networks, Ethnicity, and Entrepreneurship*, edited by A. Portes, 128–65. New York: Russell Sage Foundation, 1995.

———. "Entrepreneurship, Development, and the Emergence of Firms." Draft chapter 4 for *Society and Economy*, Northwestern University (manuscript), 1990.

———. *Getting a Job: A Study of Contacts and Careers*. Cambridge, MA: Harvard University Press, 1974.

———. "The Nature of Economic Relationships." In *Explorations in Economic Sociology*, edited by R. Swedberg, 3–41. New York: Russell Sage Foundation, 1993.

———. "The Old and the New Economic Sociology: A History and an Agenda." In *Beyond the Marketplace: Rethinking Economy and Society*, edited by R. Friedland and A. F. Robertson, 89–122. New York: Aldine de Gruyter, 1990.

Grasmuck, Sherri, and Patricia Pessar. *Between Two Islands: Dominican International Migration*. Berkeley: University of California Press, 1991.

Greenfield, Harry. *Invisible, Outlawed, and Untaxed: America's Underground Economy*. Westport, CT: Praeger, 1993.

Grootaert, Christian, and Thierry Van Bastelaer. *Understanding and Measuring Social Capital*. Washington, DC: The World Bank, 2002.

Grusky, David B., and Jesper B. Sørensen. "Can Class Analysis Be Salvaged?" *American Journal of Sociology* 103 (March 1998): 1187–234.

Guarnizo, Luis E. "Los 'Dominican Yorkers': The Making of a Binational Society." *Annals of the American Academy of Political and Social Science* 533 (1994): 70–86.

———. "The Economics of Transnational Living." *International Migration Review* 37 (Fall 2003): 666–99.

———. "One Country in Two: Dominican-Owned Firms in New York and the Dominican Republic." PhD diss., Johns Hopkins University, 1992.

Guarnizo, Luis E., and Luz M. Díaz. "Transnational Migration: A View from Colombia." *Ethnic and Racial Studies* 22 (1999): 397–421.

Guarnizo, Luis E., Alejandro Portes, and William J. Haller. "Assimilation and Transnationalism: Determinants of Transnational Political Action among Contemporary Immigrants." *American Journal of Sociology* 108 (May 2003): 1211–48.

Guarnizo, Luis E., Arturo I. Sanchez, and Elizabeth Roach. "Mistrust, Fragmented Solidarity, and Transnational Migration: Colombians in New York and Los Angeles." *Ethnic and Racial Studies* 22 (March 1999): 367–96.

Guarnizo, Luis E., and Michael P. Smith. "The Locations of Transnationalism." In *Transnationalism from Below*, edited by M. P. Smith and L. E. Guarnizo, 3–34. New Brunswick, NJ: Transaction, 1998.

Gutmann, Peter M. "Are the Unemployed Unemployed?" *Financial Analysts Journal* 25 (September/October 1978).

———. "Statistical Illusions, Mistaken Policies." *Challenge* 22 (1979): 14–17.

———. "The Subterranean Economy." *Financial Analysts Journal* 24 (1977): 27–34.

Guzmán, Rolando. "Recaudación y desarrollo: Un análisis institucional de la administración tributaria en la República Dominicana." Final report for the project "Institutions and Development in Latin America." Center for Migration and Development, Princeton University, 2008. At http://cmd.princeton.edu/papers/wp0805m.pdf.

Hall, John R. "The Reworking of Class Analysis." In *Reworking Class*, edited by J. R. Hall, 1–37. Ithaca, NY: Cornell University Press, 1997.

Hannan, Michael, and John Freeman. "The Population Ecology of Organizations." *American Journal of Sociology* 82 (1977): 929–64.

Hao, Lingxin. *Kin Support, Welfare, and Out-of-Wedlock Mothers*. New York: Garland, 1994.

Harrison, Bennett, and Barry Bluestone. *The Great U-Turn: Corporate Restructuring and the Polarization of America*. New York: Basic Books, 1988.

Hart, Keith. "The Idea of the Economy: Six Modern Dissenters." In *Beyond the Marketplace: Rethinking Economy and Society*, edited by R. Friedland and A. F. Robertson, 137–60. New York: Aldine de Gruyter, 1990.

———. "Informal Income Opportunities and Urban Employment in Ghana." *Journal of Modern African Studies* 11 (1973): 61–89.

Harvey, David. *The Condition of Postmodernity*. Cambridge, MA: Basil Blackwell, 1989.

———. *The Limits to Capital*. Chicago: University of Chicago Press, 1982.

Heilbronner, Robert. *The Worldly Philosophers: The Lives, Times, and Ideas of the Great Economic Thinkers*. 7th ed. London: Penguin, 2000.

Henken, Ted. A. "Condemned to Informality: Cuba's Experiment with Self-Employment during the Special Period." PhD diss., Department of Sociology, Tulane University, 2002.

Hill, Richard C. "Global Factory and Company Town: The Changing Division of Labor in the International Automobile Industry." In *Global Restructuring and Territorial Development*, edited by J. Henderson and M. Castells, 18–37. Beverly Hills, CA: Sage, 1988.

Hirschman, Albert O. *The Strategy of Economic Development*. New Haven, CT: Yale University Press, 1958.

Hirst, Paul, and Jonathan Zeitlin. "Flexible Specialization: Theory and Evidence in the Analysis of Industrial Change." In *Contemporary Capitalism, the Embeddedness of Institutions*, edited by J. R. Hollingsworth and R. Boyer, 220–39. Cambridge: Cambridge University Press, 1997.

Hodgson, Geoffrey M. "Institutional Blindness in Modern Economics." In *Advancing Socio-Economics: An Institutionalist Perspective*, edited by J. R. Hollingsworth, K. H. Muller, and E. J. Hollingsworth, 147–70. Lanham, MD: Rowman and Littlefield, 2002.

Hodson, Randy. "Some Considerations concerning the Functional Form of Earnings." *Social Science Research* 14 (1985): 374–94.

Hoff, Karla, and Joseph Stiglitz. "Modern Economic Theory and Development." In *Frontiers of Development Economics*, edited by G. Neier and J. Stiglitz, 389–460. New York: Oxford University Press, 2001.

Hollingsworth, J. Rogers. "On Institutional Embeddedness." In *Advancing Socio-economics: An Institutionalist Perspective*, edited by J. R. Hollingsworth, K. H. Muller, and E. J. Hollingsworth, 87–107. Lanham, MD: Rowman and Littlefield, 2002.

Homans, George C. *Social Behavior: Its Elementary Forms*. New York: Harcourt, Brace, and World, 1961.

Hopkins, Terence K., and Immanuel Wallerstein. "Patterns of Development in the Modern World-System." *Review* 1 (1977): 111–45.

Hout, Michael, Clem Brooks, and Jeff Manza. "The Persistence of Classes in Post-Industrial Societies." *International Sociology* 8 (September 1993): 259–77.

Howe, Irving. *World of Our Fathers*. New York: Harcourt, Brace, Jovanovich, 1976.

Hufbauer, Gary, and Jeffrey J. Schott. *NAFTA: An Assessment*. Washington, DC: Institute for International Economics, 1993.

International Labour Organization (ILO)/Lima. "Panorama laboral: La estructura del empleo urbano en el periodo 1990–1998." Report of the ILO Regional Office, 2000. At www.ilolim.org.pe/panorama/1999.

Itzigsohn, José, Carlos Dore Cabral, Esther Hernandez Medina, and Obed Vázquez. "Mapping Dominican Transnationalism: Narrow and Broad Transnational Practices." *Ethnic and Racial Studies* 22 (March 1999): 316–39.

Itzigsohn, José, and Silvia G. Saucido. "Immigrant Incorporation and Sociocultural Transnationalism." *International Migration Review* 36 (Fall 2002): 766–98.

Jacobson, William. "Risk in the Mortgage Industry Spurred Meltdown." *Ithaca Journal*, September 27, 2008.

Jaffee, David. "The Political Economy of Job Loss in the United States, 1970–1980." *Social Problems* 33 (1986): 297–318.

Jencks, Christopher, Marshall Smith, Henry Acland, Mary Jo Bane, David Cohen, Herbert Gintis, Barbara Heyns, and Stephan Michelson. *Inequality: A Reassessment of the Effect of Family and Schooling in America*. New York: Harper and Row, 1972.

Jenkins, J. Craig, and K. Leicht. "Class Analysis and Social Movements: A Critique and Reformation." In *Reworking Class*, edited by J. R. Hall, 369–97. Ithaca, NY: Cornell University Press, 1997.

Karoleff, Vladimir, Rold Mirus, and Roger S. Smith. "Canada's Underground Economy Revisited: Update and Critique." Paper presented at the 49th Congress of the International Institute of Public Finance, Berlin, August 1993.

Kaztman, Ruben, Gabriel Corbo, Fernando Filgueira, Madgalena Furtado, Denise Gelber, Alejandro Retamoso, and Federico Rodriguez. "La ciudad fragmentada: Mercado, territorio y marginalidad en Montevideo." Final report for the project "Latin American Urbanization in the Late Twentieth Century," delivered at the final project conference, Montevideo, Uruguay, August 2003.

Kempe, Ronald Hope. "Growth and Impact of the Subterranean Economy in the Third World." *Futures* 1 (October 1993): 864–76.

Kennedy, Paul. *The Rise and Fall of the Great Powers*. New York: Random House, 1987.

Kepel, G. *Les banlieus de l'Islam*. Paris: Ed. Du Seinl, 1987.

Kim, Ilsoo. *New Urban Immigrants: The Korean Community in New York*. Princeton, NJ: Princeton University Press, 1981.

Kircheman, Joleen, and Kathryn M. Neckerman. "We Love to Hire Them But . . . : The Meaning of Race to Employers." In *The Urban Underclass*, edited by C. Jencks and P. E. Peterson, 203–34. Washington, DC: Brookings Institution, 1991.

Kivisto, Peter. "Theorizing Transnational Migration: A Critical Review of Current Efforts." *Ethnic and Racial Studies* 24 (July 2001): 549–77.

Klein, Emilio, and Victor Tokman. "La estratificación social bajo tensión en la era de la globalización." *Revista de la CEPAL* 72 (December 2000): 7–30.

———. "Sector informal: Una forma de utilizar el trabajo como consecuencia de la manera de producir y no viceversa." *Estudios Sociológicos* 6 (16 January–April 1988): 205–12.

Korzeniewicz, Roberto, and William C. Smith. "Poverty, Inequality, and Growth in Latin America: Searching for the High Road to Globalization." *Latin American Research Review* 35 (2000): 7–54.

Kyle, David. *Transnational Peasants: Migration, Networks, and Ethnicity in Andean Ecuador*. Baltimore: Johns Hopkins University Press, 2000.

Lamarche, François. "Property Development and the Economic Foundations of the Urban Question." In *Urban Sociology: Critical Essays*, edited by C. G. Pickvance, 85–118. New York: St. Martin's Press, 1976.

Landolt, Patricia. "The Causes and Consequences of Transnational Migration: Salvadorans in Los Angeles and Washington, DC." PhD diss., Department of Sociology, Johns Hopkins University, 2000.

Landolt, Patricia. "Salvadoran Economic Transnationalism: Embedded Strategies for Household Maintenance, Immigrant Incorporation, and Entrepreneurial Expansion." *Global Networks* 1 (2001): 217–42.

Landolt, Patricia, Lilian Autler, and Sonia Baires. "From 'Hermano Lejano' to 'Hermano Mayor': The Dialectics of Salvadoran Transnationalism." *Ethnic and Racial Studies* 22 (1999): 290–315.

Latin American Weekly Report. "Corred Redefines Meaning of Full Powers." WR-07-49, December 13, 2007, 4.

———. "Fernandez: An Era of Continuity and Change." WR-07-49, December 13, 2007, 6–7.

———. "MAS Approves New Constitution in Bolivia." WR-07-49, December 13, 2007, 1–2.

Lenin, Vladimir I. *What Is to Be Done? Burning Question of Our Movement*. New York: International Publishers, 1929.

Leonard, Madeleine. *The Informal Economy in Belfast*. Aldershot, Ireland: Avebury, 1994.

Lerner, David. *The Passing of Traditional Society: Modernizing the Middle East*. New York: Free Press, 1958.

Lévi-Strauss, Claude. *The Elementary Structures of Kinship*. 1949. Reprint, Boston: Beacon Press, 1969.

Levitt, Peggy. "Transnational Migration and Development: A Case of Two for the Price of One?" Working Paper, Center for Migration and Development, Princeton University, 2000.

———. *The Transnational Villagers*. Berkeley: University of California Press, 2001.

Levitt, Peggy, and Nina Glick Schiller. "Conceptualizing Simultaneity: A Transnational Social Field Perspective on Society." *International Migration Review* 38 (Fall 2004): 1002–39.

Light, Ivan. "Asian Enterprise in America: Chinese, Japanese, and Koreans in Small Business." In *Self-Help in Urban America*, edited by Scott Cummings, 33–57. New York: Kennikat Press, 1980.

———. "Disadvantaged Minorities in Self-Employment." *International Journal of Comparative Sociology* 20 (1979): 31–45.

———. *Ethnic Enterprise in America: Business and Welfare among Chinese, Japanese, and Blacks*. Berkeley: University of California Press, 1972.

———. "Immigrant and Ethnic Enterprise in North America." *Ethnic and Racial Studies* 7 (1984): 195–216.

Light, Ivan, and Edna Bonacich. *Immigrant Entrepreneurs: Koreans in Los Angeles, 1965–1982*. Berkeley: University of California Press, 1988.

Light, Ivan, and Steven J. Gold. *Ethnic Economies*. San Diego, CA: Academic Press, 2000.

Lin, Nan, Walter M. Ensel, and J. C. Vaugh. "Social Resources and Strength of Ties: Structural Factors in Occupational Attainment." *American Sociological Review* 46 (1981): 393–405.

Linton, Ralph. *The Cultural Background of Personality*. New York: Appleton, Century, Crofts, 1945.

Lomnitz, Larissa. "Informal Exchange Networks in Formal Systems: A Theoretical Model." *American Anthropologist* 90 (1988): 42–55.

Lopreato, Joseph. *Vilfredo Pareto*. New York: Thomas Y. Crowell, 1965.

Lozano, Beverly. *The Invisible Work Force: Transforming American Business with Outside and Home-Based Workers*. New York: Free Press, 1989.

Lungo, Mario, and Susan Kandel. *Transformando El Salvador: Migración, sociedad y cultura*. San Salvador: Fundación Nacional para el Desarrollo, 1999.

Luxembourg, Rosa. *The Accumulation of Capital*. London: Routledge and Kegan Paul, 1951.

MacDonald, R. "Fiddly Jobs, Undeclared Working, and the Something for Nothing Society." *Work, Employment, and Society* 8 (1994): 507–30.

MacIver, R. H., and Charles H. Page. *Sociología*. Translated from English by J. Cazorla Perez. 1949. Reprint, Madrid: Tecnos Editores, 1961.

MacKenzie, Donald. *An Engine, Not a Camera: How Financial Models Shape Markets*. Cambridge, MA: MIT Press, 2006.

MacLeod, Dag. *Downsizing the State: Privatization and the Limits of Neoliberal Reform in Mexico*. University Park: Pennsylvania State University Press, 2004.

Makaria, Kinuthia. *Social and Political Dynamics of the Informal Economy in African Cities*. Lanham, MD: University Press of America, 1997.

Mandel, Ernest. *Late Capitalism*. London: Verso Books, 1978.

Margolis, Maxine. *Little Brazil: An Ethnography of Brazilian Immigrants in New York City*. Princeton, NJ: Princeton University Press, 1994.

Marqués, Maria M., Rui Santos, and F. Araújo. "Ariadne's Thread: Cape Verdean Women in Transnational Webs." *Global Networks* 1 (2001): 283–306.

Marx, Karl. *Capital, Volume 1*. 1867. Reprint, New York: International Publishers, 1967.

———. *The Class Struggles in France, 1848–50*. 1871. Reprint, New York: International Publishers, 1964.

———. *The Eighteenth Brumaire of Louis Bonaparte*. 1869. Reprint, New York: International Publishers, 1963.

———. *The Grundrisse*. Edited and Translated by D. McLellan. 1939. Reprint, New York: Harper and Row, 1970.

Marx, Karl, and Friedrich Engels. "Manifesto of the Communist Party." In *Marx and Engels: Basic Writings on Politics and Philosophy*, edited by L. S. Fener, 1–41. 1847. Reprint, Garden City, NY: Doubleday, 1959.

Massey, Douglas S. *Categorically Unequal*. New York: Russell Sage Foundation, 2007.

———. "Understanding Mexican Migration to the United States." *American Journal of Sociology* 92 (1987): 1372–403.

Massey, Douglas S., Joaquín Arango, Grame Hugo, Ali Kouaouci, Adela Pellegrino, and J. Edward Taylor. *Worlds in Motion: Understanding International Migration at the End of the Millennium*. Oxford: Clarendon Press, 1998.

Massey, Douglas S., Jorge Durand, and Nolan J. Malone. *Beyond Smoke and Mirrors: Mexican Immigration in an Era of Economic Integration*. New York: Russell Sage Foundation, 2002.

Massey, Douglas S., and Felipe Garcia España. "The Social Process of International Migration." *Science* 237 (1987): 733–38.

Matute-Bianchi, Maria Eugenia. "Ethnic Identities and Patterns of School Success and Failure among Mexican-Descent and Japanese-American Students in a California High School." *American Journal of Education* 95 (1986): 233–55.

Mauss, Marcel. *The Gift: The Form and Reason for Exchange in Archaic Societies*. 1925 Reprint, New York: Norton, 1990.

Mayer, Susan. "A Comparison of Poverty and Living Conditions in the United States, Canada, Sweden, and Germany." In *Poverty, Inequality, and the Future of Social Policy*, edited by K. McFate, R. Lawson, and W. J. Wilson, 109–51. New York: Russell Sage Foundation, 1993.

McCrohan, Kevin, James D. Smith, and Terry K. Adams. "Consumer Purchases in Informal Markets: Estimates for the 1980s, Prospects for the 1990s." *Journal of Retailing* 67 (1991): 22–50.

McKeever, Matthew. "Reproduced Inequality: Participation and Success in the South African Informal Economy." *Social Forces* 76 (June 1998): 1209–41.

Meagher, Kate. "Crisis, Informalization, and the Urban Informal Sector in Sub-Saharan Africa." *Development and Change* 26 (April 1995): 259–84.

Menjívar, Cecilia. *Fragmented Ties: Salvadoran Immigrant Networks in America.* Berkeley: University of California Press, 2000.

Merton, Robert K. "Manifest and Latent Functions." In *Social Theory and Social Structure*, edited by R. K. Merton, 73–138. New York: Free Press, 1968.

———. "On Sociological Theories of the Middle Range." In *Social Theory and Social Structure*, edited by R. K. Merton, 39–72. New York: Free Press, 1968.

———. "The Role-Set: Problems in Sociological Theory." *British Journal of Sociology* 8 (June 1957): 106–20.

———. "The Self-Fulfilling Prophecy." *Antioch Review* 8 (1948). 193–210.

———. "Social Structure and Anomie." In *Social Theory and Social Structure*, edited by R. K. Merton, 185–214. New York: Free Press, 1968.

———. *Social Theory and Social Structure*. Enlarged ed. New York: Free Press, 1968.

———. "Unanticipated Consequences and Kindred Sociological Ideas: A Personal Gloss." In *L'Opera di R. K. Merton e la Sociologia Contemporanea*, edited by C. Mongardini and S. Tabboni, 307–29. Genoa, Italy: Edisioni Culturali Internazionali, 1989.

Merton, Robert K. "The Unanticipated Consequences of Purposive Social Action." *American Sociological Review* 1 (1936): 894–904.

Meyer, John. "The World-Policy and the Authority of the Nation-State." In *Institutional Structure: Constituting State, Society, and the Individual*, edited by George M. Thomas et al., 41–70. Beverly Hills, CA: Sage, 1987.

Meyer, John, John Boli, George M. Thomas, and Francisco Ramirez. "World Society and the Nation State." *American Journal of Sociology* 103 (July 1997): 144–81.

Meyer, John, and Michael T. Hannan. *National Development and the World System: Educational, Economic, and Political Change, 1950–1970*. Chicago: University of Chicago Press, 1979.

Meyer, John, and Francisco O. Ramirez. "World Expansion of Mass Education, 1870–1980." *Sociology of Education* 65 (1992): 128–49.

Meyer, John, and Brian Rowan. "Institutionalized Organizations: Formal Structure as Myth and Ceremony." *American Journal of Sociology* 83 (1977): 340–63.

Meyer, John, and Richard Rubinson. "The World Educational Revolution, 1950–1970." *Sociology of Education* 50 (1977): 242–58.

Michels, Robert. *Political Parties: A Sociological Study of the Oligarchical Tendencies in Modern Democracy.* 1915. Reprint, New York: Free Press, 1968.

Millman, Joel. "New Mex City." *New York* 7 (1992): 37–42.

Mills, C. Wright. *The Sociological Imagination.* London: Oxford University Press, 1959.

Min, Pyong Gap. "Factors Contributing to Ethnic Business." *International Journal of Comparative Sociology* 28 (1987): 173–93.

Mingione, Enzo. "The Case of Greece." In *Underground Economy and Irregular Forms of Employment, Final Report,* edited by P. Barthelemy, P. Migueliz, E. Mingione, R. Pahl, and A. Wenig. Luxembourg: Commission of the European Communities, 1990.

Molefsky, Barry. "American's Underground Economy." Report #81-181E, Congressional Research Service, The Library of Congress, Washington DC, 1981.

Money. "Everyone's Getting Rich." *Money* 28 (May 1999).

Moore, Barrington. *Social Origins of Dictatorship and Democracy.* Boston: Beacon Press, 1966.

Morrill, Calvin. "Conflict Management, Honor, and Organizational Change." *American Journal of Sociology* 97 (1991): 585–621.

Nee, Victor. "The New Institutionalisms in Economics and Sociology." In *The Handbook of Economic Sociology,* 2nd ed., edited by N. J. Smelser and R. Swedberg, 49–74. New York: Russell Sage Foundation; Princeton, NJ: Princeton University Press, 2005.

Nee, Victor, and Brett de Bary Nee. *Longtime Californ': A Documentary Study of an American Chinatown.* New York: Pantheon Books, 1992.

Nee, Victor, and Paul Ingram. "Embeddedness and Beyond: Institutions, Exchange, and Social Structure." In *The New Institutionalism in Sociology,* edited by M. C. Brinton and V. Nee, 19–45. Stanford, CA: Stanford University Press, 1998.

Newcomb, Theodore M. *Social Psychology.* New York: Holt, Rinehart, and Winston, 1950.

Newcomb, Theodore M., Ralph H. Turner, and Philip E. Converse. *Social Psychology: The Study of Human Interaction.* New York: Holt, Rinehart, and Winston, 1965.

Nicolson, H. G. *The Congress of Vienna: A Study in Allied Unity, 1812–1822.* New York: Harcourt, 1946.

North, Douglass C. *Institutions, Institutional Change, and Economic Performance.* Cambridge: Cambridge University Press, 1990.

Nun, José. Superpoblación relativa, ejército industrial de reserva y masa marginal." *Revista Latinoamericana de Sociología* 5 (1969): 178–235.

O'Connor, James. *Fiscal Crisis of the State.* New York: St. Martin's Press, 1973.

O'Donnell, Guillermo. "The State, Democratization, and Some Conceptual Problems." In *Latin American Political Economy in the Age of Neoliberal Reform,* edited by W. C. Smith, C. H. Acuña, and E. A. Gamarra, 157–79. New Brunswick, NJ: Transaction, 1994.

Office of Immigration Statistics. *2002 Annual Report*. Washington, DC: Department of Homeland Security, 2003.

Ostergaard-Nielsen, Eva K. "Transnational Practices and the Receiving State: Turks and Kurds in Germany and the Netherlands." *Global Networks* 1 (2001): 261–81.

Ostrom, Elinor. *Governing the Commons: The Evolution of Institutions for Collective Action*. Cambridge: Cambridge University Press, 1990.

Pahl, Raymond E. "Employment, Work, and the Domestic Division of Labor." *International Journal of Urban and Regional Research* 4 (1980): 1–20.

Parsons, Talcott, and Neil J. Smelser. *Economy and Society*. New York: Free Press, 1956.

Passel, Jeffrey S. "The Economic Downturn and Immigration Trends: What Has Happened and How Do We Know." Lecture delivered at the Center for Migration and Development, Princeton University, March 26, 2009.

Peattie, Lisa. "What Is to Be Done with the 'Informal Sector'? A Case Study of Shoe Manufacturers in Colombia." In *Towards a Political Economy of Urbanization in Third World Countries*, edited by H. Safa. Delhi: Oxford University Press, 1982.

Pedraza-Bailey, Silvia. "Cuba's Exiles: Portrait of a Refugee Migration." *International Migration Review* 19 (1985): 4–34.

Pérez, Lisandro. "Cuban Miami." In *Miami Now!* edited by Guillermo J. Grenier and Alex Stepick, 83–108. Gainesville: University Press of Florida, 1992.

Pérez-Sáinz, Juan Pablo. 1992. *Informalidad urbana en América Latina: Enfoques, problemáticas e interrogantes*. Caracas: Editorial Nueva Sociedad.

Petersen, William. *Japanese Americans: Oppression and Success*. New York: Random House, 1971.

Piore, Michael J., and Charles F. Sabel. *The Second Industrial Divide*. New York: Basic Books, 1984.

Polanyi, Karl. "The Economy as Instituted Process." In *Trade and Market in the Early Empires*, edited by K. Polanyi, C. Arensberg, and H. Pearson, 243–69. 1957. Reprint, Chicago: Regnery, 1971.

———. *The Great Transformation*. 1944. Reprint, Boston: Beacon Press, 1957.

———. "Our Obsolete Market Mentality: Civilization Must Find a New Thought Pattern." *Commentary* 3 (1947): 109–17.

———. "Our Obsolete Market Mentality." In *Primitive, Archaic, and Modern Economics: Essays of Karl Polanyi*, edited by G. Dalton, 59–77. 1947. Reprint, Boston: Beacon Press, 1971.

Porter, Richard D., and Amanda S. Bayer. "A Monetary Perspective on Underground Economic Activity in the United States." *Federal Reserve Bulletin* 70 (1984): 177–89.

Portes, Alejandro. "The Debates and Significance of Immigrant Transnationalism." *Global Networks* 1 (2001): 181–93.

———. "Economic Sociology and the Sociology of Immigration: A Conceptual Overview." In *The Economic Sociology of Immigration: Essays on Networks, Ethnicity, and Entrepreneurship*, edited by Alejandro Portes, 1–41. New York: Russell Sage Foundation, 1995.

———. "Global Villagers: The Rise of Transnational Communities." *The American Prospect*, 25 (1996): 74–77.

———. "The Hidden Abode: Sociology as Analysis of the Unexpected." *American Sociological Review* 65 (2000): 1–18.

———. "Institutions and Development: A Conceptual Re-Analysis." *Population and Development Review* 32 (June 2006): 233–62.

———. "Neoliberalism and the Sociology of Development: Emerging Trends and Unanticipated Facts." *Population and Development Review* 23 (June 1997): 229–59.

———. "On Grand Surprises and Modest Certainties." *American Journal of Sociology* 100 (May 1995): 1620–26.

———. "The Resilient Significance of Class: A Nominalist Interpretation." *Political Power and Social Theory* 14 (2000): 249–84.

———. "Social Capital: Its Origins and Applications in Modern Sociology." *Annual Review of Sociology* 24 (1998): 1–24.

———. "The Social Origins of the Cuban Enclave Economy of Miami." *Sociological Perspectives* 30 (1987): 340–72.

———. "Theoretical Convergencies and Empirical Evidence in the Study of Immigrant Transnationalism." *International Migration Review* 37 (Fall 2003): 874–92.

———. "The Two Meanings of Social Capital." *Sociological Forum* 15 (2000): 1–12.

Portes, Alejandro, and Robert L. Bach. *Latin Journey: Cuban and Mexican Immigrants in the United States*. Berkeley, CA: University of California Press, 1985.

Portes, Alejandro, Manuel Castells, and Lauren Benton. "The Policy Implications of Informality." In *The Informal Economy: Studies in Advanced and Less Developed Countries*, edited by A. Portes, M. Castells, and L. A. Benton, 298–311. Baltimore: Johns Hopkins University Press, 1989.

Portes, Alejandro, Cristina Escobar, and Renelinda Arana. "Bridging the Gap: Transnational and Ethnic Organizations in the Political Incorporation of Immigrants in the United States." *Ethnic and Racial Studies* 31 (September 2008): 1056–90.

Portes, Alejandro, Cristina Escobar, and Alexandria Walton Radford. "Immigrant Transnational Organizations and Development: A Comparative Study." *International Migration Review* 41 (Spring 2007): 242–81.

Portes, Alejandro, and Luis E. Guarnizo. "Tropical Capitalists: U.S.-Bound Immigration and Small Enterprise Development in the Dominican Republic." In *Migration, Remittances, and Small Business Development: Mexico and Caribbean*

Basin Countries, edited by S. Díaz-Briquets and S. Weintraub, 101–31. Boulder, CO: Westview Press, 1991.

Portes, Alejandro, Luis E. Guarnizo, and Patricia Landolt. "Transnational Communities: Pitfalls and Promise of an Emergent Research Field." *Ethnic and Racial Studies* 22 (1999): 217–37.

Portes, Alejandro, and William Haller. *Handbook of Economic Sociology*, 2nd ed. New York: Russell Sage Foundation; Princeton, NJ: Princeton University Press, 2005.

———. "The Informal Economy." In *Handbook of Economic Sociology*, 2nd ed., edited by N. J. Smelser and R. Swedberg, 403–25. New York: Russell Sage Foundation; Princeton, NJ: Princeton University Press, 2005.

Portes, Alejandro, William Haller, and Luis E. Guarnizo. "Transnational Entrepreneurs: An Alternative Form of Immigrant Adaptation." *American Sociological Review* 67 (April 2002): 278–98.

Portes, Alejandro, and Kelly Hoffman. "Latin American Class Structures: Their Composition and Change during the Neoliberal Era." *Latin American Research Review* 38 (February 2003): 41–81.

Portes, Alejandro, and Leif Jensen. "The Enclave and the Entrants: Patterns of Ethnic Enterprise in Miami before and after Mariel." *American Sociological Review* 54 (1989): 929–49.

Portes, Alejandro, Donald Light, and Patricia Fernández-Kelly. "The American Health System and Immigration: An Institutional Interpretation." *Sociological Forum* (forthcoming 2009).

Portes, Alejandro, and Robert D. Manning. "The Immigrant Enclave: Theory and Empirical Examples." In *Competitive Ethnic Relations*, edited by Joanne Nagel and Susan Olzak, 47–68. Orlando, FL: Academic Press, 1986.

Portes, Alejandro, and Margarita Mooney. "Social Capital and Community Development." In *The New Economic Sociology: Developments in an Emerging Field*, edited by M. F. Guillen, R. Collins, P. England, and M. Meyer, 303–29. New York: Russell Sage Foundation, 2002.

Portes, Alejandro, and Bryan R. Roberts. "The Free Market City: Latin American Urbanization in the Years of the Neoliberal Experiment." *Studies in Comparative and International Development* (Spring 2005): 43–82.

Portes, Alejandro, and Rubén G. Rumbaut. *Immigrant America: A Portrait*, 3rd ed. Berkeley: University of California Press, 2006.

———. *Legacies: The Story of the Immigrant Second Generation*. New York: Russell Sage Foundation; Berkeley: University of California Press, 2001.

Portes, Alejandro, and Saskia Sassen. "Making It Underground: Comparative Materials on the Informal Sector in Western Market Economies." *American Journal of Sociology* 93 (1987): 30–61.

Portes, Alejandro, and Richard Schauffler. "Competing Perspectives on the Latin American Informal Sector." *Population and Development Review* 19 (1993): 33–60.

Portes, Alejandro, and Julia Sensenbrenner. "Embeddedness and Immigration: Notes on the Social Determinants of Economic Action." *American Journal of Sociology* 98 (1993): 1320–50.

Portes, Alejandro, and Steven Shafer. "Revisiting the Enclave Hypothesis: Miami Twenty-Five Years Later." *Research in the Sociology of Organizations* 25 (2007): 157–90.

Portes, Alejandro, and Lori D. Smith. "Institutions and Development in Latin America: A Comparative Study." *Studies in Comparative and International Development* 43 (Summer 2008): 101–28.

Portes, Alejandro, and Alex Stepick. *City on the Edge: The Transformation of Miami*. Berkeley: University of California Press, 1993.

Portes, Alejandro, and John Walton. *Labor, Class, and the International System*. New York: Academic Press, 1981.

Portes, Alejandro, and Min Zhou. "Entrepreneurship and Economic Progress in the 1990s: A Comparative Analysis of Immigrants and African Americans." In *Immigration and Ethnicity in the United States*, edited by F. Bean and S. Bell-Rose, 143–71. New York: Russell Sage Foundation, 1999.

———. "Self-Employment and the Earnings of Immigrants." *American Sociological Review* 61 (1996): 219–30.

Poulantzas, Nicos. *Classes in Contemporary Capitalism*. London: New Left Books, 1975.

Pozas, Maria de los Angeles. "Sociología económica y migración internacional: Convergencias y divergencias." In *El país transnacional*, edited by M. Ariza and A. Portes, 619–49. Mexico City: Institute for Social Research, National Autonomous University of Mexico, 2007.

Programa Regional de Empleo para America Latina (PREALC). *Mas alla de la crisis*. Santiago, Chile: International Labour Organization, 1985.

Putnam, Robert D. *Bowling Alone: The Collapse and Revival of American Community*. New York: Simon and Schuster, 2000.

———. "The Prosperous Community: Social Capital and Public Life." *American Prospect* 13 (Spring 1993): 35–42.

Ramos, Carlos Guillermo. "Rapporteurs' Comments." Delivered at the Conference on Immigrant Transnationalism and Its Impact on Sending Nations." Sponsored by the Center for Migration and Development, Princeton University and Latin American School of Social Science (FLACSO), Santo Domingo, Dominican Republic, January 2002.

Reich, Robert. *The Work of Nations: Preparing Ourselves for 21st-Century Capitalism*. New York: Vintage Books, 1992.

Repak, Terry. *Waiting on Washington: Central American Workers in the Nation's Capital*. Philadelphia: Temple University Press, 1995.

Reskin, Barbara. "Sex Segregation in the Workplace." *Annual Review of Sociology* 19 (1993): 241–70.

Rev, Ivan. "The Advantages of Being Atomized." Working Paper. The Institute for Advanced Study, Princeton University, 1986.

Rischin, Moses. *The Promised City: New York Jews, 1870–1914.* Cambridge, MA: Harvard University Press, 1962.

Roberts, Bryan R. "Employment Structure, Life Cycle, and Life Chances: Formal and Informal Sectors in Guadalajara." In *The Informal Economy: Studies in Advanced and Less Developed Countries*, edited by A. Portes, M. Castells, and L. A. Benton, 41–59. Baltimore: Johns Hopkins University Press, 1989.

———. "The Other Working Class: Uncommitted Labor in Britain, Spain, and Mexico." In *Cross-National Research in Sociology*, edited by M. L. Kohn, 352–72. Newbury Park, CA: Sage, 1989.

Roberts, Kenneth. "Social Inequalities without Class Cleavages in Latin America's Neoliberal Era." *Studies in Comparative International Development* 36 (Winter 2002): 3–33.

Robinson, William. *Promoting Polyarchy: Globalization, U.S. Intervention, and Hegemony.* Cambridge: Cambridge University Press, 1996.

Rodríguez Garavito, César. "De club de caballeros a foro electrónico de negociación: Un análisis institucional de la Bolsa de Valores de Colombia." Final report to the project "Institutions and Development in Latin America." Center for Migration and Development, Princeton University, 2006. At http://cmd .princeton.edu/papers/wp0608f2.pdf.

Rodríguez Garavito, César, and Diana Rodríguez Franco. "Entre el clientelismo y la modernización: Una etnografía institucional de la administración de impuestos de Colombia." Final report to the project "Institutions and Development in Latin America." Center for Migration and Development, Princeton University, 2008. At http://cmd.princeton.edu/papers/wp0805h.pdf.

Rogers, Joyce. "Is Everyone Getting Really Rich?" *Money* 28 (July 1999): 20.

Roig, Alexandre. "La Dirección General Impositiva de la Agencia Federal de Ingresos Públicos (AFIP) de la Argentina." Final report to the project "Institutions and Development in Latin America." Center for Migration and Development, Princeton University, 2008. At http://cmd.princeton.edu/papers/wp0805d .pdf.

Roland, Gerard. "Understanding Institutional Change: Fast-Moving and Slow-Moving Institutions." *Studies in Comparative International Development* 38 (Winter 2004): 109–31.

Romo, Frank P., and Michael Schwartz. "The Structural Embeddedness of Business Decisions: The Migration of Manufacturing Plants in New York State, 1960–1985." *American Sociological Review* 60 (December 1995): 874–907.

Roof, Wade Clark. *Spiritual Marketplace: Baby Boomers and the Remaking of American Religion.* Princeton, NJ: Princeton University Press, 1999.

Roque, Martha Beatriz. "Economía Informal en Cuba." Report commissioned by the Center for Migration and Development, Princeton University (May 2002).

Rosenblum, Gerald. *Immigrant Workers: Their Impact on American Radicalism.* New York: Basic Books, 1973.

Rosenfeld, Michael J., and Marta Tienda. "Mexican Immigration, Occupational Niches, and Labor Market Competition: Evidence from Los Angeles, Chicago, and Atlanta 1970 to 1990." In *Immigration and Opportunity*, edited by F. D. Bean and S. Bell-Rose, 64–105. New York: Russell Sage Foundation, 1999.

Rumbaut, Rubén G. "Assimilation and Its Discontents: Between Rhetoric and Reality." *International Migration Review* 31 (1997): 923–60.

———. "Ties That Bind: Immigration and Immigrant Families in the United States." In *Immigration and the Family: Research and Policy on U.S. Immigrants*, edited by A. Booth, A. C. Crouters, and N. Landale. Mahwah, NJ: Lawrence Erlbaum, 1997.

Sabatini, Francisco, and Guillermo Wormald. "Santiago de Chile bajo la nueva economía." In *Ciudades latinoamericanas: Un análisis comparativo en el umbral del nuevo siglo*, edited by A. Portes, B. R. Roberts, and A. Grimson, 217–98. Buenos Aires: Prometeo Libros, 2005.

Sabel, Charles. "Changing Modes of Economic Efficiency and Their Implications for Industrialization in the Third World." In *Development, Democracy, and Trespassing: Essays in Honor of Albert O. Hirschman*, edited by A. Foxley, M. S. McPherson, and G. O'Donnell, 27–55. Notre Dame, IN: Notre Dame University Press, 1986.

———. "Flexible Specialization and the Re-Emergence of Regional Economies." In *Reversing Industrial Decline? Industrial Structure and Policy in Britain and Her Competitors*, edited by P. Hirst and J. Zeitlin, 28–29. New York: Berg, 1989.

———. "Learning by Monitoring: The Institutions of Economic Development." In *The Handbook of Economic Sociology*, edited by N. J. Smelser and R. Swedberg, 137–65. New York: Russell Sage Foundation; Princeton, NJ: Princeton University Press, 1994.

Sassen, Saskia. *The Global City.* Princeton, NJ: Princeton University Press, 1991.

———. *The Mobility of Labor and Capital: A Study in International Investment and Labor Flow.* New York: Cambridge University Press, 1988.

———. "New York City's Informal Economy." In *The Informal Economy: Studies in Advanced and Less Developed Countries*, edited by A. Portes, M. Castells, and L. A. Benton, 60–77. Baltimore: Johns Hopkins University Press, 1989.

Sassen, Saskia, and Robert C. Smith. "Post-Industrial Growth and Economic Reorganization: Their Impact on Immigrant Employment." In *U.S.-Mexico Relations, Labor Market Interdependence*, edited by C. W. Reynolds, J. Bustamante, and R. Hinojosa. Stanford, CA: Stanford University Press, 1992.

Schiff, Maurice. "Social Capital, Labor Mobility, and Welfare." *Rationality and Society* 4 (1992): 157–75.

Schom, Alan. *Napoleon Bonaparte.* New York: HarperCollins, 1997.

Schumpeter, Joseph A. "An Economic Interpretation of Our Time: The Lowell Lectures." In *Joseph A. Schumpeter: The Economics and Sociology of Capitalism*, edited by R. Swedberg, 338–63. 1941. Reprint, Princeton, NJ: Princeton University Press, 1991.

Scott, Richard W. *Institutions and Organizations*. Thousand Oaks, CA: Sage, 1995.

Selznick, Philip *TVA and the Grassroots*. 1949. Reprint, Berkeley: University of California Press, 1966.

Sen, Amartya. *Development as Freedom*. New York: Alfred A. Knopf, 1999.

———. "Rational Fools: A Critique of the Behavioral Foundations of Economic Theory." *Philosophy and Public Affairs* 6 (1977): 317–44.

Sennett, Richard, and Jonathan Cobb. *The Hidden Injuries of Class*. New York: Norton, 1972.

Sethuraman, S. V. *The Urban Informal Sector in Developing Countries*. Geneva: International Labour Organization, 1981.

Shaiken, Harley. "Advanced Manufacturing and Mexico: A New International Division of Labor?" *Latin American Research Review* 29 (1994): 39–72.

——— 1990. *Mexico in the Global Economy*. Monograph Series #33. San Diego: Center for U.S.-Mexican Studies, University of California.

Simmel, Georg. "The Metropolis and Mental Life." In *The Sociology of Georg Simmel*, edited by and translated by K. H. Wolff, 409–24. 1902. Reprint, New York: Free Press, 1964.

———. "The Significance of Numbers in Social Life." in *The Sociology of Georg Simmel*, edited and translated by K. H. Wolff, 87–99. 1908. Reprint, New York: Free Press, 1964.

———. "The Sociology of Conflict." *American Journal of Psychology* 9 (1903): 490–525.

———. "The Stranger." In *The Sociology of Georg Simmel*, edited and translated by K. H. Wolff, 402–8. 1908. Reprint, New York: Free Press, 1964.

Smelser, Neil J., and Richard Swedberg, eds. *Handbook of Economic Sociology*, 1st ed. New York: Russell Sage Foundation; Princeton, NJ: Princeton University Press, 1994.

———. *Handbook of Economic Sociology*, 2nd ed. New York: Russell Sage Foundation; Princeton, NJ: Princeton University Press, 2005.

Smith, Adam. *The Wealth of Nations*. 1776. Reprint, Baltimore: Penguin, 1979.

Smith, James P., and Barry Edmonston. *The Immigration Debate: Studies on the Economic, Demographic, and Fiscal Impacts of Immigration*. Washington, DC: National Academy Press, 1998.

Smith, Michael P., and Luis E. Guarnizo. *Transnationalism from Below*. New Brunswick, NJ: Transaction, 1998.

Smith, Philip M. "Assessing the Size of the Underground Economy: The Statistics Canada Perspective." In *The Underground Economy: Global Evidence of*

Its Size and Impact, edited by O. Lippert and M. Walker, 11–36. Vancouver, Canada: The Fraser Institute, 1997.

Smith, Robert C. "Diasporic Memberships in Historical Perspective: Comparative Insights from the Mexican, Italian, and Polish Cases. *International Migration Review* 37 (Fall 2003): 724–59.

———. *Mexican New York: Transnational Worlds of New Immigrants*. Berkeley: University of California Press, 2005.

Sowell, Thomas. *Ethnic America: A History*. New York: Basic Books, 1981.

Stack, Carol. *All Our Kin*. New York: Harper and Row, 1974.

Standing, Guy. "The 'British Experiment': Structural Adjustment or Accelerated Decline?" In *The Informal Economy: Studies in Advanced and Less Developed Countries*, edited by A. Portes, M. Castells, and L. Benton, 279–97. Baltimore: Johns Hopkins University Press, 1989.

Stark, David. "Bending the Bars of the Iron Cage: Bureaucratization and Informalization in Capitalism and Socialism." *Sociological Forum* 4 (December 1989): 637–64.

Stark, Oded. "Migration Decision Making." *Journal of Development Economics* 14 (1984): 251–59.

Stepick, Alex. "Miami's Two Informal Sectors." In *The Informal Economy: Studies in Advanced and Less Developed Countries*, edited by A. Portes, M. Castells, and L. A. Benton, 111–34. Baltimore: Johns Hopkins University Press, 1989.

———. "The Refugees Nobody Wants: Haitians in Miami." In *Miami Now!* edited by G. J. Grenier and A. Stepick, 57–82. Gainesville: University Press of Florida, 1992.

Stepick, Alex, Guillermo Grenier, Max Castro, and Marvin Dunn. *This Land Is Our Land: Immigrants and Power in Miami*. Berkeley: University of California Press, 2003.

Stepick, Alex, and Carol Dutton Stepick. "Power and Identity: Miami Cubans." In *Latinos: Remaking America*, edited by M. M. Suárez-Orozco and M. M. Páez, 75–92. Berkeley: University of California Press, 2002.

Stewart, James B. *African-Americans and Post-Industrial Labor Markets*. New Brunswick, NJ: Transaction, 1997.

Storper, Michael, and Allen J. Scott. "Work Organization and Local Labour Markets in an Era of Flexible Production." Working Paper #30, World Employment Programme, Geneva: International Labour Organization, 1989.

Suárez-Orozco, Marcelo M. "Towards a Psychosocial Understanding of Hispanic Adaptation to American Schooling." In *Success or Failure? Learning and the Languages of Minority Students*, edited by H. T. Trueba, 156–68. New York: Newbury House Publishers, 1987.

Sunkel, Osvaldo. "The Unbearable Lightness of Neoliberalism." Paper presented at the Conference on Latin American Sociology. University of Florida, Gainesville, April 2001.

Swedberg, Richard. "Markets as Social Structures." In *Handbook of Economic Sociology*, 1st ed., edited by N. J. Smelser and R. Swedberg, 255–82. New York: Russell Sage Foundation; Princeton, NJ: Princeton University Press, 1994.

———. *Principles of Economic Sociology*. Princeton, NJ: Princeton University Press, 2003.

Swidler, Ann. "Culture in Action: Symbols and Strategies." *American Sociological Review* 51 (1986): 273–86.

Tanzi, Vito. *The Underground Economy in the United States and Abroad*. Lexington, MA: D. C. Health, 1980.

Tilly, Charles. *The Contentious French: Four Centuries of Popular Struggle*. Cambridge, MA: Harvard University Press, 1986.

———. *Durable Inequality*. Berkeley: University of California Press, 1998.

———. "To Explain Political Processes." *American Journal of Sociology* 100 (May 1995): 1594–1610.

———. "Invisible Elbow." *Sociological Forum* 11 (1996): 589–601.

Tokman, Victor. "Unequal Development and the Absorption of Labour: Latin America 1950–1980." *CEPAL Review* 17 (1982): 121–33.

Treml, Vladimir. "Purchases of Food from Private Sources in Soviet Urban Areas." Berkeley-Duke Occasional Papers on the Second Economy, #3, September 1985.

Updegrave, Walter. "Assessing Your Wealth." *Money* 28 (July 1999): 63–73.

Valladares, Licia, Edmond Preteceille, Bianca Freire-Medeiros, and Filipina Chinelli. "Río de Janeiro en el viraje hacia el nuevo siglo." in *Ciudades latinoamericanas: Un análisis comparativo en el umbral del nuevo siglo*, edited by A. Portes, B. R. Roberts, and A. Grimson, 149–215. Buenos Aires: Prometeo Libros, 2005.

Veblen, Thorstein. *The Theory of the Leisure Class*. 1899. Reprint, Amherst, NY: Prometheus Books, 1998.

Velasco, José Luis. "Servicio de Administración Tributaria de México." Final Report to the Project "Institutions and Development in Latin America." Center for Migration and Development, Princeton University, 2008. At http://cmd .princeton.edu/papers/wp0805k.pdf.

Vertovec, Steven. "Migrant Transnationalism and Modes of Transformation." *International Migration Review* 38 (Fall 2004): 970–1001.

Wacquant, Loic, and William J. Wilson. "The Cost of Racial and Class Exclusion in the Inner City." *Annals of the American Academy of Political and Social Science* 501 (1989): 8–26.

Wadhwani, Sushil. "How Efficient Market Theory Gave Rise to Policy Mistakes." *Financial Times*, December 17, 2008.

Waldinger, Roger. "The 'Other Side' of Embeddedness: A Case Study of the Interplay between Economy and Ethnicity." *Ethnic and Racial Studies* 18 (1995): 555–80.

Waldinger, Roger, and David Fitzgerald. "Transnationalism in Question." *American Journal of Sociology* 109, no. 5 (2004): 1177–96.

Waldinger, Roger, and Michael I. Lichter. *How the Other Half Works*. Berkeley: University of California Press, 2003.

Wallerstein, Immanuel. *Geopolitics and Geoculture: Essays on the Changing World-System*. Cambridge: Cambridge University Press, 1991.

———. *The Modern World-System: Capitalist Agriculture and the Origins of the European World-Economy in the Sixteenth Century*. New York: Academic Press, 1974.

———. "The Rise and Future Demise of the World Capitalist System: Concepts for Comparative Analysis." *Comparative Studies in Sociology and History* 16 (September 1974): 387–415.

———. "Semi-Peripheral Countries and the Contemporary World Crisis." *Theory and Society* 3 (1976): 461–83.

Waters, Mary. "West Indian Immigrants, African Americans, and Whites in the Workplace: Different Perspectives on American Race Relations." Paper presented at the meetings of the American Sociological Association. Los Angeles, 1994.

Weber, Max. "Capitalism and Rural Society in Germany." In *From Max Weber: Essays in Sociology*, edited and translated by H. H. Gerth and C. Wright Mills, 363–85. 1906. Reprint, New York: Oxford University Press, 1946.

———. "Class, Status, Party." In *From Max Weber: Essays in Sociology*, edited and translated by H. H. Gerth and C. Wright Mills, 180–95. 1922. Reprint, New York: Oxford University Press, 1946.

———. "Objectivity in Social Science." In *The Methodology of the Social Sciences*, edited by M. Weber, 49–112. Translated by E. A. Shils and H. A. Finch. 1904. Reprint, New York: Free Press, 1949.

———. *The Protestant Ethic and the Spirit of Capitalism*. Originally published a two-part article in "Archiv fur Sozialwissenschaft und Sozialpolitick, 1904–1905." Boston, 1985.

———. "Religious Rejections of the World and Their Directions." In *From Max Weber: Essays in Sociology*, edited by H. H. Gerth and C. Wright Mills, 323–59. 1915. Reprint, New York: Oxford University Press, 1958.

———. "Social Stratification and Class Structure." In *The Theory of Social and Economic Organization*, edited by T. Parsons, 424–29. 1922. Reprint, New York: Free Press, 1947.

———. *The Sociology of Religion*. Translated by E. Fischoff. 1922. Reprint, Boston: Beacon Press, 1964.

———. *The Theory of Social and Economic Organization*. Edited by T. Parsons. 1922. Reprint, New York: Free Press, 1965.

Western, Bruce, and Katherine Beckett. 1999. "How Unregulated Is the U.S. Labor Market? The Penal System as a Labor Market Institution." *American Journal of Sociology* 104 (January 1999): 1030–60.

Western, Bruce, Katherine Beckett, and David Harding. "Système pénal et marché du travail aux États-Unis." *Actes de la Recherche en Sciences Sociales* 124 (September 1998): 27–35.

White, Harrison. "Where Do Markets Come From?" *American Journal of Sociology* 81 (November 1981): 517–47.

Williamson, John. *The Political Economy of Policy Reform.* Washington, DC: Institute for International Economics, 1994.

Williamson, Oliver. *The Economic Institutions of Capitalism.* New York: Free Press, 1985.

———. *Markets and Hierarchies.* New York: Free Press, 1975.

Wilson, William J. *When Work Disappears: The World of the New Urban Poor.* New York: Knopf, 1996.

Wolff, Kurt H. *The Sociology of Georg Simmel.* New York: Free Press, 1964.

Wolpe, Harold. "The Theory of Internal Colonialism: The South African Case." In *Beyond the Sociology of Development: Economy and Society in Latin America and Africa,* edited by I. Oxaal, T. Barnett, and D. Booth, 252–79. London: Routledge and Kegan Paul, 1975.

Wormald, Guillermo, and Daniel Brieba. 2006. "La Bolsa de Comercio de Santiago de Chile: Un análisis institucional." Final report to the project "Latin American Institutions and Development." Center for Migration and Development, Princeton University, 2006. At http://cmd.princeton.edu/papers/wp0608c2.pdf.

Wormald, Guillermo, and Ana Cárdenas. "Formación y desarrollo del Servicio de Impuestos Internos (SII) en Chile: Un análisis institucional." Final report to the project "Institutions and Development in Latin America." Center for Migration and Development, Princeton University, 2008. At http://cmd.princeton.edu/papers/wp0805f.pdf.

Wright, Erik O. *Classes.* London: Verso, 1985.

———. "Rethinking Once Again the Concept of Class Structure." In *Reworking Class,* edited by J. R. Hall, 41–72. Ithaca, NY: Cornell University Press, 1997.

———. 1980. "Varieties of Marxist Conceptions of Class Structure." *Politics and Society* 9 (1980): 299–322.

Wright, Erik O., and Luca Perrone. "Marxist Class Categories and Income Inequality." *American Sociological Review* 42 (1976): 32–55.

Wrong, Dennis. "The Oversocialization Conception of Man in Modern Sociology." *American Sociological Review* 26 (1961): 183–93.

Wuthnow, Robert. *After Heaven: Spirituality in America since the 1950s.* Berkeley: University of California Press, 1998.

———. *Meaning and Moral Order: Explorations in Cultural Analysis.* Berkeley: University of California Press, 1987.

Zelizer, Viviana. *The Purchase of Intimacy.* Princeton, NJ: Princeton University Press, 2005.

Zhou, Min. *New York's Chinatown: The Socioeconomic Potential of an Urban Enclave.* Philadelphia: Temple University Press, 1992.

———. "Revisiting Ethnic Entrepreneurship: Convergencies, Controversies, and Conceptual Advancements." *International Migration Review* 38 (Fall 2004): 1040–74.

Zhou, Min, and Carl L. Bankston. "Entrepreneurship." In *Asian American Almanac*, edited by I. Natividad, 511–28. Columbus, OH: Gale Research, 1995.

———. "Social Capital and the Adaptation of the Second Generation: The Case of Vietnamese Youth in New Orleans." In *The New Second Generation*, edited by A. Portes, 197–220. New York: Russell Sage Foundation, 1996.

Index